THE THEORY
OF
UNEMPLOYMENT

MACMILLAN AND CO., Limited
LONDON · BOMBAY · CALCUTTA · MADRAS
MELBOURNE

THE MACMILLAN COMPANY
NEW YORK · BOSTON · CHICAGO
DALLAS · ATLANTA · SAN FRANCISCO

THE MACMILLAN COMPANY
OF CANADA, LIMITED
TORONTO

THE THEORY
OF
UNEMPLOYMENT

BY

A. C. PIGOU, M.A.

PROFESSOR OF POLITICAL ECONOMY IN THE UNIVERSITY OF CAMBRIDGE

AUTHOR OF
"THE ECONOMICS OF WELFARE", ETC.

MACMILLAN AND CO., LIMITED
ST. MARTIN'S STREET, LONDON
1933

COPYRIGHT

PRINTED IN GREAT BRITAIN
BY R. & R. CLARK, LIMITED, EDINBURGH

PREFACE

THIS book is addressed to students of economics. Its aim is to clarify thought, not to advocate a policy. While it is natural and right in the present deplorable state of the world's affairs that many economists should seek to play a part in guiding conduct, that is not their primary business. They are physiologists, not clinical practitioners; engineers, not engine-drivers. The main part of such contribution as they may hope to make must be indirect; in the study, not in the pages of newspapers or even in the council chamber. I offer no apology, therefore, for publishing, in a period when the tragedy of unemployment is of unexampled magnitude, a book on that subject strictly academic in tone and content.

It is possible to study the problem of unemployment either from the money end or from what I shall call, in contrast, the real end. The two studies, if made complete and carried through correctly, must necessarily come to the same thing, their analyses meeting in the middle. There can, therefore, be no question of the one way of approach being right and the other wrong. Both are right, and both can be used with profit. In recent years, as is to be expected in a period of monetary disorganisation, economists have been inclined to concentrate attention on the money end. The result, in my opinion, has been to overstress somewhat the rôle that money plays in more normal times, and to put in the background very important factors of a non-monetary character. For this reason, among others, I have chosen to write my book from the real end, and to bring in the monetary factor only at a fairly late stage.

Addressing myself to economists, I have made use without disguise of whatever tools have appeared to me, in different

v

parts of the analysis, to be helpful. In some chapters of Parts II. and III. this method has involved the employment of a little elementary differential calculus. I am aware that there are writers on economic subjects, unacquainted with this tool, who resent its use by others. To them it is sufficient to reply with Pareto that persons ignorant of the German language are ill-qualified to criticise German literature. There are, however, other writers, themselves masters of all the relevant technique, who, nevertheless, deprecate the introduction of mathematical symbols into economic discussions. Marshall, for example, a great part of whose work was built up round a mathematical skeleton, was at extreme pains to keep the skeleton concealed. By so doing he made his *Principles of Economics*, not only a great work of science, but also a great instrument of general education. None the less, I venture a doubt how far those many readers of Marshall, who leave the skeleton unwrapped—who perhaps are even unaware of its existence—really grasp his thought. Would they not in the end have been better off had mathematical ideas been presented to them in mathematical form: and had they been advised to acquire a mastery of these few and simple tools? However that may be, I have in this book deliberately discarded cotton-wool and said what I had to say in a direct manner.

Though this volume is of substantial size, it does not claim to be exhaustive. What I have studied is a simplified model of the economic world rather than that world itself in its full completeness. Neither our analytic apparatus nor our statistical information is at present adequate for that. In particular many complications of detail associated with the imperfection of markets are left aside: and the concept of wage-goods is employed in a manner which cannot, in the nature of things, yield more than a rough approximate picture of the facts. The work is thus tentative in character and, as no one knows better than the author, in many respects unsatisfactory. Moreover, on a number of relevant matters, including some of the broader influences that govern movements of demand, I have said little. The reason is that they have already been discussed at length in my *Industrial*

Fluctuations. In some degree this book and that are complementary to one another.

Part I. is general and introductory. Part II. is concerned with the form of the real demand functions for labour in particular occupations and in the aggregate: Part III. with alterations in these demand functions brought about otherwise than through the monetary factor: Part IV. with alterations in whose genesis or development that factor is concerned. All these Parts are, in a sense, preliminary. Finally, in Part V. the results obtained are brought together and utilised in a direct discussion of the causation of unemployment and its fluctuations. Mr. Denis Robertson, of Trinity College, Cambridge, has very kindly read all these Parts in manuscript and has helped me with many valuable suggestions ; and Mr. Sraffa has done me a like service for Parts I. and II. In each Part, when reference is made to a chapter in another Part, both Part and chapter are named; when reference is made to a chapter in the same Part, the number of the chapter only is given.

A. C. P.

KING'S COLLEGE, CAMBRIDGE,
April 1933.

ANALYTICAL TABLE OF CONTENTS

PART I

GENERAL CONSIDERATIONS

CHAPTER I

CHAPTER II

CHAPTER III

CHAPTER IV

ix

CHAPTER VII

CHAPTER VIII

CHAPTER IX

CHAPTER III

THE PRINCIPAL FACTORS OF CHANGE IN THE REAL DEMAND
FOR LABOUR IN PARTICULAR OCCUPATIONS . .

CHAPTER IV

STATE STIMULATION OF EMPLOYMENT IN PARTICULAR OCCUPA-
TIONS . . . .

CHAPTER V

THE INTERDEPENDENCE OF DEMAND CHANGES IN RESPECT OF
SUBSTITUTES AND COMPLEMENTS . . . .

PART V

THE CAUSATION OF UNEMPLOYMENT AND OF CHANGES IN UNEMPLOYMENT

CHAPTER I

CHAPTER II

§ 1. The real rates of wage for which workpeople stipulate adjust themselves to the average state of real demand for labour, and therefore differences in the average states of real demand between various places and times are not correlated with differences in the percentage of unemployment.
§ 2. Hence long-run Government policies affecting the real demand for labour in a permanent manner are not relevant.
§ 3. This, of course, is no argument against the temporary adoption of expansionist Government policies as "remedies" for unemployment in times of exceptional depression:
§ 4. Nor yet against devices—if such were practicable—designed to make the real demand for labour undergo continuous and progressive expansion.

CHAPTER III

§§ 1–2. In so far as wage policy aims at establishing rates of real wage in excess of what, in the ruling state of demand, would allow of full employment, it is a factor making for unemployment.
§ 3. In industries sheltered from foreign competition, particularly if a State system of unemployment insurance exists, a wage policy of this kind is not unlikely to be adopted.
§ 4. Collective bargains under time-wage systems involve "by accident" the adoption of this policy in respect of specially slow workers:
§ 5. And the pressure of public opinion or minimum wage legislation has a like tendency in respect of low-grade industries.
§ 6. This long-run factor in the causation of unemployment is probably much more important now than it used to be in pre-war times.

CHAPTER IV

§§ 1–2. The adjustment rate of real wages is defined.
§ 3. Wage-rates elsewhere being assumed to be held rigid, the effect of establishing a wage-rate in particular occupations in excess of the adjustment wage is studied, first, on the assumption that labour is perfectly mobile:

CHAPTER VIII

CHAPTER IX

§ 4. Since upward price movements often accompany rises in the aggregate real demand function for labour, this implies that the real rate of wage stipulated for often falls when the aggregate real demand function for labour is rising, and rises when it is falling. This association causes the aggregate volume of employment to fluctuate more widely than it would do if there were no such association.

§ 5. An analytical point is examined.

PART I
GENERAL CONSIDERATIONS

CHAPTER I

§ 1. THE volume of *employment* in any occupation over any assigned period can be defined unambiguously as the number of man-hours of work performed during that period. It is recognised that the quality of the men at work may vary from time to time and also the energy with which they perform their work. But this does not spoil the statistical measure any more than the fact that the quality and age distribution of the persons constituting a community varies prevents us from stating unambiguously the number of the population.

§ 2. *Unemployment*, however, is not an equally clear-cut conception. If it meant simply the number of man-hours that exist over a period, during which people are *not* employed, it would be so. But nobody seriously proposes to define unemployment in such a way as to make a man unemployed during the whole of the time (*e.g.* while he is asleep at night) that he is *not* employed. A man is only unemployed when he is *both* not employed and *also* desires to be employed. Moreover, the notion of desiring to be employed must be interpreted in relation to established facts as regards (1) hours of work per day, (2) rates of wage and (3) a man's state of health.

Thus, first, if the normal hours of work in a particular factory are eight, and a specially strong man would have liked to be at work for nine, nobody would say that he is, therefore, "unemployed" for one hour a day. In fact, for the purpose of measuring unemployment, the normal hours of work per day must be taken as given. This must be done even when the normal hours are different at different seasons of the year, as they are in the building trade. Awkward questions may,

3

indeed, arise if this line of thought is pursued to its logical conclusion. Thus, obviously, it is in substance much the same thing if a cotton mill closes three days a week as if it cuts down its daily hours from eight to four. If the idleness due to the former act is to be called unemployment, it is arbitrary to refuse that name to the idleness due to the latter. But, if we do not refuse it, we are not interpreting the notion of desiring to be employed in relation to established facts as regards hours of work.

Secondly, desire to be employed must be taken to mean desire to be employed at current rates of wages in an establishment not engaged in an industrial dispute. A man is not unemployed because he would like to work if the current wage were £1000 a day but does not so like when the current wage is 5s. a day. There are here, of course, certain ambiguities about the meaning of current rates of wage. If the wage in a man's own town is 5s. a day, whereas in another town it is 6s., a man is not unemployed if he stays in his own town and refuses to work because the wage there is not 6s. The same thing is true if a man of poor quality, such that the current rate for one of his ability is 3s., refuses to work for that, because the current rate for stronger men is 5s.

Thirdly, desire to be employed means desire subject to the facts of a man's own health. A man is not unemployed because he desires to work but is prevented from doing so by sickness. In the terminology current in England that type of non-employment is carefully separated from unemployment.

§ 3. We thus conclude that the number of persons unemployed at any time is equal to the number of persons who desire employment in the above sense—the number of would-be wage-earners—*minus* the number of persons employed. The task of obtaining a correct record of the difference between these two numbers is rendered difficult by the fact that some persons, who are not in fact desirous of employment in our sense, are, nevertheless, enumerated as though they were. It is well known that casual labourers often do not desire, and do not offer themselves for, work on more than three or four days in a week. Moreover, it is alleged that some men on occasions, possibly even for considerable periods, prefer to

draw unemployment pay rather than make difficult efforts to
find a job, particularly if this would require a shift in dwelling-
place and, still more, a shift in occupation. Such men do not
in fact desire employment in any effective sense; and yet in
current statistics they are always classed as unemployed. With
a well-organised system of Employment Exchanges, reasonable rules about conditions of benefit and rates of benefit not
too high relatively to normal wages, we need not, indeed, fear
that from this cause any appreciable number of available
vacancies will be left unfilled. But in a period of depression,
when all available vacancies are filled, the fact that these men
do not desire employment does not cause them to act otherwise than they would do if they did desire it; and, since it is
impossible to look directly into people's minds, there are,
therefore, no means of discovering or enumerating them. When
records are based on the number of persons eligible for benefit
under Unemployment Insurance schemes, and when the test
of eligibility is such as to include persons who *were* desirous
of employment at some date in the past but are not necessarily so desirous now, there is further scope for the type of
error we are here considering. Before the amendment of the
Insurance Act in 1931 there were a number of persons recorded
as unemployed who did not in fact desire employment. Thus
in the *Labour Gazette* of November 1930 we read: "If the
average rate of exit (from the Insurance scheme) experienced
during the three years 1925–8 had continued during the
subsequent two years, while the number of new entrants remained the same, there would have passed out of the Insurance scheme approximately 185,000 males and 130,000
females, who are now included in the figures for July
1930".[1] It appears further that the number in insurance in
the northern section of the country took a spurt upwards in
1929–30. The *Labour Gazette* writes: "This change in the trend
is attributable in the main to the retention within the scheme
of unemployment insurance, in areas where unemployment
has been heavy, of numbers of persons who would have
passed out of the scheme if the changes in the conditions
for the receipt of benefit introduced by the Unemployment

[1] *Loc. cit.* p. 397.

Insurance Act, 1930, had not been made".[1] Under the
technique of the English scheme, as it then stood, women
who had married and in effect withdrawn from industry,
were, nevertheless, legally entitled to claim benefit for a considerable period, and a fair number of them did so. These
women were clearly not would-be wage-earners and not unemployed in the terms of my definition. For the purposes
of a general view, however, the proportion of "unemployment" that is affected by difficulties of this character is
too small to make unemployment as here defined seriously
different from unemployment as recorded in British official
statistics.

§ 4. With this definition it is plain that one very important
type of cause, namely alterations in the rate of wages offered
by employers, coming about while other things remain the
same, may affect employment and unemployment in different
degrees. They will affect them in equal degrees if, and only
if, they leave the number of men desiring to be employed, and
so the number liable to be "unemployed" in our sense, unaltered. It may happen, however, if the rate of wage is raised,
that a few men, who, at the lower rate, would have been in retirement, living on pensions or on their savings or with friends,
and a few who would have been engaged in non-wage work,
will become seekers after wage work. *Per contra*, it may happen
that a rise in the rate of wage, if the effort demand of workers
for stuff is inelastic, may cause a few men to seek employment
on fewer days in the week. But the generality of occupations
in the real world are so organised that men cannot do this
except on pain of dismissal, so that this point is not practically important. Of more weight is the tendency of a rise
in the rate of wage, by enabling the husband to support his
family, without his wife working, to cause a certain number
of women to withdraw from the labour market. This tendency and the tendency for men to be drawn back from
retirement, and so on, work in opposite directions. In any
event neither tendency is likely to manifest itself on a large
scale. It is not probable, therefore, that on this account the
amount—or the proportion—of unemployment caused by a

[1] *Loc. cit.* p. 399.

rise in the rate of wages will be appreciably different from the amount, or proportion, of employment that is destroyed.

§ 5. It should be noted further that in certain conditions a given reduction in the number of persons employed is associated with an equal transfer of persons from inside the class of would-be wage-earners to outside that class, and so leaves the number of unemployed, in my sense, unaltered. This will happen if women, who have been employed, leave their jobs on marriage, and the vacancies that their withdrawal creates are not filled because acceptable candidates are not available. In times of general depression, however, it is very improbable that vacancies thus created will remain unfilled for any appreciable length of time. In England in the post-war slump domestic service has probably been the only large-scale occupation in which unfilled vacancies have played any significant part. In such circumstances withdrawal from employment by particular persons merely means the entrance into employment of others. The volume of employment is not affected. The voluntary idleness of A is a substitute for, not an addition to, the involuntary idleness of B. Thus this type of reaction is not likely to prove practically important in bad times. In good times it conceivably might do so. But even then its scope is probably not great.

§ 6. In sum, then, we may conclude that the number of would-be wage-earners and the number of persons employed are in the main independent of one another, so that, if the first decreases or the second increases in a given measure, the number of persons unemployed, in the sense of my definition, will decrease in an approximately equal measure. There are thus available two main types of "remedy for unemployment": those that seek to diminish the number of would-be wage-earners by inducing old men to retire on pensions, by raising the school age, or by stimulating emigration, and those that seek to increase the number of persons employed. In popular discussions of unemployment the vital distinction between these two types of remedy is not always perceived —or at all events expounded—with perfect clarity. In this book in the main I shall take the number of would-be wage-earners in a given situation as a fixed datum, so that the quantity of unemployment and the quantity of employment are simple complements of one another. It is obvious, of course, that, if the number of the would-be wage-earning population expands and employment remains unchanged, the absolute and the proportionate quantity of unemployment must both increase. If employment grows with population, the absolute quantity of unemployment will increase, but the proportionate quantity will remain constant.

CHAPTER II

§ 1. THE quantity of unemployment is, as we have seen, equal to the number of would-be wage-earners *minus* the quantity of employment. At first blush it is natural to add that the quantity of employment is equal to the quantity of labour demanded; so that the quantity of unemployment is equal to the number of would-be wage-earners *minus* the quantity of labour demanded. A moment's reflection, however, shows that the second step in this chain of analysis is faulty.

§ 2. The quantity of employment ruling at any time is equal, not to the quantity of labour demanded *simpliciter*, but to this quantity *minus* the quantity of unfilled vacancies —that is to say, of posts that in each occupation, at the wage-rate ruling there, employers desire, but are unable, to fill. Thus, if we write for the aggregate quantity of employment E, for the aggregate quantity of labour demanded D and for the aggregate quantity of unfilled vacancies V, in all circumstances $E = (D - V)$. When $V = 0$, the number of men employed in the aggregate is equal to the number of men demanded in the aggregate: and also, it will be observed, the number of men employed in each centre separately is equal to the number of men demanded there. When, however, $V > 0$, these constraints are removed. It follows that, in these circumstances, though differences in wage-rates or demand conditions still imply differences in the aggregate quantity of labour demanded, they do not imply differences in the aggregate quantity of employment. An expansion in general demand or a fall in wage-rates all round must lead to an expansion of D, that is of $(E + V)$: but it need not lead to any

9

change in E. *Per contra*, alterations in the relative demand
schedules or the relative wage-rates ruling in different occupations, that leave D unchanged, may, nevertheless, involve
an alteration in E.

§ 3. Thus the quantity of unemployment prevailing at any
time is equal to the number of would-be wage-earners *minus*
the quantity of labour demanded *plus* the number of unfilled
vacancies: so that, if the number of would-be wage-earners
and the quantity of labour demanded are both constant, the
quantity of unemployment may still fluctuate, provided that
the quantity of unfilled vacancies also fluctuates in the same
direction and to an equal extent.

CHAPTER III

§ 1. THE phrase cost of unemployment may be used in two senses, according as we are considering cost to the community in a wide sense inclusive of unemployed persons or cost to the community in a narrower sense exclusive of these persons. Clearly the former sense is the more important of the two, and to that attention will be confined. It is further necessary to distinguish between objective cost and subjective cost. The purpose of the present chapter is to study these two kinds of cost in turn. To make the issue precise I shall suppose that the percentage of unemployment is 10 per cent, and that this means, as it does in this country, some 1,200,000 persons.

§ 2. The objective cost to the community of those persons being unemployed may, it would seem, be measured by the quantity of goods and services, which, had they been employed, they would have produced, or, more exactly, by the difference to the inventory of goods and services forthcoming which their being employed would have made. This postulates, of course, that the general conditions of productive technique and so on are not altered: for, if we imagine these people brought into employment *in consequence of improvements* in these conditions, a part of the altered output of goods and services will be due, not to increased employment, but to something entirely different. Even, however, with this proviso there is an ambiguity. The difference that would be made by these persons being employed depends in part on *how* they would be employed. For example, do we contemplate, as the alternative situation against which the actual situation is to

11

be compared, the displaced coal miners of this country returned to work in the depressed coal industry or moved across into some other occupation where the outlook is less poor? It is best, I think, to imagine them employed in such a way that openings in which the demand for their services is higher are filled before those in which the demand is lower.

§ 3. The inventory of hypothetical goods and services, which the 10 per cent unemployed men might have produced but do not, must, if we are to measure it in a single figure, be expressed as a sum of money value. This money value will not, in general, be the difference between the actual money value of the community's output and the money value which the community's output would have if the 10 per cent unemployed men were at work. For the addition made to output by their efforts would affect the price level: and it is even conceivable, under a very rigid money system, that the money value of the enlarged output would not be any larger than that of the actual output. The figure we require rather is the inventory of these men's hypothetical output valued at current prices. This figure can be set against the money value of actual output: and we can say in a rough way that 10 per cent unemployment is responsible for a percentage contraction in output of goods and services measured by the percentage which our money figure makes of the money value of actual output. This method fails to take account of some of the reactions involved, and is not ideal. But it is, I think, the best that is available.

§ 4. In order to make an estimate of what the required money figure, reckoned on the above plan, works out at in any given case, we ought, in strictness, to know for what reason our 10 per cent unemployed men are out of work. In so far as they are out of work because obstructions to movement prevent their going to jobs in which employers, at the current rate of wage, are asking for hands, the value of their output, if they contrived to get to these jobs, would exceed the value of the wages paid to them. But, in so far as they are out of work because employers do not want their services at the current rate of wages, the value of their output would fall short of their wages if they were paid at current rates.

In fact, at all events in a serious depression, it is very unlikely that the number of vacancies which employers wish
to fill but cannot will be appreciable. *Prima facie*, therefore, we
may incline to conclude that the value of the output of our
unemployed men, if they were employed, would be less than
their number multiplied by the wages they would receive if
paid at current rates. Thus, if we reckon current wages in this
country at a rough average—it must be remembered that
many of the unemployed are women—of £2 per week, and
10 per cent unemployment at 1,200,000 persons, we get an
upper limit for the money value of loss involved of some
£125 million in a year. To reason in this way, however, is to
ignore the fact that the withdrawal from work of 1,200,000
workpeople carries with it also the withdrawal of a large
amount of plant. In view of this, the upper limit of loss,
though certainly much less than 10 per cent of the national
income, may well be more than 10 per cent of the national
wages bill.

§ 5. What has just been said concerns the objective cost of
10 per cent unemployment to the community as a whole. The
subjective cost is the loss of the satisfaction which would have
been yielded by the consumption, or other use, of the goods
that might have been, but were not, produced *minus* the dissatisfaction that would have been involved in their production. This conception is not a precise one until we have
specified how far unemployed persons, who produce nothing,
are assisted out of the real income accruing to other persons:
for, obviously, the non-appearance of their product involves
a much greater loss of satisfaction if it means that these
men are reduced to the verge of starvation than if it means
merely that the superfluities of some rich men are cut a little
to finance the unemployed. In England roughly half the loss
of product due to unemployment is borne by the unemployed
man himself and half by other people. Even with this datum,
however, we have no means of settling quantitatively how
big the loss of satisfaction associated with a given reduction
of output will be. *Prima facie*, when account is taken of the
fact that an unemployed man escapes the dissatisfaction involved in work, it might seem doubtful whether there is any

net subjective cost at all. Thus, if it be the fact that a man working ten hours a day would produce more stuff than the same man working eight hours, the objective cost of his not working the two extra hours is measured by the associated reduction of output. But if, as may well happen, the man gets more satisfaction out of the two hours' extra leisure than he would have got out of the proceeds of the stuff he could have produced by working these two hours, there is no subjective cost, even though our man receives no unemployment pay at the expense of richer men. In like manner, if a man does not work for a week, the satisfaction of his week's leisure must be set against the satisfaction that would have been yielded to him by a week's worth of stuff. If his week's idleness is voluntary, the presumption is that the gain of leisure outweighs, in respect of satisfaction, the loss of stuff. If it is enforced, though the presumption is the other way, the gain of leisure may still offset a considerable part of the loss of stuff. Whether it in fact does this depends upon the proportion of a man's working time that the enforced leisure covers. If it lasts only for a day or two, the offset will be substantial; but, if it continues over a long period, there will be no offset; the leisure will itself become an evil.

§ 6. The practical moral of this is that the relation between the objective cost of unemployment and the subjective cost of it to the community in the widest sense depends in great measure upon the size of the lumps in which unemployment is served out to individual unemployed men. With even distribution an average of 6 per cent unemployment over the year would mean that everyone was involuntarily idle for about one work-day in every three weeks, or, say, for a spell of four or five days once every quarter. Plainly this would not be a very serious matter. If the idle days could be foreseen and arranged for beforehand, the net subjective cost, even though there were no unemployment pay contributed by other people, might well be nil. Even 10 per cent unemployment evenly distributed only means a little over five weeks a year for everybody of holidays without pay—a serious matter no doubt, for some poor men, but not a devastating calamity. In real life, however, unemployment is not distributed evenly over everybody. While leaving the larger part of the wage-earning population untouched or but lightly touched, it falls with tremendous force on a relatively small group. Thus, under the instructions of the Ministry of Labour, 1 per cent sample inquiries were held on March 18 and September 16, 1929—in each of which months the aggregate percentage of unemployment was 10 per cent—into the period of unemployment of men then unemployed. Averaging the two sets of numbers, which are fairly close, we obtain the following table.[1]

	Men.		Women.
	All Industries.	All Industries other than Coal Mining.	All Industries.
	%	%	%
Less than 3 months .	30·8	33·5	51·1
3-6 months . .	29·5	31·3	30·9
6-9 ,, . .	20·2	20·95	11·65
9-12 ,, . .	14·5	11·95	5·55
12 months or more .	5·0	2·3	0·8

Thus, even apart from coal mining, two-thirds of the men unemployed had been out of work for more than three months and more than one-third for over six months. Among the women unemployed nearly half had been out of work for over three months and one-fifth for over six months. In a sample count taken on February 2, 1931, the situation was not substantially different.[2] Nobody can suppose that, with a distribution of this sort, the leisure associated with unemployment is an asset to be weighed against the loss of what work would have produced. It is an aggravation, not a mitigation, of the subjective cost involved.

§ 7. The discussion so far has been confined to direct contemporary cost, for which alone there is hope of obtaining a rough statistical measure. This direct contemporary cost is not, however, the most important part of the cost of un-

[1] *Labour Gazette*, June 1930, p. 7.
[2] Report of the Royal Commission on Unemployment Insurance [Cmd. 4185], p. 76.

employment, when the problem is viewed broadly. If a man
is subjected to unemployment for a long period of time, injurious reactions on his industrial and human quality are
almost certain to result. It is not merely that technical skill
deteriorates through lack of practice. The habit of regular
work may be lost, and self-respect and self-confidence destroyed, so that, when opportunity comes again, the man,
once merely unemployed, is found to have become unemploy-
able. Meanwhile his home life may have suffered shipwreck,
and the atmosphere in which his children are growing up may
have been poisoned. Evils of this kind do not follow from
small doses of unemployment spread over many men, even
though the aggregate amount is large. They are the fruit, in
the main, of large concentrations of unemployment upon a
small number of especially unfortunate people. It should be
noted, however, that, while, from this point of view, a distribution of unemployment that involves a moderate number
of long spells is certain to be much more injurious than one
that involves a large number of short spells, a very small
number of very long spells is not necessarily worse than a
moderate number of long spells. For it is arguable that, say,
a year's continuous unemployment does nearly as much
damage to industrial and human quality as two or even ten
years could do. If this be so, it may be a less social evil to
have the same 10,000 persons unemployed continuously for
five years than to have an equal number of man-years of unemployment spread over 50,000 people in continuous spells
of one year for each

CHAPTER IV

THE MEANING OF UNITS OF REAL WAGES

§ 1. IF the wage-earning classes always bought with their money one sort of article only, there could be no ambiguity about what is meant by real rate of wages, or real rate of unemployment pay or real demand function for labour in any occupation. In like manner if any group of wage-earners, though purchasing a number of different sorts of goods, always purchased them in the same proportions, there would be no ambiguity about what is meant by these things. We should merely have to conceive a unit of wage-goods as a packet containing the several goods or services combined in those proportions in which the group always bought them. No doubt, since groups of wage-earners with different levels of money wages buy the several sorts of goods in different proportions —not to speak of the fact that bachelors and men with families enjoying equal money wages do this—we should need to imagine differently constituted packets, *i.e.* different units of wage-goods, for different groups. We could, however, without ambiguity conceive of a definite unit of wage-goods for any assigned group of workers or for a clearly defined imaginary "representative" group: and, so long as the number of these units received by the assigned or by the representative group was unaltered, the real rate of wage or of unemployment pay—I shall not trouble henceforward in this chapter to mention this separately—to it would be constant.

§ 2. In actual life the representative wage-earner distributes his money in such a way that it buys for him packets of wage-goods in which the different items are in different proportions on different occasions. He will vary these proportions if his

tastes change. He will also vary them if, his tastes being constant, the relative prices of different wage-good items alter on
account of changes either of productive technique or of the
demand of non-wage-earners. In general, with a given money
wage, he will buy more of things that have become relatively
cheap and less of things that have become relatively dear:
though it is conceivable, in special circumstances, that, if a
cheap food—*e.g.* bread—of which he buys much, becomes
relatively dear, he may buy more and not less of it, because
its high price makes it impossible for him to get enough sus-
tenance except by concentrating nearly all his income on this
form of food. Yet again the representative wage-earner, even
though his tastes and the relative prices of different wage-
good items are unaltered, will vary the proportions in which
he buys the several items when his money wage alters. With
a rise in money wage, for example, he will augment his purchases of relative luxuries more than his purchases of those
prime necessaries that even the poorest must have. These
facts make the question what a wage-good unit is, and to
what extent, in given circumstances, the real rate of wages
has changed, very difficult to answer in a satisfactory manner.

§ 3. A solution is sometimes sought by passing behind
things to the satisfaction which their possession conveys.
Thus we may say: "The real rate of wages is unchanged between two dates if, to a representative man of given and constant tastes, the things on which he chooses to spend his
(given) money wage at the two dates yield equal satisfaction";
and we may then try to evolve a price-index number such
that the money wage divided by this number shall be unchanged when the satisfaction that our representative man
derives from his money wage is unchanged. Unfortunately it
is impossible, with our present knowledge, to accomplish,
though it is not impossible to approach,[1] this task: and, in any
event, our present purpose, which is concerned solely with the
problem of unemployment, would not be assisted by a definition of this type. What is important to us is that wage-
earners do in fact on some occasions make it an object of
policy to "keep real wages constant" or to "prevent them

[1] Cf. *The Economics of Welfare*, Part I. chap. vi.

from falling". Our definition must be one that interprets this aim in the way that it is in fact interpreted in the wage discussions of real life. No doubt, in these discussions the idea of utility or satisfaction lies somewhere concealed in the background; but the foreground is occupied by something much less recondite.

§ 4. The solution commonly adopted by practical men is, of course, well known. We select in an arbitrary manner a particular more or less average or typical wage-earner, ascertain the way in which at some—also arbitrarily selected —date he distributes his money wages, and treat this packet or some fractional multiple of it, not as a simple physical unit of wage-goods, but as a mixed physical and value unit. We then say that the real rate of wage is constant if the money rate of wage divided by the price of this arbitrarily selected packet is constant. Thus, in England, we say that the real rate of wage is constant if the money rate of wage divided by the Ministry of Labour's cost-of-living index number is constant. In like manner we say that the real rate of wage has risen or fallen 10 per cent when this quotient is increased or diminished by 10 per cent.

§ 5. If, between the dates we are comparing, the proportions in which our representative wage-earner purchases different wage-good items has not altered, this method is in effect the same as that described in § 1, and there is no difficulty or ambiguity. But, if these proportions have altered, the procedure outlined contains an arbitrary element. There is no reason for using as our base the workmen's budget of wage-good items which represents the facts of one year rather than that which represents the facts of another: and it may easily happen, if the constitution of the budgets is changing, that a calculation based on one budget would show wage-rates constant between two years, whereas one based on another budget would show them varying. Calculations on the two bases would generally indicate changes measured by different percentages; and sometimes one calculation would show a rise and the other a fall in the rate of real wage. A compromise between the two calculations can, of course, if we wish, be set up in preference to either of them singly:

but this too must depend on arbitrary choice. It may, indeed, be replied that, as a matter of practice, for comparisons between neighbouring dates, the proportions of different wage-good items embraced in a representative worker's budget do not alter substantially; so that these difficulties do not arise, and all reasonably plausible methods of calculation yield nearly identical results. I have no quarrel with this reply as a defence of current practice. But it gives no help towards the solution of the theoretical difficulty. We are asking what does a wage-good unit mean and what does a 10 per cent change in real wages mean when the constitution of the representative workman's budget is altered. The reply that over short periods its constitution frequently is not altered—or not altered much—is interesting but irrelevant.

§ 6. I suggest that the correct answer is simply this: when, between two dates, there has occurred any sensible change in the proportions in which the representative wage-earner buys different sorts of wage-goods, the term a unit of wage-goods has no exact meaning. Except in the unlikely event of the relative prices of the several wage-good items having remained unaltered, this implies that changes of real wage-rates are incapable of exact measurement. We know that the representative wage-earner's money wage at the second date buys, say, 10 per cent less than before of the packet of goods contained in his first budget and, say, 12 per cent less of the packet contained in his second. We may rightly infer that his real wage has been reduced by not less than 10 per cent and by not more than 12 per cent. But we must not infer that it has been reduced by some percentage intermediate between these two. For the limits 10 per cent and 12 per cent display an objective ambiguity, such as, in relativity theory, attaches to the idea of simultaneity, not a gap in our knowledge. Hence, when, in Part II., we endeavour to relate proportionate changes in rates of real wages to proportionate changes in quantities of labour demanded, and specify, for this purpose, precise proportionate changes in rates of real wages, we shall be ignoring an ambiguity which in fact exists and asking questions to which, in the nature of the case, only approximate answers are possible.

CHAPTER V

§ 1. In any week, year or other interval of time the quantity of employment and the quantity of wage-goods or wage-good units, as here defined, that are paid out in wages, are correlated together in such wise that, if we start with a given volume of employment, that volume can only be varied in accordance with variations either in the rate of real wages or in the flow of wage-good units handed over per (say) week to wage-earners. More generally, if we write E for the quantity of employment, w for the average rate of real wage and F for the flow of wage-good units handed over to wage-earners in wages, in any week $E = \dfrac{F}{w}$.

§ 2. Let us begin by supposing that wage-goods consist of a single sort of item only. The total flow of wage-goods available in a country in any week or other interval is made up of the following items:

(1) Item P, the output of wage-goods in the country in that interval:

(2) Item $(I_1 + I_2 - M)$, the claims (I_1) on wage-goods abroad created by exports, *plus* the claims (I_2) on wage-goods abroad due as interest on previous investments, *minus* that part (M) of these claims that is utilised to buy non-wage-goods or securities, *i.e.* to take up new investments, abroad:

(3) Item S, the flow of wage-goods extracted net during the interval out of stocks held in shops and warehouses.

The first of these three items, P, is necessarily positive. The second, $(I_1 + I_2 - M)$, would be negative if the country were a net exporter of wage-goods: but, so far as England is con·

cerned, it is in fact always positive. The third item, S, may be either positive or negative, and is likely sometimes to be the one, sometimes the other.

§ 3. Of the total flow of wage-goods thus composed, namely the sum $(P + I_1 + I_2 - M + S)$, not all is devoted to paying wages to employed wage-earners. A portion C is reserved by non-wage-earners for their own personal consumption, and a portion $(G - B)$ is transferred by them to the wage-earning classes otherwise than in wage-payments, namely as income from investments, old-age pensions, sickness benefit and so on. In this last item the positive element G represents the total of non-wage payments accruing to wage-earners, and the negative element B the contributions towards pensions and sickness benefit made by wage-earners themselves. If then no payments were made to unemployed workers as such, the net flow of wage-goods, which pays the wages of employed workpeople, would be

$$P + (I_1 + I_2 - M) - C + S - (G - B);$$

and the volume of employment

$$E = \frac{P + (I_1 + I_2 - M) - C + S - (G - B)}{w}.$$

§ 4. There has also to be taken into account unemployment benefit and other payments (through Poor Law, private charity and so on) made specifically to unemployed persons as such, and, on the other side, the contributions made by employed workers towards providing for these things. If we write r for the benefit paid per unemployed man, t for the contribution per head of employed wage-earners, A for the total would-be wage-earning population, employed and unemployed together, we obtain a final general equation as follows:

$$E = \frac{P + I_1 + I_2 - M - C + S - (G - B)}{w} + \frac{Et}{w} - \frac{(A - E)r}{w}: . \qquad \text{(i)}$$

or

$$E = \frac{P + I_1 + I_2 - M - C + S - (G - B) - Ar}{w - t - r}. \qquad \text{(ii)}$$

§ 5. For the quantity of unemployment write U.

Then $U = (A - E)$.

$$\therefore U = \frac{A(w - t) - \{P + I_1 + I_2 - M - C + S - (G - B)\}}{w - t - r}. \quad . \quad (iii)$$

The percentage of unemployment

$$\frac{100 \, U}{A} = 100 \left\{ \frac{w - t}{w - t - r} - \frac{P + I_1 + I_2 - M - C + S - (G - B)}{A(w - t - r)} \right\}. \quad (iv)$$

Hence, obviously, unemployment is nil when, A being given, the average wage-rate w and the various other elements involved in our equation are so adjusted to one another that

$$w - t = \frac{P + I_1 + I_2 - M - C + S - (G - B)}{A}. \quad . \quad (v)$$

It will be observed that this condition is independent of the value of r, except in so far as r reacts to determine the values of some of the other variables, but not of the value of t. If $\{w - t\} > \dfrac{P + I_1 + I_2 - M - C + S - (G - B)}{A}$, some unemployment necessarily exists.

If r and t are both equal to 0, that is, if there is no unemployment benefit and, consequently, no wage-earners' contribution towards it, equations (iii) and (iv) reduce to

$$U = A - \frac{P + I_1 + I_2 - M - C + S - (G - B)}{w} \quad . \quad (vi)$$

$$\frac{100 \, U}{A} = 100 \left\{ 1 - \frac{(P + I_1 + I_2 - M - C + S - (G - B))}{Aw} \right\}. \quad (vii)$$

§ 6. Up to this point we have supposed that there is only a single sort of wage-good. This implies that each of the letters in the above formula represents so many completed wage-good units. In fact, of course, this is not so. The items P and so on are not necessarily numbers of completed wage-good units, but the values, in terms of wage-good units, of assorted bundles of wage-good items. The aggregate $\{P + I_1 + I_2 - M - C + S - (G - B)\}$, however, *is* necessarily a defined number of actual completed wage-good units, not merely a collection of diverse things having the value of this number.

§ 7. The propositions embodied in the equations of §§ 3-6, equally whether we allow there to be only one sort of wage-good or admit many sorts, are propositions, not of economics, but of arithmetic. Nevertheless, it will be found, they provide a convenient skeleton for analysis. It is essential, however, in making use of them to remember that, of the elements represented by the several letters, the most important are not independent quantities, such that we can isolate each of them in turn for separate study and then, adding together our separate results, exhaust the problem. On the contrary, the structure represented in the formula is complex, in such wise that changes in certain elements imply changes in others also. In particular it is vital to remember that the quantities P and I_1 are dependent on the rate of real wages. Moreover, we must note, they are dependent, not merely on the average rate of wages, but also on the way in which this average is constituted. Thus, if people's desire for home-made non-wage-goods expands, and if, as an indirect consequence, the real rate of wages asked for in the wage-good industries is raised, employment and output in these industries will be diminished. In the net result, though employment in non-wage-good industries must be increased, aggregate employment may remain exactly what it was before. Employment may be simply transferred from wage-good to non-wage-good industries, the reduction in the output of wage-goods together with the increase in the consumption of wage-goods by wage-earners being offset by a corresponding reduction in the use of wage-goods by non-wage-earners, namely in $(C + M)$. When these characteristics of our symbols are clearly understood, a certain resistance, which the reader may have felt to the above formulae on the ground that they seem to assert a modernised form of fixed wage-fund theory, may be expected to disappear. The arithmetical equations are not a substitute for, nor do they exercise any constraint upon, analysis. On the contrary, they merely set out in summary form certain consequences of the fundamental causal factors which analysis studies. The whole complex of relevant conditions, people's desires, the state of productive technique in the several centres, the state of foreign demand and so on, together with the rates of real wage established in the several centres, determine the elements denoted by the letters in our formulae. These are merely mediating channels *through* which, not *by* which, the process of the economic cosmos is ruled.

CHAPTER VI

THE CAUSATION OF UNEMPLOYMENT

§ 1. STATISTICS for this country demonstrate—and the same thing is known to be true in a general way elsewhere—that the percentage of unemployment varies somewhat between different seasons, and greatly between different years, but that there is always, over any long period, a certain intractable minimum below which the volume of unemployment, or, better, the percentage of unemployment, never falls. This intractable minimum, moreover, is not necessarily the same for all periods. Thus, whereas over the thirty years before the war the lowest annual figure for unemployment in this country was 2 per cent, for the ten years following the post-armistice boom the lowest was 8·1 per cent. These facts suggest that attempts to disentangle the causation of unemployment must be directed, not towards one, but towards two objectives. We wish to discover, if we can, both why the unemployment that exists at any time does exist and also why the amounts of it that exist are different at different times. It will not be found practicable to keep our treatment of the two questions rigidly separate. In this preliminary chapter, however, which is concerned to state, and not to attack, the problem, to distinguish between them makes for clarity.

§ 2. In popular discussions it is often tacitly assumed that the question why such and such an amount of unemployment exists at a particular time can be answered by naming some single "cause": high direct taxation, the absence—or presence—of a protective tariff, the presence in office of a Socialist government—or a Conservative government,—the return to the gold standard, or whatever the cry of the moment may be. No reflective person is entrapped by these crudities. He recognises, perforce, that not one, but many factors are at work. For him, as a plain man, such unemployment as prevails at any time is the consequence of a large number of separate causes, each of which is responsible for a part of it; responsible in the sense that, if it were removed, that part of unemployment would disappear, and if it is not removed, no matter what else is done, that part will not disappear. This view, though, of course, a great improvement on any "single cause" theory, is, none the less, seriously misleading. The unemployment that exists at any time is not the summed effect of a number of causes acting independently: it arises because a number of factors are balanced against one another in a particular way. To speak of the state of one of these factors as the cause, or even as *a* cause, is arbitrary; for that factor might remain as it is and yet the relevant part of unemployment disappear, provided that the state of one or more of the others was modified. When a ship is too low in the water, this effect is a combined result of the weight of the cargo and of the capacity of the ship. If the capacity of the ship is taken as given, the excess weight of the cargo is called the cause; but, if the weight of the cargo is taken as given, the inadequate capacity of the ship is called the cause. In truth neither of these things taken by itself is the cause, but the maladjustment between them. The evil will be cured if the maladjustment is removed either by decreasing the cargo in sufficient measure or by enlarging the ship in sufficient measure, or by decreasing the cargo and enlarging the ship in such measures that adjustment between them is attained. The effects of the various relevant factors in promoting unemployment are thus, in general, not independent of one another. We cannot say that A is responsible for so much and B for so much. For A is responsible for different amounts according to the state of B. If both A and B are removed together, the quantitative result will not be equal to the sum of the result of removing A while B is left and of removing B while A is left. It may even happen that, in a situation where by reducing both of two causal factors we should lessen unemployment, if one is

not reduced, by reducing the other we should make unemployment larger. Thus, if, in an industry where the method
of engaging labour is of the casual type, the wage-rate is
held artificially high and also some physical barrier hinders
workpeople from entering the industry from outside, to
remove the barrier, while leaving the artificial rate, would add
nothing to employment there and might draw people to unemployment there away from employment elsewhere. What
we have to look for, therefore, is not a sum of separate
causes of unemployment, each accountable for so much of it,
but rather a system of interconnected *factors* jointly responsible for the whole of it. As will appear presently, the
elements involved in this complex are numerous: the set, or
rather the interrelated scheme, of employers' real demand
functions for labour in various occupations and places; the
set of real wage-rates stipulated for by the workpeople; the
distribution of workpeople at different centres; and the degree of their mobility. It is not enough to know the state
of real demand for labour and the state of real wages. For
the quantity of employment is equal, not simply to the
quantity of labour demanded, but to this quantity minus
the number of unfilled vacancies, *i.e.* the posts for which, at
the ruling wage, employers wish to, but are not able to
find men. For the present, however, I am not concerned to
analyse the causal complex, but to drive home the point
that it *is* a complex and not a sum of causes.

§ 3. So far we have been considering the causation of unemployment conceived as a certain quantity at a certain
time. Let us now turn to the causation of differences in the
quantity of unemployment between two times. Since at each
time such unemployment as exists is the result of a causal
complex as described above, the difference between the two
quantities of unemployment is clearly the result of the
difference between the two complexes. This difference may
consist in a single item. If it does, we are able to find for a
change in unemployment a single cause, such as it is impossible ever to find for a *state* of unemployment. Moreover,
when the difference between the two complexes consists of
more than one item, it may be that the effects of the several

items are independent, so that the difference between the
quantities of unemployment prevailing in the two periods
can be attributed, so much to one item, so much to another.
On the other hand, it may be that the effects of the several
items are *not* independent. When that is so, the change in
unemployment is not attributable to separate causes, but to
a complex of causal factors. It will be found that the distinction between the state and changes in the state of unemployment has relevance to certain attempts, that have
recently been made, to determine by reference to statistics
the relation of wage-policy to unemployment in this country
during the post-war period.

§ 4. There remains a final point. When a magnitude
fluctuates on both sides of a zero line, if the fluctuations are
symmetrical about that line, the average value of the magnitude and the total net value of it, over periods covering equal
numbers of positive and negative fluctuations, are nil. The
range of the fluctuations makes no difference to these things.
But, when a magnitude cannot fall below the zero line, an
enlargement of the range of the fluctuations, if pressed
beyond a certain point, will carry with it an enlargement of
the average value of the magnitude and of the total net
amount of it. Unemployment obviously cannot fall to less
than nil. Hence any factor whose presence causes unemployment to fluctuate more widely than it would otherwise do
may—not must—also cause the average and the aggregate
amount of unemployment to be larger than they would
otherwise be.

PART II

THE SHORT PERIOD ELASTICITY OF THE REAL DEMAND FOR LABOUR

CHAPTER I

THIS Part is preliminary. Its general purpose is to investigate the differences, or variations, in quantity of labour demanded that are associated with given differences, or variations, in the rates of real wages for which workpeople stipulate, *when the relevant real demand functions for labour are given.* In Chapter II. the fundamental ideas involved in the inquiry will be set out. The ground thus prepared, in Chapters III.-V., the relation between given wage variations and variations in the quantity of labour demanded will be studied in particular occupations, without reference to any reactions that may be set up in other occupations and on the assumption that other things remain the same. In Chapters VI.-VII. it will be shown that the relation between differences, or variations, in the general wage-rate (assumed uniform) of all occupations and associated variations in the aggregate quantity of labour demanded cannot be ascertained by simply adding together independent studies of the type carried out in earlier chapters. In Chapters VIII. and IX. the problem presented by this more general relation is directly attacked. Finally, in Chapter X. the relation between the elasticity of the demand for labour in real terms and the elasticity in terms of money is examined. Over the main part of the discussion abstraction is made of the distinction between the several kinds of manual labour and of the fact that variations in the scale of output in an occupation may cause the comparative quantities of the several kinds that are employed to change. I have not followed Marshall's convention of making the elasticity of demand positive by defining it as $\dfrac{dx}{x} \div \dfrac{-dy}{y}$. I define it as $\dfrac{dx}{x} \div \dfrac{dy}{y}$. It is, therefore, in general, a negative quantity. Where, therefore, Marshall would say simply that one elasticity is larger than another, I am obliged, when there is any chance of ambiguity, to say that it is numerically larger.

CHAPTER II

DEMAND FUNCTIONS AND ELASTICITY OF DEMAND

§ 1. In an ideally simplified world we should be able to say, alike for particular occupations and for industry as a whole: There exists a certain definite real demand function for labour in any period, such that to each rate of real wage asked for by workpeople there corresponds a definite quantity of labour demanded. Hence the difference between any one given rate of real wage asked for and any other involves, other things being equal, a definite associated difference in the quantity of labour demanded. If we represent the demand function for labour by F, the two alternative wage-rates by W and W′, and the associated quantities of labour demanded by X and X′, we can write $F(X') - F(X) = W' - W$. If we know what the form of F is, *i.e.* what the shape of the demand curve is, over the relevant range, we can always calculate what percentage difference, as from a given starting-point, in the quantity of labour demanded is associated, other things being equal, with a given percentage difference in the real rate of wage for which workpeople stipulate.

§ 2. For very small—strictly for infinitesimal—differences in real wage-rate asked for the ratio

$$\frac{\text{proportionate change in quantity of labour demanded}}{\text{proportionate change in real rate of wage}}$$

is called the elasticity of demand for labour in respect of the initial quantity of labour or the initial real wage-rate. To determine this ratio for finite differences in the real wage asked for, it is not sufficient to know what the elasticity of demand in respect of the initial quantity or initial wage is.

We need to know the elasticities for every point over the range separating the two end-points in which we are interested. Write W and X for the original rate of real wage and quantity of labour demanded; and $W(1 - m)$ and $(X + h)$ for the new rate and new quantity. Write η for the elasticity of demand in respect of wage-rate W and quantity X. Let us first assume that the demand function is linear. Then we have

$$F(X) = W,$$
$$F(X + h) = W(1 - m).$$
$$\therefore h = -\frac{mW}{F'} = -\frac{mF(X)}{F'}.$$

But
$$\eta = \frac{F(X)}{XF'}.$$

$$\therefore \frac{h}{X} = -\eta m.$$

Alternatively let us assume that the demand function is not linear, but is, over the relevant range, a constant elasticity function. Again the relation between finite wage differences and finite demand differences can be calculated. With given wage differences, the proportionate excess of demand is somewhat smaller than it would be with a linear function for elasticities less than unity, and somewhat larger for elasticities greater than unity. The relation is given by the equation $w^{-\eta}x = C$. That is to say, if the real wage-rate falls from W to $W(1 - m)$, and the quantity of labour demanded consequently rises from X to $X(1 + r)$, we have

$$-\eta \log W + \log X = -\eta \log W(1 - m) + \log X(1 + r).$$

For small differences of wage or of quantity demanded the two assumptions of linearity and of constant elasticity give nearly the same result, except when the elasticities are very low. Unless we have special knowledge to the contrary, it is reasonable to suppose that over small ranges one or other of them is likely to approximate to the fact. With either of them, apart from very low elasticities, the ratio

$$\frac{\text{proportionate change in quantity}}{\text{proportionate change of wage}}$$

works out, for small differences, at approximately the value of the elasticity itself. Therefore, for finite differences, as well as for infinitesimal ones, provided they are small, we may treat the elasticity of demand in respect of either of the two wage-rates under review as a rough measure of this ratio.[1] For substantial proportionate differences either of wage-rate or of quantity demanded we are not, of course, entitled to assume that the above ratio will approximate to the elasticity at either end of the relevant demand range. Nor have we any reason to suppose that at different points on the demand curve substantially separate from one another the elasticity of demand will be nearly the same. Hence we must not infer, from the fact that a 2 per cent wage cut starting from one level carries, say, a 3 per cent expansion in the quantity of labour demanded, that an equal per cent cut starting from a different level will do this.

§ 3. The ideally simplified world, to which the foregoing observations refer, is unfortunately far removed from the world of real life. One difficulty is that the quantity of labour demanded within a given period is not necessarily a simple function of the wage-rate then ruling. It may be also a function of the wage-rate which is expected to rule in the near future. Thus, if the wage-rate falls from one level to another in an industry engaged in making goods that are durable and (or) the purchase of which can be easily postponed, the consequential change in the quantity of labour

[1] The following table gives the percentage deficiency in wage-rates associated with a 10 per cent excess of demand for various elasticities of demand in respect of the initial (lower) quantity of labour demanded, upon the assumptions that over the relevant range the demand function is (1) linear, (2) a constant elasticity function.

Elasticity.	Percentage Wage Deficiency associated with a 10 % Excess of Demand with Linear Functions.	Percentage Wage Deficiency associated with a 10 % Excess of Demand with Constant Elasticity Functions.
	%	%
$-\frac{1}{10}$	[100]	74
$-\frac{1}{2}$	20	33
-1	10	9·1
-2	5	4·6
-5	2	1·8
-10	1	·95

demanded will be different according as the wage-rate is expected (1) quickly to revert to the old level, (2) to stay for a long while at the new level, or (3) soon to fall still further. When the last sort of expectation prevails, we may easily be confronted with the apparent paradox of a large drop in the wage-rate associated with a large contraction in the quantity of labour demanded. Similar considerations apply, of course, to upward movements in the wage-rate. It follows that the type of analysis indicated in § 1 cannot claim generality. It is only appropriate when conditions are such that the actual wage differences are the dominant influences at work and the part played by expected changes can be disregarded.

§ 4. There is, however, a more far-reaching difficulty than this. In § 1 it was supposed that a given wage-rate carried with it demand for a given quantity of labour, so to speak, *sub specie aeternitatis*. In fact this is not so. No doubt, for a stationary state in long-period equilibrium a single rate of real wage would always rule everywhere and a single quantity of labour per week or year would always be demanded in each several occupation. But even in a state initially stationary, if we suppose the real wage-rate asked for in any particular occupation to be shifted from the equilibrium position, the consequence will not be a single new quantity of labour demanded eternally. The new real wage-rate will be associated with different quantities of labour demanded at different intervals after it has been established. Originally, *ex hypothesi*, conditions were such that capital equipment in the occupation, as it became worn out, was always exactly made good in identical form—neither more nor less. Suppose that the shift of real wage-rate has been an upward shift. This implies, in general, that advantage can be gained by altering some of the forms of capital equipment in the occupation, and substituting, in some measure, equipment for labour. While this process is going on, the quantity of labour demanded in the industry will be progressively contracted. Moreover, the effect of a given rise in the real price of a finished product, consequent upon a given rise in the real wage-rate asked for by the workers engaged in making it, does not, in general, produce a single effect on the quantity demanded, but a relatively small effect in the first instance followed by a larger one as alternative means of satisfying the relevant want are discovered or made use of, or, it may be, as people's tastes are modified by their new experience. Thus, when a new real rate of wage is established in a particular occupation—and the same thing is obviously true of industry as a whole,—the quantity of labour demanded is not a fixed quantity, standing in a single determinate relation to the real rate of wage, but a series of quantities falling for some time if the new wage is higher than the old, and, in like manner, rising for some time if it is lower than the old. If our starting-point is not the equilibrium position of a stationary state, but something different, the relation between real wage-rate and quantity of labour demanded is variable with time, not merely for the new wage-rate but also for the original one. In general, then, this relation cannot be properly expressed by a function of one variable. Along with the real wage-rate and the quantity of labour, there is involved the length of time for which the wage-rate has been ruling. We must write, not $w = F(x)$, but $w = F(x, t)$. In the language of elasticities there is not, in respect of any assigned volume of employment, a single elasticity of demand for labour, but a whole family of elasticities with different members referred to different time intervals. In given conditions, when one real wage-rate has been ruling for a certain time and another is substituted for it, there is, when any given interval has been allowed for adjustment, a definite associated change in the quantity of labour demanded. But it is impossible to specify what the change will be without reference to this time interval.

§ 5. For the purposes of this book we are primarily interested in the relation between wage-rate and quantity demanded in respect of what may be called the short period—more roughly, in short-period elasticities of demand. The short period does not mean a certain defined number of days, the same for all occupations, but a period such that, in respect of it, over the field of any particular investigation, industrial equipment, both in form and quantity, may properly be regarded as more or less fixed. Short-period elasticities are, in general, limiting elasticities, in the sense that, if a given variation in real wage-rate is associated with such and such a variation in quantity of labour demanded in respect of the short period, it will be associated with a larger variation in respect of periods long enough to allow of complete adjustment being made to the new conditions. Hence, in general, whenever we see reason to conclude that the short-period elasticity of demand for labour is (numerically) large, or exceeds some specified figure, this conclusion will hold *a fortiori* for the elasticities relevant to longer periods.

CHAPTER III

THE DETERMINATION OF THE SHORT-PERIOD ELASTICITY OF
DEMAND FOR LABOUR IN PARTICULAR OCCUPATIONS, IN
RESPECT OF A GIVEN REAL WAGE-RATE, IN CONDITIONS
OF FREE COMPETITION

§ 1. PROVIDED that employers in any centre are not in a position to exercise monopolistic power against their customers, the quantity of labour demanded there at any given rate of real wage is such that the value in terms of wage-goods of its marginal net product (*i.e.* of the difference made to the total physical yield by the marginal man with the help of existing equipment)[1] approximates to that rate of wage *plus* the rate of employers' contribution to sickness and unemployment insurance. Henceforth, for economy of language, I shall use the term wage to include these elements, so that reference to them need not again be made. If, then, conditions of competition being assumed, we write x for the quantity of labour employed in any occupation and $F'(x)$ for the rate of wage, as above defined, in terms of wage-goods, the elasticity of the real demand for labour in respect of a quantity x may be written $E_d = \dfrac{F'(x)}{xF''(x)}$. The purpose of this chapter is not to provide any concrete information, but to set out in an orderly way the questions that must be answered if we are to determine the value of E_d, not in industry in general, but in any given occupation.

---

[1] It should be noted that this is not the same as the marginal net product of long-period analysis. That allows for an adjustment in the form, though not in the quantity, of capital equipment. (Cf. *Economics of Welfare*, Part II. chap. ii.)

§ 2. To make this task reasonably simple, abstraction is made of the fact that, in general, several different sorts of labour will be at work. It is postulated that there is only one sort. It is further postulated that each unit of finished product uses the same amount, say one unit, of raw material, whatever the quantity of finished product that is being produced. Each unit of finished product then consists of one unit of raw material *plus* one unit of what I shall call *processing*, namely, work done on it by labour with the help of the available capital equipment. The differences in the quantity of wear-and-tear suffered by equipment and in the costs of non-manual labour employed, that are associated with differences in output, are ignored, as being, in general, of secondary importance. Moreover, in the present and following chapters the fact that production occupies time is ignored; the consequences of this fact being postponed for consideration in Chapter V. In the short period the demand price per unit, in terms of wage-goods, of y units of *processing* is then equal to the demand price per unit of y units of new output at works of the finished product *minus* the supply price per unit of y units of raw material. Thus, if $\psi'(y)$ be the demand price of y units of new output at works of finished product and $f'(y)$ the supply price of y units of raw material, the demand price of y units of *processing* is $\{\psi'(y) - f'(y)\}$. Let us write x for the number of units of labour that yield y units of processing, so that $y = \phi(x)$.[1] It follows that the demand price per unit of labour, that is, the payment per unit in terms of wage-goods, that is offered

$$= w = \left\{ \frac{d\psi\{\phi(x)\}}{dx} - \frac{df\{\phi(x)\}}{dx} \right\}. \qquad . \qquad . \qquad \text{(i)}$$

[1] It appears at first sight that the concept of this—as we may say—productivity function of labour in respect of processing is wholly unambiguous. In fact, however, it is not. The output of service of 500 men working 8 hours a day is not exactly the same as that of 1000 men working equally hard for 4 hours a day: nor is the output of 500 men working slackly for 8 hours a day exactly the same as that of the same number of men working proportionately harder over a shorter day or a shorter week. There is not, indeed, likely to be much difference between these several outputs. Nevertheless for strict accuracy we ought to postulate a certain length of working day and a certain degree of working speed—the length of working day and degree of working speed that in fact exist—and conceive the productivity function of labour as relative to these things.

If, therefore, thus far modifying the notation of the preceding chapter, we write $F'(x)$ for the demand price per unit of x units of labour, we have the equation

$$F'(x) = \left\{ \frac{d\psi\{\phi(x)\}}{dx} - \frac{df\{\phi(x)\}}{dx} \right\}. \qquad . \qquad . \quad \text{(ii)}$$

On this basis a formula for the (short-period) elasticity of demand for labour in terms of wage-goods in respect of any given real wage-rate, or, what comes to the same thing, in respect of any given quantity of labour demanded, is easily obtained. The elasticity in respect of x units of labour—called here E_d—by definition $= \dfrac{F'(x)}{xF''(x)}$. Hence, in respect of x labour, the elasticity of demand may be written

$$E_d = \left\{ \frac{d\psi\{\phi(x)\}}{dx} - \frac{df\{\phi(x)\}}{dx} \right\} \div x \left\{ \frac{d^2\psi\{\phi(x)\}}{dx^2} - \frac{d^2f\{\phi(x)\}}{dx^2} \right\}$$

$$= \left\{ \frac{d\psi\{\phi(x)\}}{d\phi(x)} - \frac{df\{\phi(x)\}}{d\phi x} \right\} \phi'(x) \div x \left[\left\{ \frac{d\psi\{\phi(x)\}}{d\phi(x)} \right. \right.$$

$$\left. - \frac{df\{\phi(x)\}}{d\phi(x)} \right\} \phi''(x) + \left\{ \frac{d^2\psi\{\phi(x)\}}{d\phi(x)^2} - \frac{d^2f\{\phi(x)\}}{d\phi(x)^2} \right\} \{\phi'(x)\}^2 \left. \right].$$

§ 3. This ungainly general formula can be reduced to more intelligible shape as follows. Write E_f for the elasticity of the demand, in terms of wage-goods, for new output at works of the finished product, E_s for the elasticity of the supply of the raw material—of which, *ex hypothesi*, one unit is always used in one unit of finished product—and E_p for the elasticity of demand for units of *processing*, of which, also *ex hypothesi*, one unit is always used in one unit of finished product, in respect of $\phi(x)$ units of finished product. Further write η for the elasticity of the (short-period) productivity function of labour in respect of *processing* when x units are being employed: and finally write m for the demand price per unit of finished product at works divided by the price of the raw material used in it when $\phi(x)$ units are being produced. Then we have the following equations:

(1)
$$\mathrm{E}_f = \frac{1}{\phi(x)} \cdot \frac{d\psi\{\phi(x)\}}{d\,p(x)} \div \frac{d^2\psi\{\phi(x)\}}{d\phi(x)^2}.\ ^1$$

(2)
$$\mathrm{E}_s = \frac{1}{\phi(x)} \cdot \frac{df\{\phi(x)\}}{d\phi(x)} \div \frac{d^2f\{\phi(x)\}}{d\phi(x)^2}.$$

(3)
$$\mathrm{E}_p = \frac{1}{\phi(x)} \left\{ \frac{d\psi\{\phi(x)\}}{d\phi(x)} - \frac{df\{\phi(x)\}}{d\phi(x)} \right\} \div \left\{ \frac{d^2\psi\{\phi(x)\}}{d\phi(x)^2} - \frac{df^2\{\phi(x)\}}{d\phi(x)^2} \right\}.$$

(4)
$$\eta = \frac{\phi'(x)}{x\phi''(x)}.$$

By algebraical manipulation of these expressions we obtain

(5)
$$\frac{1}{\mathrm{E}_p} = \frac{1}{m-1} \cdot \left\{ \frac{m}{\mathrm{E}_f} - \frac{1}{\mathrm{E}_s} \right\}.$$

(6)
$$\frac{1}{\mathrm{E}_d} = \frac{1}{\mathrm{E}_p} \cdot \left\{ \frac{x\phi'(x)}{\phi(x)} \right\} + \frac{1}{\eta}.$$

Hence, (7)
$$\frac{1}{\mathrm{E}_d} = \frac{1}{m-1} \left[\left\{ \frac{m}{\mathrm{E}_f} - \frac{1}{\mathrm{E}_s} \right\} \cdot \frac{x\phi'(x)}{\phi(x)} \right] + \frac{1}{\eta}.$$

§ 4. Now $\dfrac{x\phi'(x)}{\phi(x)}$ is the marginal amount of *processing* done by x men multiplied by x and divided by the total quantity of *processing* done by x men. In competitive conditions, where the wage is equal to the value of the marginal net product as defined in § 1,[2] this fraction is obviously equal to the total money wages of the x men divided by the money value of their total net product—that is, by the money value of the finished goods into which the *processing* enters *minus* the money value of the raw material employed. This in turn is equal to the money rate of wage divided by the money value of the net output per head. Write then w for the money wage and q for the money value of net output per head. Then equation (7) becomes our final equation

(8)
$$\frac{1}{\mathrm{E}_d} = \frac{1}{m-1} \cdot \left[\left\{ \frac{m}{\mathrm{E}_f} - \frac{1}{\mathrm{E}_s} \right\} \cdot \frac{w}{q} \right] + \frac{1}{\eta}.$$

[1] For $\dfrac{d\phi(x)}{d\phi(x)} \div \phi(x)$ reduces to $\dfrac{1}{\phi(x)}$.

[2] When employers act as monopolists towards their customers that condition is not satisfied. Cf. *post*, Chap. IV.

§ 5. The general inferences deducible from this equation may be set out as follows. We know that E_d, E_f and η are negative, that E_s may be either positive or negative, and that $m > 1$. Hence we may conclude that E_d is (numerically) larger,

(1) the larger (numerically) is E_f: *i.e.* the more elastic is the demand for the finished commodity at works:

(2) the larger, if positive, and the smaller, if negative, is E_s: *i.e.* the more elastic is the supply of the relevant raw material:

(3) the larger is m:[1] *i.e.* the less important is the part played by the raw material in the cost of the finished product:

(4) the larger (numerically) is η:

(5) the smaller is $\dfrac{w}{q}$:

(6) Finally, if $\eta = 0$, E_d also $= 0$. That is, if the productivity function of labour in the occupation under review is perfectly inelastic, so also is the demand for labour in terms of wage-good units.

§ 6. These, however, are only qualitative statements. Is it possible to obtain data that will enable us, from equation (8), to determine quantitatively the value of E_d for the group of workpeople engaged in a particular industry at any given time? Some of the required *data* are accessible. Thus there should be no difficulty, for most occupations, in ascertaining the value of m, which, *ex hypothesi*, does not vary over short periods. Further, $\dfrac{w}{q}$ is often obtainable. For the Census of Production records the average money rate of wages paid and the average money value of output per head both in 1907 and 1924 for a large number of industries. Of course these values vary from time to time, but the ratio between them is probably fairly stable: so that, apart from abnormal disturbances, Census of Production figures could probably be used without serious error for a considerable period after

[1] Subject to the condition, as found by differentiation, that E_s is positive, or, if negative, is numerically greater than E_f. If E_s is negative and equal to E_f, the magnitude of m is immaterial to E_d.

they had been calculated. The evaluation of E_f, E_s and η, which are, of course, different in respect of different amounts of output, is, however, a more difficult matter.

§ 7. For commodities in the nature of direct personal services the demand function ψ *for new output at works of the finished product* is identical with the contemporary demand function of the final buyers for their total purchases of the product, and the elasticity E_f, in respect of any given quantity, is thus identical with the final buyers' elasticity of demand for their total purchases. For other commodities, however, this is not so. Write E'_f for the elasticity of the final buyers' demand for the commodity. This differs from E_f. For the final buyers' purchases comprise, along with the commodity as issuing from works, a quantity of wholesalers', transporters' and retailers' services, which varies greatly for different commodities, but constitutes, for some of them, a very large part of their total value. For purposes of a rough approximation we may postulate that the proportion of the total value contributed by the cost of these services remains constant in the face of the short-period variations in consumption that follow from changes in the wage-rate. Let us call the total value divided by the cost of distributors' services k. Then, if there were no variations in the stocks of the commodity held by dealers, E_f would obviously be equal to $\frac{1}{k} \cdot E'_f$. For a number of commodities the statistical task of ascertaining roughly the value of k need not, I think, present any insuperable difficulty.

§ 8. Again, for commodities that are not instantly perishable, variations occur in the stocks held by dealers and, in some cases, by manufacturers themselves. In normal conditions the quantity of these stocks will be approximately constant, so that neither additions to, nor subtractions from, them are made. But, if, through a wage cut—of a sort, that people do not regard as permanent—real cost of production is reduced below the normal, some absorption into stocks is likely to take place; in the converse case some emission out of stocks. Moreover, it is to be expected in general that, even when we do not start from a position of normality, until stocks are, on the one hand reduced to nearly nothing, or on the other hand expanded to near the maximum that people are in any event prepared to hold, a given percentage change in price will cause the inflow to or outflow from stocks to vary by a larger percentage than that by which consumption varies. It follows that, over a range of prices not too far on either side of the normal, the elasticity of demand for new output at works of the finished product—our E_f—will not be equal to, but will be somewhat larger than, $\frac{1}{k} E'_f$.

The excess of E_f above this quantity will be larger or smaller according as the commodity in question is more or less well adapted to be made for stock. It is easy to see that those commodities are best adapted for this that do not perish rapidly in the physical sense and are not subject to the vagaries of fashion; and also that standardised parts, capable of being used in many different types of some finished good, can sometimes be safely made for stock though the finished goods could not be.[1] But no statistical machinery is available for measuring the gap between E_f and $\frac{1}{k} E'_f$ with precision. Moreover, it must be remembered, in so far as high elasticity of demand for labour is due to changes in stocks, the effect of a wage reduction in increasing the quantity of labour demanded at the time is in part offset by a contrary effect later on, when output that has been temporarily absorbed into stocks is discharged on to the market.[2]

---

[1] Cf. Douglas and Director, *The Problem of Unemployment*, p. 101.

[2] Suppose that the supply function of a commodity in respect of each successive year is $f(p)$, and the demand function $\phi(p)$: that in equilibrium the price is p and that the cost of carrying a unit of the commodity from one year to the next is r. In consequence of a reduction in the wage-rate in a certain year, which is not, and is not expected to be, repeated, the supply function in that year becomes $f(p+t)$. Let us make the assumption that both functions are linear and that f' is positive and ϕ' negative. Write h for the fall in price to consumers below p in the initial year and n for the number of times that r exactly divides into h with or without remainder. We have then the following equalities:

(1) the addition to production which the wage-reduction in the initial year would bring about then if the price were unaltered = tf';

(2) the contraction in aggregate production over the $(n+1)$ relevant years due to contraction of price below p.

§ 9. The problem of determining, from statistics for particular commodities, the elasticity of demand *in terms of money* for consumers' purchases of these commodities in the neighbourhood of the quantities that are currently purchased, is one to which in America and Germany considerable attention has recently been paid. The present writer is responsible for two suggested methods, one depending on general price and quantity figures,[1] the other on the facts collected in family budgets.[2] There is some hope that, by these or other methods, rough approximations for this elasticity may gradually be obtained for a number of commodities. It is obvious that for any ordinary individual commodity the money elasticity for various stages in the trade cycle of demand is approximately equal to the elasticity E'_f in terms of wage-goods. It is equally obvious that, when E'_f is determined, an important step will have been taken towards determining E_f.

§ 10. The determination of E_s, the elasticity of supply of the relevant raw material for any given quantity of output, is subject to the same kind of difficulty, when the material is capable of being made for stock, as the determination of E_f. There is an elasticity E'_s, from which E_s is derived. For the

$$= \left\{ (n+1)h - \frac{(n+1)n}{2}r \right\} f';$$

(3) the addition to aggregate consumption over the $(n+1)$ relevant years due to the contraction of price below p

$$= \left\{ (n+1)h - \frac{(n+1)n}{2}r \right\} \left\{ -\phi' \right\}.$$

Since the sum of (2) and (3) must obviously be equal to (1), it follows that the aggregate addition to consumption, and so also to production, over the whole of the $(n+1)$ years $= tf' \cdot \dfrac{\phi'}{f' - \phi'}$. Hence in the conditions postulated the aggregate effect on production over all the $(n+1)$ years of the reduction in wage-rate in the first year is independent of the value of r. That is to say, *it is the same whether the commodity is capable of being made for stock or not*. In conditions of diminishing return this implies that the total quantity of labour demanded (and employed) is somewhat larger if the commodity can be made for stock than if it cannot. It should be noted that, if f' is nil or negative, the conditions proper to the above analysis fail; and the aggregate effect on production of the supposed wage reduction is larger for a commodity that can than for a similar commodity that cannot be made for stock.

[1] The statistical determination of demand curves, *Economic Journal*, December 1930.

[2] *The Economics of Welfare*, Appendix II.

evaluation of E'_s statistical methods have been proposed. But the difficulties, principally connected with the element of time, are more serious than they are with E_f, and, in my opinion, have not yet been overcome. It should be observed, however, that, when m is large, that is to say when the price of raw material is only a small part of the price of the finished product, considerable divergencies in our estimate of the value of E_s will make little difference to the figure we arrive at for E_d.

§ 11. There remains η, the elasticity of the productivity of labour in an industry in respect of *processing*, derived from the function ϕ. If we were entitled to assume that the productivity function in our occupation was linear, so that $\phi''(x)$ was constant for all values of x, and likewise if we were entitled to assume that this function was a constant elasticity function throughout, the value of η, in respect of the quantity of labour actually employed at any time, could—conditions of competition being assumed—be calculated directly from a knowledge of w, the money wage-rate, and q, the value of net output per head. On the assumption of linearity $\eta = -\dfrac{w}{2(q-w)}$;[1] on the assumption of constant elasticity—an assumption which is only permissible if η is (numerically) greater than 1, since otherwise it would imply infinite cost per unit for all outputs—$\eta = -\dfrac{q}{q-w}$.[2] Plainly, however, though it may well be a legitimate approximation to posit linearity or constant elasticity over small pieces of the productivity function, *i.e.* between points on the curve depicting this function that are fairly close together, we have no right to postulate either condition for the whole length of the curve, or rather—for

---

[1] For $\eta = \dfrac{\phi'(x)}{x\phi''(x)} = -\dfrac{\phi'(x)}{2\dfrac{\phi(x)}{x} - \phi'(x)} = -\dfrac{w}{2q-w}$.

[2] I am indebted for this calculation to Mr. R. F. Kahn, of King's College, Cambridge. It will be noticed that, since q is always $>w$, the elasticity, as calculated on the constant elasticity hypothesis, is always (numerically) larger than the elasticity as calculated on the straight-line hypothesis. Therefore, when the straight-line hypothesis gives an elasticity (numerically) greater than unity, the hypothesis of a constant elasticity function is always a possible one.

E

that is all we require—for that part of the length that covers all values of x less than the value actually attained. We cannot, therefore, make use of this method of deduction. Nor is there available any other machinery of statistical technique. It is necessary to rely on those rough generalisations from experience that are called common sense.

§ 12. Proceeding along this route, we observe that, if in a given occupation there was no capital equipment and no work of non-wage-earners, but the services of workpeople consisted exclusively of running so many yards or lifting so many pounds through ten feet per day, the productivity function would clearly have an infinite elasticity for all quantities of labour. The "output" of 1000 men would be exactly 1000 times that of one man (of given quality). An infinite number of new men might be added to the labour force without the marginal output diminishing in any degree. When there is capital equipment, this is not so. Two broad general statements may, however, be made.

The first refers to the comparative elasticities of the short-period productivity functions for labour in different occupations in respect of outputs in the neighbourhood of "normal capacity". Normal capacity for any occupation means the rate of output which the equipment is designed to yield at least average supplementary *plus* prime cost per unit. In respect of normal capacity the short-period elasticity of the productivity function is different in different occupations. In general it is likely to be larger the larger is the part played by capital equipment relatively to labour. Consider, for example, an enormous electric power plant operated by 100 men. A given change in the number of men at work will evidently make a larger difference to marginal output than would be made by an equal change in a concern normally adjusted to the same number of workpeople but with smaller capital equipment. This fact is of more than mere abstract interest. For it is well known, on the one hand, that this country's industry is much more heavily capitalised than it was a hundred years ago, on the other hand, that it is much less heavily capitalised—there is much less horse-power per wage-earner—than in the industries of the United States at the present time.

The second general statement refers to the comparative elasticities of the productivity function in a given occupation in respect of different outputs. In all sorts of occupations, whether heavily capitalised or not, if at any time a quantity of labour is at work substantially greater than that adapted to capacity, the marginal productivity of labour will plainly increase rapidly as the quantity of labour is reduced. That is to say, the short-period productivity function of labour in respect of such quantities will be highly inelastic. But, if we start with a quantity of labour substantially below that adapted to "capacity", this is not so. Even if reduction of the quantity of labour employed means a thinner spreading of labour over the whole body of existing equipment, all of which is retained in use, marginal productivity need not, over this range, rise very much as employment declines. In fact, as labour is withdrawn from work, bits of equipment are withdrawn also. In these circumstances there is, *a fortiori*, little reason for believing that variations in the quantity of labour employed, within the range intervening between something less than capacity output and a very deep depression, will involve other than small variations in marginal productivity. In other words, over this range, in a great many occupations, the (short period) productivity function seems likely to be very elastic.

§ 13. We have thus considered in turn all the elements which were found in § 4 to determine the value of E_d for the labour employed in any particular industry on any given occasion. The result is meagre. It may be hoped, however, that, with the progress of statistical analysis, better means for calculating these several elements will gradually be evolved, so that approximate estimates of E_d, at all events in some occupations, will become obtainable.

§ 14. One further point may be added. Throughout the foregoing discussion we have supposed that changes in the rate of real wages do not involve changes in the physical or psychical capacity—willingness to work—of the wage-earners. They may, however, involve such changes. If they do, certain further complications are introduced. In the simplest case let us suppose that a given wage reduction involves an exactly proportionate reduction in capacity. In these circumstances the wage-rate per capacity unit is unchanged, but the number of capacity units per man is reduced. The same quantity of capacity units being employed, this implies that the number of man-hours of work that are employed is increased; and unemployment correspondingly diminished. Conversely, when the real wage-rate is raised and, as a consequence, capacity rises proportionately, employment is diminished and unemployment is increased. In the general case let us suppose that a reduction of wage-rate per man from w to $w(1 - m)$ involves a decrease in the number of capacity units per man from 1 to $(1 - h)$. This means that the wage-rate per capacity unit changes from w to $w \cdot \dfrac{1 - m}{1 - h}$. Then, $\phi(w)$ being written for the aggregate quantity of employment at wage w, the number of capacity units employed changes from $\phi(w)$ to $\phi\left\{w \cdot \dfrac{1 - m}{1 - h}\right\}$. The number of men employed, therefore, changes from $C\phi(w)$ to $\dfrac{C}{1 - h} \phi\left\{w \cdot \dfrac{1 - m}{1 - h}\right\}$. There is, therefore, an increase in employment if $\phi\left\{w\dfrac{1 - m}{1 - h}\right\} > (1 - h)\phi(w)$. This condition may or not be realised according to the relative values of m and h and the form of ϕ.

CHAPTER IV

VARIATIONS IN THE QUANTITY OF LABOUR DEMANDED IN PARTICULAR OCCUPATIONS IN RELATION TO VARIATIONS IN THE REAL RATE OF WAGE UNDER MONOPOLY

§ 1. If the employers in any occupation are in a position to exercise monopolistic power against the purchasers of their goods, it will, in general, pay them to restrict output and so to restrict employment. Consequently, the number of men demanded at a given wage-rate is no longer that number the value of whose marginal net product, in the sense of Chapter II. § 1, is equal to the wage-rate. In general the number is smaller than this, and is expressed by a formula different from that appropriate to conditions of free competition. Using the same notation as before, we find that employers seek to maximise their net monopoly revenue expressed in wage-goods, namely

$$\left\{\frac{d\psi\{\phi(x)\}}{d\phi(x)} - \frac{df\{\phi(x)\}}{d\phi(x)}\right\}\phi(x) - wx.$$

$$\therefore \ \left\{\frac{d\psi\{\phi(x)\}}{d\phi(x)} - \frac{df\{\phi(x)\}}{d\phi(x)}\right\}\phi'(x)$$

$$+ \left\{\frac{d^2\psi\{\phi(x)\} - d^2f\{\phi(x)\}}{d\phi(x)^2}\right\}\phi'(x).\phi(x) = w. \quad . \quad (i)$$

When the demand for new output at works of the finished product of our occupation in terms of wage-goods is perfectly elastic and the supply of the raw material is also perfectly elastic, that is, when $\dfrac{d^2\psi\{\phi(x)\}}{d\phi(x)^2}$ and $\dfrac{d^2f\{\phi(x)\}}{d\phi(x)^2} = 0$, the second half of the left-hand side of the foregoing

53

expression vanishes; and the above equation is identical with equation (i) given in Chapter III. § 2 for conditions of free competition. In these conditions the employees in the industry cannot possibly gain by restricting output below the amount at which marginal yield and marginal cost are equal, any more than they could do if they were producing their commodity, not for sale, but for their own use. When, however, employers in one occupation are selling their commodity against the output of many occupations, the demand for it in terms of this output is sure to have some degree of negative elasticity.[1] Therefore $\left\{ \dfrac{d^2\psi\{\phi(x)\}}{d\phi(x)^2} - \dfrac{d^2f\{\phi(x)\}}{d\phi(x)^2} \right\}$ is negative: and the root of equation (i) above is necessarily smaller than the root of equation (i) on p. 42. That is to say, less labour will be demanded than would be demanded if free competition among employers prevailed.

§ 2. To determine the comparative quantities of labour that will be demanded under free competition and monopoly respectively in certain artificially simplified conditions is not difficult. Thus it is easy to show that, if ψ'' and f'' are both constant, that is to say if the functions ψ and f are both linear, and if also ϕ' is constant, that is to say if the *processing* contributed by labour is provided under conditions of constant return, the root of equation (i) above is one-half of the root of equation (i) on p. 42. That is to say, in these conditions the quantity of labour demanded under monopoly is, at every wage-rate, one-half of the quantity demanded under free competition. This same result—it being remembered that ϕ' is constant—can be derived directly from the familiar proposition that, with linear demand and supply functions, *output* under monopoly is always one-half of output under free competition. But, if these artificially simplified conditions do not rule, the proportion of labour demanded under monopoly to labour demanded under free competition is different for different rates of real wage. When the func-

---

[1] This is in accordance with the general principle that, as against changes in the purchase of any commodity on which only a small part of people's incomes are spent, the marginal utility of money may be regarded as approximately constant (cf. Marshall, *Principles of Economics*, Book V. chap. ii. § 3).

tions ψ and f are linear, but ϕ' is not constant, we can say further that the proportionate difference in quantity of labour demanded, associated with a given proportionate shift from an initial wage W, is smaller under monopoly than under free competition if ϕ'' is negative (*i.e.* with diminishing returns), and larger if ϕ'' is positive (*i.e.* with increasing returns). With non-linear functions the problem is more complex and the above proposition is not necessarily true. There is in all circumstances a presumption that a given wage deficiency will be associated with a smaller absolute excess of labour demanded in an industry where monopolistic restriction is at work than in a similar industry where it is not at work; since the scale of activity of the monopolistic industry is smaller. But there is no general presumption about the proportionate excess demanded.

§ 3. If we choose, we may proceed in the manner of Chapter III. and derive the elasticity of demand for labour, in respect of any quantity x, when employers are exercising monopoly power against their customers, and then use this elasticity as a means of ascertaining the variations in quantity of labour demanded that will be associated with given small variations in wage-rates. The general formula for this elasticity, derived from equation (i) on page 53, is very complex and cumbrous. If we make the assumption that the functions ψ and f are linear, so that ψ'' and f'' are constant, a number of terms in the denominator of the general formula disappear. In order, however, to obtain a reasonably simple expression, it is necessary to assume further that ϕ' is constant, that is to say that the *processing* contributed by labour is provided under conditions of constant return. With this assumption we find, writing E'_d for the elasticity of demand for x labour in respect of wage w under monopoly and E_d for the elasticity in respect of this wage under competition, that $E'_d = E_d$. This implies that the elasticity of demand in respect of quantity x of labour under monopoly is equal to the elasticity of demand in respect of quantity $2x$ under competition. It is easy to show further that, if ϕ'' is positive, *i.e.* under conditions of diminishing return, E'_d is less than E_d; in opposite conditions greater than E_d.

CHAPTER V

THE DEFERRED CHARACTER OF THE RETURN TO LABOUR

§ 1. IN the preceding chapters we have assumed that, when, in any occupation, labour is set to work, the resultant product is instantaneously available on the market. In real life, however, in all occupations except the rendering of direct services, for which no preparation has to be made, the process of production is not instantaneous, but takes a certain time. There is always an interval between the setting to work of a man and the emergence, in consequence of his work, of any finished product, whether for consumption or as a productive instrument for the machine of industry. If wages are paid contemporaneously with work, this implies that *some* interval between wage payments and associated output is bound to elapse. Even if wages are paid weekly, *i.e.* if work is paid for on the average three days after it has been performed, there will, for most sorts of commodities, be an interval. For complete production processes that occupy a period so short as three days are not common. Hence, in general, we may properly postulate the existence of some interval, which we may call, if we will, the period of gestation, and the length of which will vary in different occupations. The term period of gestation in this connection is not, however, a really appropriate one. It suggests that an act of work takes place and that then, after an interval, during which Nature alone has been labouring, fruit emerges. This represents the facts fairly well in some agricultural occupations. There is the work of ploughing and sowing, and then, some months later, the grain is ready for harvest. But in mechanical industries this kind of thing does not happen. The material that is being developed

into some product useful to man is being handled and worked
at throughout the whole of this so-called period of gestation.
Moreover, the quantity of labour required may vary considerably at different stages of the process; so that the distance between the completion of that process and the laying
of the first stone may bear all sorts of different relations to
the distance between this completion and, so to speak, the
moment at which the centre of gravity of the labour employed
is situated.[1] What is essential here is the time interval between the centre of gravity of the labour employed and the
output (or, more strictly, the sale) of the finished product. I
shall call this interval the period of production. Obviously,
when work is done on the commodity continually by the same
quantity of labour from its start to its completion, the period
of production for the purpose of these calculations is, not the
whole time during which work has been going on—the whole
period of gestation—but approximately one-half of that time.

§ 2. In consequence of the existence of this period of production the demand price in terms of wage-goods for any x
units of labour per day, as reckoned in Chapters III. and IV.,
is subject to a correction that depends on the length of the
period of production and the rate of interest in terms of
wage-goods. Let us suppose that the raw material used in
each unit of product is paid for at the time that the finished
product containing it is sold; or, if it is not paid for then, let
the supply price of it for the purpose of our analysis be the
supply price that would rule for it if it were paid for then.
Let it be postulated further that the rate of interest in terms
of wage-goods is independent of the quantity of labour demanded (and employed) in the occupation we are considering
—which, for individual occupations, is approximately true.
The correction that has to be made to allow for the deferred
nature of the return to labour is thus very simple. The uncorrected demand equation for conditions of free competition
was given in Chapter III. § 2, as $w = \dfrac{d\psi\{\phi(x)\}}{dx} - \dfrac{df\{\phi(x)\}}{dx}$. The
corrected demand equation is the same, with the right-

---

[1] Cf. *Industrial Fluctuations*, Part I. chap. x.

hand expression decreased by a percentage equal to the rate of interest in terms of wage-goods for the time covered by the period of production. Thus, roughly, if the period of production is six months and the rate of interest in terms of wage-goods is 5 per cent, the demand price in respect of each quantity of labour is $2\frac{1}{2}$ per cent less than it would otherwise have been. More exactly, if the period of production is k days and the rate of interest per day is i, the corrected demand price in respect of each quantity of labour is equal to the uncorrected demand price multiplied by $\left(\dfrac{1}{1+i}\right)^k$. That is to say, the demand equation for labour is

$$w = \left(\frac{1}{1+i}\right)^k \cdot \left\{\frac{d\psi\{\phi(x)\}}{dx} - \frac{df\{\phi(x)\}}{dx}\right\}.$$

It is easy to see that, for conditions of monopoly, the correcting factor is also $\left(\dfrac{1}{1+i}\right)^k$. In Chapter VIII. it will be shown that, in the more general problem there discussed, this correcting factor plays an important rôle. So far, however, as the elasticity of the demand for labour, in respect of any given quantity in particular industries is concerned, it has no significance. For, for any given value of x, the elasticity of the demand for labour, namely $\left\{\dfrac{x}{x} \div \dfrac{w}{w}\right\}$, is obviously the same for all values (other than 0) of $\left(\dfrac{1}{1+i}\right)^k$.[1]

§ 3. For conditions of competition this conclusion can be elucidated from a different angle as follows. When the centre of gravity of the work done in respect of any commodity stands six months prior to the emergence and sale of the product, so that each unit of product emerges six months after the middle point (as reckoned

---

[1] This result, of course, would not be reached if the raw material was not paid for at the time the finished good was sold and if we took for its supply price the actual, not, as supposed in the text, the appropriately corrected supply price. For in that case the factor m in the equations of Chapter III. §§ 3-4 would be different with different rates of interest.

by weighted average) of the work done on it, this implies, under a system of continuous production, that those items of finished commodity, on which a total of one day's labour by the marginal man has, in the aggregate, been expended, emerge, so to speak, out of a tube, where there are lying a series of goods in process, on which respectively $\frac{364}{365}, \frac{363}{365}$

$\ldots \frac{1}{365}$ of a day's labour of one man has been engaged. That is to say, in the production of each item of finished commodity, embodying in the aggregate (over and above the raw material contained in it) one day's labour of the marginal man, there is associated a structure of working capital embodying 182 days', or six months', labour of one man. With interest at 5 per cent, $2\frac{1}{2}$ per cent of the value in wage-goods of the emerging commodity *minus* its raw material content has to be handed over in payment for the services of this structure of working capital, without which the continuous process of production could not take place. Thus there is only available, to pay for the one day's labour of our marginal man, distributed over 365 days, that is embodied in the commodity *minus* its raw material, not the whole, but $97\frac{1}{2}$ per cent of the value of the said commodity *minus* its raw material. We may then, if we will, regard the remaining $2\frac{1}{2}$ per cent as payment that has to be made for the services of the structure of working capital; the demand price for labour being the demand price for the commodity produced by an increment of it *minus* the supply price of the raw material and of the services of the structure of working capital. For conditions of monopoly an analysis on similar lines is easily worked out.

§ 4. Alike in conditions of competition and of monopoly, the demand price for labour, in terms of wage-goods, calculated on the above plan, is, of course, identical with the demand price in wage-goods found by the alternative plan of direct discounting. By following either plan we find that the demand curve, as against what it would have been had production been instantaneous, is lowered throughout, not by the same absolute amount, but *in the same proportion*.

This implies that, in respect of any given quantity of labour, the elasticity of demand is the same as it would have been with instantaneous production.[1]

§ 5. It will have been observed that, throughout this chapter, we have always spoken, not of the rate of interest simply, but of the rate of interest in terms of wage-goods. This is essential, because, contrary to what is sometimes vaguely supposed, there is no such thing as a rate of interest in general, irrespective of the commodity (or composite commodity) in terms of which it is specified, save only in the very special case where all relative values are, and are expected to remain, constant. The illusion that there is a single rate of interest is generated by the fact that in practice we always think and speak of interest in terms of one particular thing, money, so that the existence of many different rates is never brought to our notice. Suppose, however, that there are a number of commodities or composite commodities, A, B, C and so on, measured in units such that one unit of each one is worth now one unit of each other one. If it is expected that, after a time interval t, their values will stand in the ratio 1, v_b, v_c and so on, and if the rate of interest in terms of A over the interval t is i, so that one unit of A now is worth the promise of $(1 + i)$ units at the end of that interval, it necessarily follows that the rate of interest in terms of B over the time interval $= \{(1 + i)v_b - 1\}$, that is $\{(v_b - 1) + v_b i\}$; and so on. Thus the rate of interest is different according to what the commodity or composite commodity is in terms of which it is being reckoned. There is no such thing as a rate of interest except *in* some defined object, just as there is no such thing as a price except *of* some defined object.[2]

---

[1] Should anybody be perplexed that no reference is here made to interest on fixed capital, he may be reminded that this is cared for out of the balance of total selling price over total wage cost *plus* material cost, and so, even from the standpoint of the long period, does not enter into the demand price for labour at the margin.

[2] This consideration, which should be familiar to students of Professor Irving Fisher's writings, is brought out very clearly by Mr. Sraffa in his article entitled "Dr. Hayek on Money and Capital" (*Economic Journal*, March 1932).

CHAPTER VI

§ 1. I NOW pass from variations in the rate of wages in particular occupations to variations in the rate of wages, assumed to be uniform, over the whole body of occupations. We have to relate these variations to variations in the aggregate quantity of labour demanded in all occupations. It is tempting at first sight to suppose that the problem can be resolved by studying the position in each centre separately and adding together the results obtained. This is equivalent to supposing that the demand functions of the separate centres are independent of one another, so that the demand function for labour in the aggregate is derived by simple addition from the demand functions of the several centres. This supposition, even when it is not explicitly entertained, often colours our thought. Thus, in speculating upon the probable effect on the aggregate volume of employment that would be produced by, say, a 5 per cent reduction of real wage-rates everywhere, we instinctively think of a number of separate industries and ask ourselves how a 5 per cent wage cut confined to any one of them would affect employment there; and then slide into the view that a rough average of our results will give the effect on aggregate employment of a 5 per cent wage cut all round. Since, from a short-period standpoint, the elasticity of the demand for labour in many important industries viewed in isolation is, we may suppose, substantially less than unity, so that a large percentage variation in wage-rate means only a small percentage variation in the quantity of labour demanded, the inference is often

61

drawn that the elasticity of demand for labour in the aggregate is probably also less than unity, so that a large percentage variation in the whole body of wage-rates would only
carry with it a small percentage variation in the total quantity of labour demanded.

§ 2. Before inquiring as to the validity of this supposition
it will be convenient to set out its implications in precise
form. With independent functions, let A, B, C be the quantities of labour initially demanded at a common wage-rate
W in the several centres, and let η_a, η_b, η_c be the elasticities
of demand in respect of these quantities. Then, if we write
E for the general elasticity of demand for labour in the aggregate in respect of a quantity $(A + B + C \ldots)$, it is readily
found that

$$E = \frac{\eta_a A + \eta_b B + \eta_c C \ldots}{A + B + C + \ldots}.$$

If initially different wage-rates rule in the several centres,
we can still derive, in the same manner as above, a general
elasticity of demand, in the sense of percentage change in
quantity of labour demanded divided by the associated uniform (small) percentage change in all the different wage-rates.
We may write

$$E' = \frac{\eta_a' A' + \eta_b' B' + \eta_c' C'}{A' + B' + C'}.$$

Even though $(A + B + C) = (A' + B' + C')$ and $\eta_a = \eta_a'$, $\eta_b = \eta_b'$,
etc., it is clearly not necessary that $E' = E$, except in the
special case where *also* $\eta_a = \eta_b = \eta_c = \ldots$

§ 3. We have now to inquire into the validity of the supposition that the demand functions for labour in different
centres are in fact independent—an inquiry which, as we shall
find, involves several stages. Before it is attacked directly,
however, it will be well to clear out of the way a somewhat
troublesome complication. In the course of the discussion that
follows it will be argued that frequently the quantity of labour
demanded at a given wage-rate in one centre partly depends
on the quantity that is demanded in some other centre or set
of centres; for example, in those that produce substitutes for

the commodities produced by our centre or centres. Now, as is easily seen, all arguments of this type depend on the condition that the quantity of labour demanded in the other centres is the same as, or at all events varies with, the quantity of labour employed there. Obviously, for example, what is relevant to the demand for labour to produce wheat is not the quantity of labour demanded in barley-making but the quantity of labour *employed* in barley-making. That part of the demand there which is filled, to speak paradoxically, with unfilled vacancies has no relevance; only that part which is filled with employment has relevance. Hence, when two commodities are substitutes for one another, and similarly over the whole complex range of cases to be studied in this chapter, the quantity of labour demanded in the centres that make the first commodity is partly dependent, not merely on the quantity of labour demanded in the second, but on this quantity *minus* the quantity of unfilled vacancies there, and so indirectly on the distribution of labour and the mobility of labour over the relevant part of industry. This complication does not matter so long as attention is confined to conditions in respect of which it may be postulated that wage-rates for labour of given quality are uniform over all occupations. For this condition cannot in practice be satisfied unless labour is perfectly mobile, and, if labour is perfectly mobile and a uniform wage-system prevails, it is very unlikely that wage-earners will allow the rate at any time to stand so low that employers would be willing to take on more men at that rate than are actually available. Hence, so long as attention is confined to the hypothetical case of uniform wage-rates, the difficulty here set out need not trouble us. When, however, non-uniform wage-rates are brought into account, some way will have to be found for meeting or evading it. For the purpose of this and the following chapter, which are primarily critical and directed to show that a general demand function for all labour cannot be obtained by adding together the demand functions for different sets of centres, no matter how these sets are made up, I shall ignore this complication. I shall postulate, in fact, that there are no unfilled vacancies, or, in other words, that the quantity of labour demanded and the quantity employed are everywhere the same.

§ 4. So much being understood, let us consider first a number of different centres engaged in providing a single commodity. Let us, for simplicity, ignore the fact that the production process is not instantaneous, so that complications of the kind described in Chapter V. need not be taken into account. For short-period problems it is reasonable to suppose that the productivity functions of the several centres are independent, *i.e.* that they are not linked together by the presence of external economies or diseconomies. In these conditions the demand function for labour in all the centres jointly *in terms of the thing which they produce, i.e.* the productivity function of all of them jointly, is derived by simple addition from independent demand functions proper to the several centres. It follows that the supposition set out in § 1 above is correct and the inferences to which it leads warranted, provided that either (1) the centres in question produce wage-good units, so that the demand functions for labour in them in terms of their product are identical with the demand functions in terms of wage-goods, or (2) that, while they do not produce wage-good units, the aggregate demand for their product in terms of wage-good units is, over the relevant range, absolutely elastic.

§ 5. Now, since there are a great number of different items that enter into wage-good units, the former of the above two provisos *cannot* be satisfied. The latter is extremely unlikely to be satisfied; for absolute elasticity of demand is a thing practically unheard of. In practice, therefore, there do not arise independent demand functions in terms of wage-goods for labour in the several centres producing any (the same) thing, that can be added together to constitute an aggregate demand function. This is particularly obvious in the extreme case where the aggregate demand is absolutely fixed. In that case the elasticity of demand for the output of each single firm is infinite, but the elasticity of demand for the product of the industry as a whole is nil. A cut in price restricted to one firm would enable it to expand its output enormously—in such wise as to cut out all the others: but a cut extended over all the firms would not enable any of them to expand their output at all. Anyone who tried to gauge the elasticity of demand for the labour engaged in an industry by considering how a cut confined to particular firms would affect employment there would thus obtain a very exaggerated idea of the magnitude of this elasticity. In truth the demand in terms of wage-goods for labour in one centre can only be derived when the productivity functions of labour in all the other centres are given. The difference between the quantities of labour demanded in the one centre at two different wage-rates depends in part on the form of the productivity functions in the others. None the less, there is, so far as the present argument has gone, a demand function for labour, in terms of wage-goods, in respect of all the centres of production taken together, in any one occupation providing any one thing.

§ 6. Are we then entitled to conclude, for labour engaged in separate occupations, though not for the labour engaged in separate centres in the same occupation, that separate and independent demand functions exist? If this conclusion were correct it would follow that the effect of a 10 per cent reduction in real wage-rates on labour demand in two occupations together is equal to the effect on labour demand in occupation A of a 10 per cent reduction restricted to A *plus* the effect on labour demand in occupation B of a 10 per cent reduction restricted to B. This inference would hold good also about employment, provided only that there was, so to speak, sufficient employment to go round; that is to say, that a wage reduction confined to one occupation did not cause men to leave that occupation to attach themselves (in unemployment) to other occupations in sufficient numbers to create, under the new wage, unfilled vacancies, or a shortage of labour, in the first occupation. This condition is necessarily satisfied when labour is prevented by obstacles from moving between different occupations, and may be satisfied, should we start with sufficient unemployment everywhere, even though movement is unhampered.

§ 7. A moment's reflection shows, however, that, at best, demands can only be independent in occupations whose

F

products are neither competitive nor complementary with the products of any other occupation. The product of occupation A is completely non-competitive and non-complementary if a change in its output does not affect the desire for—the utility derived from—any rth unity of output occurring in any other occupation. A relation of competition holds if an increase in the output of one occupation causes the desire for the output of some other to fall; one of complementariness if it causes this desire to rise. In both these cases there exists—so far as the present argument goes—a general demand function in terms of wage-goods for labour in the related occupations counted together. This general demand function cannot, however, be obtained by simple addition of the separate demand functions of the several occupations, for the reason that, as with different centres producing the same commodity, there do not exist separate demand functions independent of one another. Interdependence, in the two cases distinguished, assumes two different forms. In the former case it is of such a sort that a reduction in the wage-rate in the one occupation leads to diminished demand for labour in the other occupation. In the latter it is of such a sort that a reduction in the wage-rate in the one occupation affects demand for labour in the other occupation in a favourable sense.

§ 8. The former case is tolerably familiar. If two industries produce commodities that are in any degree substitutes for, or competitors with, one another, a reduction in the real wage-rate in one will lead to a fall in the demand schedule, in terms of wage-goods, for the labour employed in the other, unless the demand for the two commodities together is perfectly elastic. Hence a given percentage reduction in the real rate of wages in one of such industries, besides increasing the quantity of labour demanded there, will diminish the quantity demanded in the other. It follows that a, say, 10 per cent reduction in the real wage-rate in both the industries together will increase aggregate labour demand in the two together by less than the sum of the increase that would occur in industry A if wages were reduced there only and the increase that would occur in industry B if wages were reduced there only.

§ 9. The latter case, that of complementariness, is the contrary of the former. If two industries produce commodities that are jointly demanded, in the sense that the utility of one is increased by the presence of the other, a reduction in the real wage-rate in one of these industries leads to a rise in the demand schedule in terms of wage-goods for the labour employed in the other. It is not necessary to this result that the proportion in which the products of the two industries stand in the final product or service, which they jointly render, shall be rigidly fixed; though that is, of course, the strongest instance of this class of relation. Where the relation rules in any degree, a given percentage reduction in the real wage-rate in one of the related industries, besides increasing the quantity of labour demanded there, will also increase the quantity demanded in the other industry. It follows that a, say, 10 per cent reduction in the real wage-rate in both the industries together will increase aggregate labour demand by more than the sum of the increase that would occur in industry A if wages were reduced there only and the increase that would occur in industry B if wages were reduced there only. This case is very important, for the reason that in real life many finished commodities are highly complex, embodying the combined results of a number of different industries. Coal, iron and steel, engineering and shipbuilding are, for example, all related in this way: indeed, wherever one industry produces something that is used as material or machinery for the work of another, an element of complementariness is present.

§ 10. Thus consider a reduction in the wage-rate of workers engaged in making magnetos. Since a magneto only represents a very small part of the total cost of a motor car, the demand in money—and so in wage-goods—for the services of magneto-makers is bound to be extremely inelastic. Consequently, a 10 per cent reduction in their wage-rate could only have a very small proportional effect on the number of men demanded for making magnetos: and the same thing is true of a like reduction in the wage-rate of men engaged in making any other small item in the equipment of a motor car. But it would be wrong to infer from this that wage-reductions in respect of items of this character are unimportant from the standpoint of labour demand in general. Suppose that a 10 per cent fall in the wages of magneto-makers involves only a fall of $\frac{1}{10}$th part of 1 per cent in the total cost of motor cars, which implies, of course, that the cost of a magneto is $\frac{1}{100}$th part of that of a complete car and that there are no costs other than wages; and, for purely illustrative purposes, suppose further that the demand for motor cars has an elasticity of unity. There will then result an increase of $\frac{1}{10}$th part of 1 per cent in the output of motor cars, and so of magnetos. The labour demanded in magneto making—I assume for simplicity that labour demand and employment are equal—will expand by $\frac{1}{10}$th part of 1 per cent of the number originally demanded there—an exceedingly trivial change. But labour demand in all the other occupations that contribute towards making motor cars will also expand by $\frac{1}{10}$th of 1 per cent. The total effect on labour demand will thus be 100 times the effect in the magneto-making industry. If the original number demanded in that industry is a, the addition to labour demand there will be $\frac{1}{1000}a$: but the addition to labour demand in the aggregate will be $\frac{1}{10}a$. If we suppose a car to consist of 100 equally important parts, made by 100 separate industries, it will follow on the same assumptions that, while a 10 per cent wage reduction in any one of these industries alone would increase labour demand there by, say, $\frac{1}{10}$th of 1 per cent, a 10 per cent reduction in all the industries would increase it in them all collectively by 10 per cent. This is, of course, an extreme illustration: but the principle illustrated is a general one.

§ 11. The type of relation just described holds, it should be noticed, between the various sorts of commodities that are embodied in wage-good units—on the assumption, here made, that the constitution of these units is fixed. For, if the real wage-rate is reduced by, say, 10 per cent in an industry making one wage-good item, the quantity of this item is increased and its value in terms of wage-good units diminished. This implies that the value of each of the other items comprised in wage-goods is increased in terms of wage-good units. This means that the value in wage-good units of the marginal net product of the original number of men employed in the industries making these items is increased. Consequently, it pays employers to engage more men in them. Thus a 10 per cent wage reduction in an industry making one wage-good item causes the quantity of labour demanded to expand, not only in that industry, but in all other wage-good industries also. This implies that a 10 per cent wage reduction in all of n similar and equally large wage-good industries making different wage-good items carries with it a percentage increase in the aggregate demand for labour in all wage-good industries more than n times as large as the increase in the one wage-good industry that a 10 per cent reduction in wage-rate there produces there. This is not incompatible with the thesis that a 10 per cent wage reduction in all wage-good industries—if they are all similar—will produce n times—neither more nor less—as large an increase in labour demand in the sum of wage-good industries as a 10 per cent wage reduction in one wage-good industry would produce in this sum.

§ 12. There remains one further important consideration. When the real wage-rate in one centre of production is reduced, the damage thereby done to demand in other centres that make identical or competing products may lead indirectly to a reduction in the real wage-rate there also: while, conversely, the benefit done to demand in centres making complementary products may lead to an increase in real wage-rates there. Hitherto we have ignored these possible reactions, and the corresponding possible reactions associated with increases of wage. Plainly, however, they ought not to be ignored. In particular, when it is a question, for example, of how large an expansion in the employment of British coal-miners would be brought about by, say, a 5 per cent cut in real wages, the answer will be quite different according as the real wage-rates paid to German miners remain the same as they were before or are themselves cut correspondingly to meet the intensified British competition. When a wage cut in one region leads to a defensive wage cut in a competing region, the consequential increase in the quantity of labour demanded in the first region will be less, and may be much less, than it would have been if this had not happened. That is to say, the elasticity of demand for labour there will be less, and may be much less, than it would have been. Over the two regions together, unless the total demand for the commodity, or group of competing commodities, that they produce is absolutely inelastic, the increase in the quantity of labour demanded in consequence of the cut made in the first region will, of course, be larger than it would have been if that cut had not been followed elsewhere. When a wage cut in one region leads indirectly to a wage rise in a region making complementary goods, the increase in the quantity of labour demanded in the first region will again be less—the elasticity of demand for labour will again be smaller—than it would have been had no reaction on wages elsewhere taken place. But in this case the increase in the quantity of labour demanded over the two regions together will be smaller than it would have been. Analogous considerations hold good of reactions induced in other regions by *upward* movements in the real wage-rate ruling in one region. Reactions on wage-rates in complementary regions or occupations are, of course, much less likely to take place on a significant scale than the corresponding reactions in competing regions.

CHAPTER VII

THE INTERDEPENDENCE OF DIFFERENT CENTRES
OF PRODUCTION (*continued*)

§ 1. WHAT has been said in the last chapter will have served to show that the concept of a number of independent demand functions for labour (in terms of wage-good units) standing in relation, in the several industries, to the wage-rates, uniform or otherwise, ruling in those industries, cannot be used as an instrument for analysing the factors that determine aggregate labour demand over the whole body of industries. For this line of approach we must make our demand functions for labour refer, not to separate industries, but to separate groups of industries, so selected that no one group produces commodities competing with, or complementary to, those produced by any other. It is not, however, worth while to inquire whether or not that kind of grouping is practically feasible. For there remain two fundamental general considerations, which show that, even as between groups of industries thus constructed, the demand schedules for labour would not in fact be independent.

§ 2. The first of these has to do with the interrelations among themselves of industries engaged in making non-wage-goods. Let us suppose that these industries are broken up into groups that are neither substitutes nor complements of one another, that are, in fact, wholly independent in respect of *desire*. This does not imply that they are independent in respect of *demand* for their products, and so in respect of demand for labour in them. For demand depends, not only on desire, but also on the available quantity of the thing or things in terms of which the demand is made. Thus a high elasticity in the demand for labour in one

71

group of non-wage-good industries considered by itself may merely mean that, if the wage-rate is slightly lowered there, a large volume of demand will be *transferred* to that group from others; so that the elasticity of demand in the two together is much less than the elasticity in either singly. Suppose, to obtain a precise illustration, that we are considering demands in terms of money, and that the total quantity of money available for hiring labour in the non-wage-good industries is fixed. The demands in terms of money for labour in these industries severally are interdependent, not merely by way of desire, but also as a result of the limitation of the money fund. We might conceivably find that the elasticities of demand for the labour in each of them considered in isolation were all equal and all enormously less, or enormously greater, than unity. These findings would be quite irrelevant to the question what is the elasticity of the money demand for labour in all of them together. That elasticity, in respect of all quantities of labour, is necessarily, in the conditions supposed, precisely equal to unity. Exactly the same line of thought is applicable when demand is made, not in money, but in wage-good units. If the flow of wage-goods available for employing men in non-wage-good industries is fixed, the elasticity of demand, in terms of wage-goods, for labour in the whole body of non-wage-good industries must be equal to unity, whatever be the state of demand in the several non-wage-good industries considered in isolation. In truth, of course, a fall in the rate of wage asked for in the non-wage-good industries may be expected, as will be argued more in detail presently, to draw some wage-goods out of other uses, *e.g.* consumption by non-wage-earners or purchase by them of non-wage-goods abroad, to pay for labour in that use, so that the real demand there will have an elasticity, not equal to, but greater than unity. This, however, does not affect the point here at issue. Whatever happens in this matter, it is still true that the demand schedule for labour in the sum total of non-wage-good industries is not made up by the addition of a number of independent demand schedules proper to those industries viewed separately in isolation.

§ 3. The second fundamental consideration has to do with the interrelations between wage-good industries and non-wage-good industries. Variations in the real wage-rate asked for in the wage-good industries lead to variations in the surplus of wage-goods produced over the aggregate real wages paid to labour in these industries. Hence, if the real wage-rate is reduced in wage-good industries, a powerful reaction is set up making for an expansion in the demand for labour in the non-wage-good industries. Such reaction would come about even though no alteration were made in the amount of employment in the wage-good industries, and so in the aggregate output of wage-goods. To show this, let us call the original surplus K_1 and the surplus after the change K_2. It is open to non-wage-earners to use this increase of surplus $(K_2 - K_1)$ either for their own personal consumption of wage-goods and (or) the purchase of foreign non-wage-goods, or for hiring labour to make for them home non-wage-goods. Let us suppose that initially $(1 - q)K_1$ was used by non-wage-earners for personal consumption of wage-goods and for purchase of foreign non-wage-goods, and qK_1 for hiring labour in the aforesaid manner. Then, w being the real rate of wage, the amount of labour demand (and employment) in home non-wage-good industries was initially $\dfrac{qK_1}{w}$. When the surplus expands from K_1 to K_2, the size of the addition to labour demand (and employment) in the non-wage-good industries depends on how far the additional surplus $(K_2 - K_1)$ is used by non-wage-earners in personal consumption and the purchase of foreign non-wage-goods and how far in employing new men to make home non-wage-goods. If the whole is employed for the former purpose, the addition to labour demand and employment is nil: if the same proportion of the new surplus as of the old is so employed, the addition is $\dfrac{q(K_2 - K_1)}{w}$: if the whole of the new surplus is so employed, the addition is $\dfrac{K_2 - K_1}{w}$. It is certain in practice that the reaction will be substantial. Moreover, as a matter of fact, in consequence of the reduced wage-rate, it will pay employers to take on more men in the home wage-good industries. Presently, after a period of production has elapsed, these new men will produce more than the aggregate of wage-goods that are paid to them as wages at the new rate; and so the real fund available for employing labour in the non-wage-good industries is enlarged more than it would have been had employment in the wage-good industries remained unaffected. How much more it is enlarged will depend on the form of the productivity function in the wage-good industries. But it is bound to be enlarged to some extent. When the matter is looked at in this way, we perceive at once that the real demand for labour in the aggregate must be substantially more elastic than separate studies of wage-good and non-wage-good industries in isolation from one another would suggest.

§ 4. It might be thought at first sight that, besides this reaction from the wage-good to the non-wage-good industries, there is also a reciprocal reaction; that, just as lower wage-rates in the wage-good industries promote increased demand for labour in the non-wage-good industries, so lower wage-rates in the non-wage-good industries promote increased demand in the wage-good industries. Thus it is often argued that, if, whether as a result of reduced wage-rates there or of anything else, the number of men employed in road-making, or other sorts of capital construction, is increased, without offsetting reductions in other non-wage-good industries, a large mass of further employment will be created in the industries that make wage-goods by the expenditure of the newly employed men. This thesis must, of course, be distinguished from the different thesis that, if £1000 are spent on making roads, there will be called into work, not merely road-makers, but also people who make the various things that road-makers use in their work. That is, of course, true. But all these people are covered by the £1000. There are not £1000 worth of road-makers *plus* some further value of material-makers; there are £1000 worth of road-makers *including* material-makers. The thesis here in view is quite different from this. It asserts that an increase in employment in road-making in this wide sense will involve secondary employment in the industries that make wage-goods. It is commonly supported as follows. The people set to work on road-making, or whatever it may be, have, *pro tanto*, more money to spend; they spend it, and so set to work more makers of the wage-goods that they buy; these, by spending their money, set to work more makers of the wage-goods that *they* buy; and so on indefinitely. Indeed, according to this argument, it is only because some of the wage-earners' goods are bought from abroad that the setting of a single new man to work on road-making does not cause an infinite number of men to obtain employment in making wage-goods! This argument, in the present connection, is invalid. *When the real—not the money—rate of wages ruling in the wage-good industries is given*, the quantity of labour demanded in these industries is determined, subject to certain qualifications not here relevant, by the wage-rate in relation to their productivity functions and the rate of interest. Activity in the non-wage-good industries certainly will not *lower* the rate of interest, and cannot, therefore, by that route increase the demand for labour in the wage-good industries. Apart from that, nothing that happens in the non-wage-good industries can, from the short-period standpoint that alone is in question here, benefit the wage-good industries:[1] though, of course, from a long-period standpoint a cheapening of capital instruments used in the manufacture of wage-goods may, as was observed in Chapter II., easily do this. The money counterpart of this fact is simply that the thousand extra £s spent by the new employees taken on for road-making goes to buy wage-goods which would have been created anyhow and which, if not so

---

[1] To avoid misunderstanding it should be pointed out that the demand for labour in wage-good industries may be affected to a small extent through reactions on the activity of the non-wage-earners who co-operate with labour. Thus, if employment in, say, the whisky industry is increased and so whisky is cheapened, *non-wage-earners* in the beer trade are led, provided that their demand for whisky in terms of their own work is greater than unity, to put more hours' work into the managing of beer businesses. If they do this, the marginal net product of a given number of wage-earners making beer will be increased and, consequently, it will pay employers at the existing real wage to take on more of them. But this type of reaction is clearly, from short-period point of view, of secondary importance.

bought, would have employed other labour, have been consumed by non-wage-earners, have been exported by them
or have been placed in store. This supposed reinforcement
to the argument of § 3 is thus illusory.[1]

§ 5. In the foregoing discussion nothing has been said of
the fact that a large part of the industry of this country
is devoted to making goods for export. When this fact is
brought into account, the situation is further complicated.
In so far as additions to exports consequential upon a
reduction in wage-rates are offset by additions to imports
of foreign securities or of non-wage-goods that do not compete with native products, the industries that make them
are, from the present standpoint, on a par with industries
that make non-wage-goods for home consumption. But, in
so far as they are offset by additions to imports of wage-
goods or of raw materials, the industries that make them
are on a par with home wage-good industries. An expansion
in them indirectly promotes an expansion in the demand for
labour in home non-wage-good industries. *Per contra*, in so
far as additions to exports involve additions to imports
that compete with the products of home non-wage-good
industries, the demand for labour in those industries is
affected adversely. Here again is interdependence.

[1] For a different and valid sense in which what may be called secondary
employment occurs cf. *post*, Part IV. Chap. VIII.

CHAPTER VIII

THE ELASTICITY OF DISCOUNTING

§ 1. THE results of the two preceding chapters have been negative. We have found that, since quantities of labour demanded at given wage-rates in different centres of production, in whatever way "centre" is interpreted, are interdependent, it is not possible to construct a demand function for labour in the aggregate by adding together demand functions framed separately for different centres. Thus we cannot ascertain the effect on the aggregate quantity of labour demanded of given shifts of all wage-rates by adding together the effects that would follow in each several centre from the shifts occurring there. More direct methods of approach must, therefore, be attempted. Before, however, these are introduced, the ground must be prepared.

§ 2. It was shown in Chapter V. that, so long as the rate of interest in terms of wage-goods remains constant, the fact that a period of production intervenes between the employment of labour and the resultant output does not make any difference to the elasticity of real demand for labour in any industry. Plainly, however, if a fall in the rate of real wage carries with it a rise in the rate of interest in terms of wage-good units, this is no longer so. When the rate of interest goes up, the quantity of labour demanded, in all occupations whose output is not instantaneous, is *pro tanto* diminished. This implies that the association of a rise in interest with reductions in wage-rate renders the real demand for labour in any industry less elastic than it would have been had there been no such association. The task of the present chapter is to elucidate this matter. Readers, who will turn forward to the actuarial calculations of Part III. Chapter XV., which display the effect on the real demand for labour of given changes, other things remaining the same, in the rate of interest, will perceive that the issues to be raised are very important. In the argument that follows, since we are concerned with industry as a whole, including export industries, the short-period costs of raw materials are already counted, and need not, as in our studies of individual industries, be allowed for separately. Our *quaesitum* is the actual elasticity of demand for labour in the aggregate, in respect of the quantity actually employed. I shall call this elasticity E_d.

§ 3. Let us imagine in the first instance that the period of production in all industries is the same, namely k days, and let it be known that, apart from reactions through the rate of interest, the elasticity of the real demand for labour in the aggregate would be E_r. Write w for the real rate of wage, x for the total real wages bill, and so $\dfrac{x}{w}$ for the quantity of labour employed; and $F\left(\dfrac{x}{w}\right)$ for the total value in wage-goods of the embodied services of this labour that are due to emerge on the market at the end of the period of production. It follows that the actual demand price of $\dfrac{x}{w}$ labour is

$$\left\{\frac{1}{1+i}\right\}^k \frac{dF\left(\dfrac{x}{w}\right)}{d\left(\dfrac{x}{w}\right)}.$$

Since it is evident in a general way that the rate of interest, and so the value of $\dfrac{1}{1+i}$, is, or may be, affected by the magnitude of the quantity of wage-goods that is set aside for engaging labour in future production, let us write $\dfrac{1}{1+i} = f(x)$. Hence the actual demand price for $\dfrac{x}{w}$ labour is

$\left\{f(x)\right\}^{k} \dfrac{dF\left(\dfrac{x}{w}\right)}{d\left(\dfrac{x}{w}\right)}$. This is necessarily equal—under the competi-

tive conditions here premised—to w. Therefore we have

$$\left\{\left\{f(x)\right\}^{k} \frac{1}{w} \frac{dF\left(\dfrac{x}{w}\right)}{d\left(\dfrac{x}{w}\right)}\right\} = 1.$$

This equality obviously holds good whatever happens to the rate of wage. Hence

$$\frac{d}{dw}\left\{\left\{f(x)\right\}^{k} \frac{1}{w} \frac{dF\left(\dfrac{x}{w}\right)}{d\left(\dfrac{x}{w}\right)}\right\} = 0.$$

It follows that

$$k\frac{xf'(x)}{f(x)} \cdot \frac{dx}{dw} = x\left\{-\frac{1}{w} + \frac{\dfrac{d^{2}F\left(\dfrac{x}{w}\right)}{d\left(\dfrac{x}{w}\right)^{2}}}{\dfrac{dF\left(\dfrac{x}{w}\right)}{d\left(\dfrac{x}{w}\right)}} \cdot \frac{d\left(\dfrac{x}{w}\right)}{dw}\right\}.$$

By analogy with other elasticities we may conveniently call $\dfrac{f(x)}{xf'(x)}$ the *elasticity of discounting*, and name it e. This elasticity measures the proportionate change in $\left(\dfrac{1}{1+i}\right)$ that is due, other things being equal, to a small associated proportionate change in x, divided by that proportionate change. The above equation may, therefore, be written

$$k\frac{1}{e}\frac{dx}{dw} = x\left\{ -\frac{1}{w} + \frac{\dfrac{d^2\mathrm{F}\left(\dfrac{x}{w}\right)}{d\left(\dfrac{x}{w}\right)^2}}{\dfrac{d\mathrm{F}\left(\dfrac{x}{w}\right)}{d\left(\dfrac{x}{w}\right)}} \cdot \frac{d\left(\dfrac{x}{w}\right)}{dw} \right\} \qquad . \qquad . \qquad . \quad \text{(i)}$$

§ 4. Now

$$\frac{d\left(\dfrac{x}{w}\right)}{dw} = \frac{x}{w^2}\left\{\frac{w^2}{x}\frac{d\left(\dfrac{x}{w}\right)}{dw}\right\} = \frac{x}{w_2}\mathrm{E}_d.$$

It follows from equation (i) that, if e is infinite, that is to say, if there are no reactions through the rate of interest,

$$\mathrm{E}_d = \frac{\dfrac{d\mathrm{F}\left(\dfrac{x}{w}\right)}{d\left(\dfrac{x}{w}\right)}}{\dfrac{x}{w}\dfrac{d^2\mathrm{F}\left(\dfrac{x}{w}\right)}{d\left(\dfrac{x}{w}\right)^2}}.$$

But E_r is, by definition, the elasticity of the real demand for labour that would prevail if there were no reactions through the rate of interest. Therefore

$$\mathrm{E}_r = \frac{\dfrac{d\mathrm{F}\left(\dfrac{x}{w}\right)}{d\left(\dfrac{x}{w}\right)}}{\dfrac{x}{w}\dfrac{d^2\mathrm{F}\left(\dfrac{x}{w}\right)}{d\left(\dfrac{x}{w}\right)^2}}.$$

Now, since $E_d = \dfrac{w^2}{x} \dfrac{d\left(\dfrac{x}{w}\right)}{dw} = \left(-1 + \dfrac{w}{x}\dfrac{dx}{dw} \right)$, it follows that

$$\frac{dx}{dw} = \frac{x}{w}(E_d + 1).$$

Hence from equation (i), in the general case where e is not nil, we find

$$E_d = \frac{1 + \dfrac{k}{e}}{\dfrac{1}{E_r} - \dfrac{k}{e}}.$$

We have thus expressed E_d in terms of E_r, e and k.

§ 5. Account must next be taken of the fact that in real life different industries have, not the same, but different periods of production. Suppose that there are several sets of workpeople, in hiring whom there is initially spent x, y and z wage-goods, and whose periods of production are respectively k, q and s days. Let us write E_x, E_y and E_z for the elasticities of demand for the labour of these groups that would reign in the absence of reactions through the rate of interest: and let us, as before, write e for the elasticity of discounting. Plainly e must now be expressed as a function of $(x + y + z)$. With this understanding, the elasticity of demand for labour as a whole can evidently be written

$$E_d = \frac{x\dfrac{1 + \dfrac{k}{e}}{\dfrac{1}{E_x} - \dfrac{k}{e}} + y\dfrac{1 + \dfrac{q}{e}}{\dfrac{1}{E_y} - \dfrac{k}{e}} + z\dfrac{1 + \dfrac{r}{e}}{\dfrac{1}{E_z} - \dfrac{r}{e}}}{x + y + z}.$$

This expression is much too complex to treat directly. Its structure, however, suggests that the significance of reactions through the rate of interest on the elasticity of demand for labour in the aggregate may properly be studied by reference to a "representative" industry, whose period of production is some sort of average of the periods ruling in actual industries. With k made to measure this period, we may, therefore, concentrate on a formula of the simple type namely

$$E_d = \frac{1 + \dfrac{k}{e}}{\dfrac{1}{E_r} - \dfrac{k}{e}}.$$

§ 6. The value of k can be calculated roughly in respect of any year by dividing the value of annual income into the cost of working capital. Mr. Keynes has suggested that the working capital of this country amounts to from between 1500 and 2000 millions. If we allow for the fact that our total income comprises interest from foreign investments and earnings received for direct services, which are not relevant to working capital, the lower of these figures is round about one-half of our relevant annual income. Professor Mitchell in like manner puts the working capital of the United States at about half a year's income. On this basis the average period of production k must be about six months—180 days.

§ 7. The principal implications of the above formula may now be set out. Provided that e is positive, three consequences follow. First, since E_r cannot be positive, E_d must be negative, except in the limiting case where it is nil. That is to say, in general, a reduction in the real rate of wage *must* lead to some increase in the quantity of labour demanded. This does not, of course, imply an increase in the quantity of wage-goods that is spent on labour. Whether that increases or not depends on whether $\dfrac{dx}{dw}$, namely $(E_d + 1)$, namely $\dfrac{\dfrac{1}{E_r} + 1}{\dfrac{1}{E_r} - \dfrac{k}{e}}$, is positive or negative; which in turn depends on whether E_r is (numerically) greater or less than unity. Secondly, when e is infinite, that is to say, when changes in x make no difference to the value of $\dfrac{1}{1 + i}$, $E_d = E_r$. Thirdly, increases in e and decreases in k make for a diminution in E_d

provided that E_r is (numerically) greater than 1, but have the opposite effect if E_r is numerically less than 1. That this must be so is obvious to common sense; for, if E_r is numerically less than 1, a reduction in the wage-rate causes the quantity of resources diverted from immediate use to investment to *decrease*. Provided that e is negative, E_d *may* be positive. But this can only happen if E_r is numerically less than 1. If E_r is numerically greater than 1, E_d must be negative, and increases in e and decreases in k cause it to have a *smaller* negative value.

§ 8. In view of these results it is very important to know whether and in what conditions the elasticity of discounting e is positive or negative. This elasticity is plainly not an elementary, but a derived magnitude. Moreover, the factors which determine it are not at all those various general factors which determine the actual rate of interest that rules at any time. If, however, we postulate that the representative non-wage-earner, who invests in hiring labour, expects to have the same income and the same tastes in the future that he has now, we are able to define the required factors in a simple way. Write, as before, x for the quantity of income initially devoted to hiring labour and $\dfrac{dx}{x} \cdot \dfrac{\dfrac{1}{1+i}}{d\left(\dfrac{1}{1+i}\right)}$ for the elasticity of discounting in respect of this quantity. Write y for the quantity of income devoted by non-wage-earners to immediate use, $\phi(y)$ for the marginal utility derived from this use by the representative non-wage-earner when y is devoted to it, and ϵ for $\dfrac{\phi(y)}{y\phi'(y)}$, namely, the elasticity, in respect of this quantity, of the representative non-wage-earner's consumption-utility function. It is easy to see in a general way that, if Δy is withdrawn from the consumption use against future repayment, a burden is inflicted on the transferrer equal, on our assumptions, to $\Delta y\phi'(y)$, and that, in order to induce him to make the transfer, $\dfrac{1}{1+i}$ must be diminished in a proportion equal to $\dfrac{\phi(y)}{\phi(y) + \Delta y \phi'(y)}$. Hence, by a simple manipulation, we find

$$\frac{1}{e} = -\frac{\Delta y \phi'(y)}{\phi(y)} \cdot \frac{x}{\Delta x} = -\frac{\Delta x}{\Delta y} \cdot \frac{y}{x} \cdot \epsilon.$$

Now we know that $\dfrac{y}{x}$ is positive and that ϵ is negative. It follows that e is positive or negative according as Δy is of the same sign as or of the opposite sign to Δx.

§ 9. In order to decide that matter we need to distinguish sharply between periods too short to allow of investment in labour in the wage-good industries and in the export industries—which, as we have seen, "produce" claims on wage-goods abroad—to yield their fruits, and periods longer than this. For in the shorter type of period there is no inflow of additional wage-goods from the machine of process to offset in whole or in part additions to the wages bill, but in the longer type of period there is such an inflow. In other words, over the interval covered by the period of production, new working capital is being built up out of current income, but after the interval is over, provided that the quantity of labour is not further increased, not only is no new working capital being built up, but that just made has begun to yield interest. It will be convenient to study these two sorts of period in turn. For simplicity of exposition, I shall develop the argument for cases where Δx is positive. For cases of the opposite sort only verbal changes would be required.

§ 10. In the very short period, if there were no such thing as unemployment benefit and no possibility of adding to or subtracting from liquid stocks of wage-goods, Δy would always be equal to Δx and $\dfrac{\Delta x}{\Delta y}$ would always be equal to 1. In so far as movements in and out of liquid stocks take place, we may suppose that increases in x are in part provided out of stocks and decreases in part offset by absorptions into stock. Thus there is an element Δs with positive sign, such that $\Delta y = (\Delta x - \Delta s)$; and the fraction $\dfrac{\Delta x}{\Delta y}$ is less than unity, but still necessarily positive. The existence of a system of unemployment insurance *must*, however, render Δy negative if Δx has a sufficiently small positive value, and *may* render it negative even when the positive value of Δx, consequent upon a reduction in the wage-rate by Δw, is fairly substantial. The reason is, of course, that, for every extra man called into employment, there is a saving to non-wage-earners on unemployment benefit equal to $(r+t)$, which, *pro tanto*, reduces Δy below Δx. If the total wage bill is unchanged, that is to say if $\Delta x = 0$, there is a net saving on unemployment benefit equal to $\dfrac{\Delta w}{w} \cdot \dfrac{x}{w}(r+t)$. With Δx positive, there is a further saving equal to $\dfrac{\Delta x}{w}(r+t)$. Therefore the total saving is equal to $\Delta x \left\{ \dfrac{\Delta w}{\Delta x} \cdot \dfrac{x}{w} + 1 \right\} \dfrac{r+t}{w}$.

But

$$\frac{\Delta w}{\Delta x} \cdot \frac{x}{w} = -\frac{1}{E_d + 1}$$

$$\therefore \text{ the total saving} = \Delta x \frac{E_d}{E_d + 1} \cdot \frac{r+t}{w}.$$

This is greater than Δy. Therefore Δy, and consequently e, is negative, provided that $\dfrac{E_d}{E_d + 1} > \dfrac{w}{r+t}$, that is to say provided that E_d has a negative value numerically less than $\dfrac{w}{w-r-t}$. Thus, if the rate of unemployment benefit were equal to the wage-rate, Δy, and therefore e, would be negative for all values of E_d. If $r+t = \frac{1}{2}w$, e is negative so long as E_d has a negative value smaller than 2: if $r+t = \frac{1}{3}w$, it is negative so long as E_d has a negative value smaller than $\frac{3}{2}$. It follows that, so long as the elasticity of the real demand for labour that would prevail in the absence of reactions through the rate of interest is numerically less than 2 or $\frac{3}{2}$ as the case may be, reactions through the rate of interest do not render the actual elasticity of the real demand for labour less than it would have been without these reactions, but, on the contrary, render it greater than it would have been.

§ 11. In respect of a period longer than the period of production of labour engaged in making wage-goods and goods for export a further factor comes into play. After the lapse of the period of production there flow out every day from the machine of process extra wage-goods and claims upon wage-goods, sufficient, not only to cover the addition that has been made to the daily wages bill in the wage-good and export industries, but also to provide interest on the working capital that was created during the period of production. This does not necessarily imply that the new flow is enough to cover the whole of the addition that has been made to the daily wages bill. For what flows out of the machine of process in the instrument-making and other home non-wage-goods industries is not available to finance employment, any more than the additions that, before the period of production was over, were being made to working capital were available for that purpose. It will be suggested presently that in this country perhaps one-quarter of the total labour force is normally engaged in the service of home non-wage-good industries. If this figure is not too small, it will follow that more than three-quarters of the total extra wages bill is covered in the sort of period we are now considering by the inflow of new wage-goods and claims to wage-goods. Provided, therefore, that there exists a system of unemployment benefit with a benefit rate not less than one-quarter of the wage-rate, Δy and, therefore, e, must be positive in all circumstances. That is to say, provided this condition is satisfied, whatever the elasticity of real demand for labour that would have ruled in the absence of reactions through the rate of interest, these reactions must render the actual elasticity of real demand *more* elastic than it would otherwise have been. In the conditions ruling in this country we may safely conclude that it will have this effect.[1]

[1] It would be wrong to infer from this that, when a single period of production is over, the full effect—apart from long-period reactions through fixed capital—on the quantity of labour demanded makes itself felt immediately. The process is less simple than that. During the first production period after wage-rates have been reduced working capital is being built up, and, therefore, the rate of interest is raised; and by that fact the addition made to the quantity of labour employed is restricted. When the first production period is over, the rate of interest falls again. Equilibrium

§ 12. The practical inference of chief importance for our inquiry that emerges from this complex discussion may be set out very briefly. In respect neither of the shorter type of period distinguished above nor of the longer type can re-actions through the rate of interest in any circumstances affect adversely the elasticity of real demand unless the elasticity would otherwise have been numerically greater than unity. In the conditions prevailing in this country they cannot in the very short period have an adverse effect if the elasticity would otherwise have been numerically greater than $-\frac{3}{2}$ or -2: in periods longer than the period of production for the wage-good and export industries, they cannot in any event have an adverse effect. Hence, when we are seeking, as we shall do immediately, to determine the lowest value that the elasticity of the real demand for labour can reason-ably be expected to have, reactions through the rate of interest may be ignored altogether in studies of the longer type of period, but must be reckoned with in studies of the shorter type. These results, as the reader will perceive, might have been obtained by a more direct route without the some-what elaborate analysis of the first part of this chapter. None the less, it has seemed worth while to carry that analysis through, in the hope that, tentative and approximate as it is, it may nevertheless throw a little light on the theoretical background of the problem.

is, therefore, ruptured: and it now pays to engage a larger quantity of labour at the ruling rate of wages. The wages bill is, therefore, increased a second time, until rising interest rates make a further increase unprofitable. The happenings of the first production period are repeated in a second production period from a starting-point of higher employment; and so on. Thus the effect of the lowering of the rate of wages makes itself felt in a *succession* of additions to the quantity of labour demanded. The sum of all these successive additions eventually mounts up to what they would have been at the beginning had the elasticity of discounting been nil.

CHAPTER IX

THE ELASTICITY OF DEMAND IN TERMS OF WAGE-GOODS FOR LABOUR AS A WHOLE

§ 1. WE are now in a position to attack our main problem. To make the exposition reasonably simple I imagine that there is only a single sort of wage-good. I postulate that the rate of real wage stipulated for in respect of men of given quality is uniform in all centres; and am concerned with the relation between variations in this uniform rate of wage and in the aggregate quantity of labour demanded. The *quaesitum* is, not the actual elasticity of the real demand for labour, but a minimum figure of which we may fairly say that the actual elasticity is very unlikely to fall short. As throughout this book, the whole problem is treated as a short-period one, in the sense that slow-working reactions from changes in fixed capital equipment are left out of account; but, in accordance with what was said in the last chapter, the short period is divided into two parts. I shall study first the effect of variations of wage-rate after an interval greater than the period of production of the generality of wage-good and export industries; secondly the effect before that interval has passed. The argument will be set out in the form of an inquiry into the actual numerical values of current elasticities. This involves the introduction at critical points of certain factual estimates or, if it be preferred, guesses, that are necessarily dubious. The critical reader may, therefore, well regard the positive results attained with scepticism. From the point of view of economic science it is the method of analysis, rather than these results, to which attention is invited.

§ 2. One preliminary observation of general application must be made. It is evident that, from the standpoint either of the longer or of the shorter type of period, the elasticity of the real demand for labour must depend in large part upon the elasticity of the productivity function of labour in the several industries. It is equally evident that these elasticities will be quite different in respect of the quantities of labour at work in times of boom and in times of depression respectively. In times of boom, owing to the limitation of fixed capital equipment, it is not, in general, feasible to push employment further except at the cost of sharply decreasing physical returns. Whatever, therefore, happens to the rate of interest, it is impossible for the real demand for labour in terms of wage-goods to be other than highly inelastic. In times of depression, however, when the bulk of a country's capital equipment is working much below capacity, this is not so. As was argued in Chapter III., the elasticity of the productivity function in the generality of industries is likely to be numerically large. Hence any study of elasticity, which disregards the distinction between booms and depressions *must* be futile. It is essential to specify the sort of times to which any particular inquiry relates. Here attention will be focussed exclusively on the conditions that prevail in a marked industrial depression.

§ 3. With this understanding let us turn to the first part of our problem—that concerned with the longer type of period distinguished in § 1. Since, as was shown in the last chapter, in respect of periods greater than the period of production of the generality of wage-goods, reactions through the rate of interest make the elasticity of demand for labour numerically larger than it would otherwise have been, I shall, in my search for a minimum figure, ignore them altogether. If they were brought into account, they would strengthen and not weaken the argument. The position from which we start may be set out broadly as follows. There are engaged in making wage-goods at home and in making exports, the sale of which creates claims to wage-goods abroad, x men. The output in value of wage-goods of these men we call $F(x)$: and the general rate of wage is $F'(x)$. There are also engaged in other industries y further wage-earners, the wage payment to whom amounts, of course, to $yF'(x)$. There is thus a total wage payment $(x + y)F'(x)$: and there is left over, as, so to speak, a trading surplus to non-wage-earners in the wage-good and export industries, $\{F(x) - (x + y)F'(x)\}$ value of wage-goods. There is also available to non-wage-earners the item I_2, namely interest receipts from abroad in terms of value of wage-goods, which is not dependent on the current rate of wage: and there is withdrawn from them the item $(G - B)$, namely their contribution towards pensions and so on, also not dependent on the current rate of wage. The balance, apart from the relatively unimportant item of contribution from stocks (S), is absorbed in non-wage-earners' personal consumption of wage - goods, in financing their purchases of foreign non-wage-goods—my item M—and in making provision for the unemployed. Thus the method of expression to be employed in this chapter, and that of Part I. Chapter V., fit accurately into one another.

§ 4. Let us call the elasticity of the real demand for labour in the wage-good industries and the export industries together η: and the elasticity of the real demand for labour in the aggregate E_r. Given the surrounding conditions, we are entitled to write $(x + y) = \phi(x)$. Then clearly we have

$$\eta = \frac{F'(x)}{xF''(x)} \qquad \cdot \qquad \cdot \qquad \cdot \qquad \cdot \qquad \cdot \qquad \cdot \qquad \text{(i)}$$

$$E_r = \frac{\phi'(x)}{\phi(x)} \div \frac{F''(x)}{F'(x)} = \frac{x\phi'(x)}{\phi(x)} \cdot \eta. \qquad \cdot \qquad \cdot \qquad \cdot \qquad \text{(ii)}$$

These equations form the starting-point of the inquiry that follows.

§ 5. Our first task is to consider the value of η in respect of a period of industrial depression. This value is the same whether unemployment insurance exists or not, and, if it does exist, whatever arrangements rule under it. For, with an unemployment insurance system firmly established, the rate of real wage stipulated for by wage-earners will presumably have adjusted itself to the fact that employers have to make contributions to the unemployment fund, if in fact they have to do this. The magnitude η then is an average, of the type described in Chapter VI., between the elasticities of demand, in terms of wage-goods, for labour in home wage-good industries and for labour in export industries. When, as here, we lump wage-good items together and regard them, for simplicity, as consisting of a single sort of commodity, it is easy to see, in accordance with the reasoning of Chapter III. § 12, that the short-period demand function for labour in terms of wage-goods in the home wage-good industries— which, apart from reactions through the rate of interest, is identical with what in the chapter cited is called the productivity function—is likely to be highly elastic in respect of the output proper to a depression. The elasticity of demand for labour in terms of wage-goods in the export industries is a complex, depending on the elasticity of production of the export industries and the elasticity of the foreign demand, in terms of wage-goods, for the output of those industries. Since the foreign demand will not be perfectly elastic, the demand for labour in these export industries in terms of wage-goods will, if the elasticity of production in our export industries is the same as in our home wage-good industries, be less than the corresponding elasticity in our home wage-good industries. As will be argued presently, however, there is reason to believe, in a general way, that the foreign demand, in terms of wage-goods, for the exports of this country is considerably elastic.[1] Hence, if our starting-point is low down in a depression, both the elements on which the elasticity η depends are likely to be substantial. We conclude, therefore, that η is numerically large. It is certain to be (numerically) much larger than -1: and may well amount to -5 or more.

§ 6. I pass from the narrower elasticity η to the wider elasticity E_r. Here unemployment insurance, if present, is a relevant factor. In this and the two following sections I postulate that there is no insurance scheme. Our equation (ii) gave us $E_r = \dfrac{x\phi'(x)}{\phi(x)}\eta$. When η is known, we have, therefore, in order to determine E_r, to ascertain the values of $\dfrac{x}{\phi(x)}$ and of

---

[1] Cf. *post*, Part III. Chap. XIII. § 3.

$\phi'(x)$. Let us begin with $\dfrac{x}{\phi(x)}$, which, it will be remembered, is the same as $\dfrac{x}{x+y}$, namely, employment in the home wage-good industries and the export industries divided by aggregate employment. In a table prepared for the Macmillan Committee it was estimated that, for 1929 and 1930, workers for export constituted somewhere about one quarter of the whole occupied population of this country.[1] Any estimate of the proportion of the remainder that is engaged in home wage-good industries must be highly speculative. Still I suggest it is not unreasonable for this country, on the hypothesis of no unemployment insurance, to put, as a rough guess, $y = \frac{1}{3}x$. This makes $\dfrac{x}{\phi(x)} = \dfrac{x}{x+y} = \dfrac{3}{4}$.

§ 7. There remains the element $\phi'(x)$, that is the rate of change in $\phi(x)$ that is associated with a given small rate of change in x. For this value limits are set by two extreme conditions. The first condition is that, if the real rate of wage everywhere is reduced, non-wage-earners, having an absolutely rigid desire for home non-wage-goods, employ no extra men whatever in making them; that they not only keep the whole of the addition, which the cut in wages makes to their surplus of wage-goods, for their own use and the purchase of foreign non-wage-goods, but even withdraw for expenditure in these ways the resources set free by the wage-reductions in home non-wage-good industries. If this condition is realised, $\Delta x \phi'(x) = \Delta x$, so that $\phi'(x) = 1$. The second limiting condition is that non-wage earners have an absolutely rigid desire for wage-goods (and foreign imports purchased with them), employ none of the extra surplus of wage-goods for their own use or foreign purchases, but devote the whole of it to taking on more men in home non-wage-good industries. In this case, K being a constant, $\phi(x) = \dfrac{F(x) - K}{F'(x)}$ for all values of x over the range relevant to our problem.

---

[1] Appendix to Report, p. 308.

$$\therefore \phi'(x) = 1 - \frac{F''(x)\{F(x) - K\}}{(F'(x))^2} = \phi(x)\left\{\frac{1}{\phi(x)} - \frac{F''(x)}{F'(x)}\right\}$$

$$= \left\{1 - \frac{x+y}{x} \cdot \frac{1}{\eta}\right\}.$$

§ 8. It follows that E_r, which is equal to $\dfrac{x\phi'(x)}{\phi(x)} \cdot \eta$, necessarily lies between the limits $\eta \dfrac{x}{x+y}$ and $\left\{\eta \dfrac{x}{x+y} - 1\right\}$. If we accept the value $\frac{3}{4}$, as suggested in § 6, for $\dfrac{x}{x+y}$, these limits become $\frac{3}{4}\eta$ and $(\frac{3}{4}\eta - 1)$. We cannot, I think, get closer than this. We may, indeed, reasonably infer, from our general knowledge, that non-wage-earners desire for wage-goods for consumption in the neighbourhood of their actual holdings is likely to be inelastic relatively to their desire for non-wage-goods. But we cannot infer this about their desire for wage-goods for buying imported non-wage-goods. Hence we cannot say whether E_r probably lies nearer to the (numerically) upper or to the lower of our two limits. The middle point between the limits gives

$$E_r = \left\{\eta \frac{x}{x+y} - \frac{1}{2}\right\}, \text{ which, with } \frac{x}{x+y} \text{ put at } \tfrac{3}{4}, = (\tfrac{3}{4}\eta - \tfrac{1}{2}).$$

For particular illustrative values of η these formulae give

	Lower Limit of E_r.	Upper Limit.	Middle Point.
For $\eta = 0$	0	-1	$-\frac{1}{2}$
-1	$-\frac{3}{4}$	$-1\frac{3}{4}$	$-1\frac{1}{4}$
-2	$-1\frac{1}{2}$	$-2\frac{1}{2}$	-2
-4	-3	-4	$-3\frac{1}{2}$
$-\infty$	$-\infty$	$-\infty$	$-\infty$

Further, in order that the lower limit of E_r shall be -1, $\eta = -\frac{4}{3}$. Thus, if numerically $\eta > -\frac{4}{3}$, E_r is in all circumstances > -1.

§ 9. The foregoing results have been obtained on the assumption that there is no system of unemployment insurance or other provision for unemployed wage-earners. Let us now consider what happens when there is such a system. It is evident at once that, with a given rate of real wage, the quantity of employment y outside the home-wage-goods and export industries must now be smaller in our initial position than it would be in the conditions postulated so far. For part of the available surplus of wage-goods will be absorbed in paying unemployment benefit; and some of what is so absorbed is practically certain to be withdrawn from paying wages in home non-wage-good industries. The difference will, of course, be larger, the larger is the amount of unemployment that exists and the higher is the real rate of unemployment pay. For a definite quantity we can only make a guess. I suggest that, having put the y that is relevant in the absence of unemployment benefit at $\frac{1}{3}x$, we may not unreasonably put the y that is relevant in the presence of this benefit at $\frac{1}{4}x$. In any event, whether this guess be good or bad, it is clear that the elasticity now to be considered does not refer to the same quantity of employment as would exist if there were no unemployment pay. To avoid confusion I call the new quantity $(x + y')$ instead of $(x + y)$. To shorten the algebra I ignore the fact that a contribution, called elsewhere t, is made towards unemployment pay by workpeople in employment; as the numerical effect of this for the present purpose is very small. When a system of unemployment insurance rules, the analysis then proceeds as follows. The lower limit of E_r is, in accordance with the argument of § 8, $\eta \dfrac{x}{x + y'}$. The upper limit is found by calculation as follows :

$$\phi(x) = \frac{F(x) - K - \{A - \phi(x)\}r}{F'(x)}$$

$$= \frac{F(x) - K - Ar}{F'(x) - r}.$$

$$\therefore \phi'(x) = \frac{F'(x)}{F'(x) - r} - \frac{\{F(x) - K - Ar\}F''(x)}{\{F'(x) - r\}^2}.$$

But $E_r = \dfrac{x\phi'(x)}{\phi(x)}\eta.$

$$\therefore E_r = \eta \left\{ \frac{xF'(x)}{F'(x) - r} - \frac{xF''(x)\{F(x) - K - Ar\}}{(F'(x) - r)^2} \right\} \times \left\{ \frac{F'(x) - r}{F(x) - K - Ar} \right\}$$

$$= \eta \left\{ \frac{xF'(x)}{F(x) - K - Ar} - \frac{xF''(x)}{F'(x) - r} \right\}$$

$$= \eta \left\{ \frac{x\{F'(x) - r\}}{F(x) - K - Ar} + \frac{r(x)}{F(x) - K - Ar} - \frac{xF''(x)}{F'(x)} \cdot \frac{F'(x)}{F'(x) - r} \right\}$$

$$= \eta \left\{ \frac{x}{x + y'} + \frac{r(x)}{F(x) - K - Ar} - \frac{1}{\eta} \frac{F'(x)}{F'(x) - r} \right\}$$

$$= \eta \left\{ \frac{x}{x + y'} + \frac{r(x)}{F(x) - K - Ar} \right\} - \frac{w}{w - r}$$

$$= \eta \left\{ \frac{x}{x + y'} + \frac{r(x)}{(w - r)(x + y')} \right\} - \frac{w}{w - r} = \eta \frac{x}{x + y'} \left\{ \frac{w}{w - r} \right\} - \frac{w}{w - r}.$$

With $r = \frac{1}{3}w$, this gives $E_r = \eta \cdot \dfrac{3}{2} \cdot \dfrac{x}{x + y'} - \dfrac{3}{2}$. The middle point

between the limits is thus $\left\{ \eta \dfrac{5}{4} \cdot \dfrac{x}{x + y'} - \dfrac{3}{4} \right\}$. With $y' = \frac{1}{4}x$, and

so $\dfrac{x}{x + y'} = \dfrac{4}{5}$, the lower limit becomes $\dfrac{4}{5}\eta$, the upper limit

$\left\{ \dfrac{6}{5}\eta - \dfrac{3}{2} \right\}$, and the middle point $\left\{ \eta - \dfrac{3}{4} \right\}$. For particular

illustrative values of η the formulae translate as follows :

	Lower Limit of E_r.	Upper Limit.	Middle Point.
For $\eta = 0$ . .	0	$-1\frac{1}{2}$	$-\frac{3}{4}$
$= -1$.	$-\frac{4}{5}$	$-2\frac{3}{4}$	$-1\frac{31}{40}$
-2 .	$-1\frac{3}{5}$	$-4\frac{19}{50}$	$-2\frac{4}{5}$
-4 .	$-3\frac{1}{5}$	$-6\frac{1}{2}$	$-4\frac{17}{20}$
$-\infty$.	$-\infty$	$-\infty$	$-\infty$

Further, in order that the lower limit of $E_r = -1$, $\eta = -\frac{5}{4}$.
Thus, if η is numerically $> -\frac{5}{4}$, E_r is in all circumstances > -1.

If we put $\dfrac{x}{x + y'}$ at $\frac{3}{4}$, the value we guessed in the absence of
unemployment benefit, instead of at $\frac{4}{5}$, all these figures are,
of course, appropriately reduced. The lower limit becomes
identical with that given in § 8, but the upper limit and the
middle point are still substantially larger than those there
given.

§ 10. Since, then, it is quite certain that the actual value of E_r must lie well above the lower limit, we may conclude that, even though our y' has the same value as our y, the existence of unemployment benefit causes E_r to be substantially larger than it would have been in the absence of unemployment benefit: and, *a fortiori*, when, as must happen in fact, $y' < y$. This result is obvious to common sense. Thus, with $\eta = -4$, our calculations give for E_r without unemployment benefit a middle point value $-3\frac{1}{2}$: with unemployment benefit a middle point value $-4\frac{17}{20}$. A much more important result is that E_r is practically certain in actual conditions to be substantially greater than unity: so that a reduction of 1 per cent in the real rate of wage all round would mean an increase of substantially more than 1 per cent in the aggregate quantity of labour demanded. If, on the grounds given in § 5, we accept the view that, in times of depression η is not numerically < -4, it follows that in such times E_r cannot, on the least favourable assumption here suggested, be numerically less than -3 and may well be larger than -4.[1] This means that a 1 per cent reduction in the real rate of wage is likely to expand the aggregate demand for labour by not less than 3 per cent.

§ 11. The foregoing analysis has had in view, as was stated in § 3, a period longer than the period of production of the generality of wage-goods. The figures set out in the preceding paragraph have been found by a process in which reactions through the rate of interest have been ignored. If these reactions had been taken into account, the figures would, as was argued in the last chapter, have been (numerically) larger. I now turn to periods shorter than the period of production, in which, when more workpeople are employed, there is no extra inflow of wage-goods to finance additions to the wages bill. In this period the upper limit to which it is possible for the elasticity of demand for labour to attain must obviously be much lower than the upper limit proper to the type of period studied above. Apart from reactions

---

[1] Even if we were to assign to y' a much larger value than is given in the text—say $y' = x$,—with $\eta = -4$, we should still have the lower limit of E_r substantially greater (numerically) than unity, namely, -2.

through the rate of interest, the lower limit of elasticity will, however, be the same for this type of period as for the longer type. Thus, apart from these reactions, the elasticity of demand for labour would probably not be less (numerically) than -3. But the reactions through the rate of interest are now adverse. In view of our lack of knowledge as to the elasticity of the consumption-utility function of the representative non-wage-earner—the ϵ of Chapter VIII. § 8—we cannot say how large they will be. They *may* cut down the actual elasticity of the real demand for labour to $-\frac{3}{2}$: but if the argument of Chapter VIII. § 12 is valid, they cannot in any event cut it down below this, and it is exceedingly improbable that they will cut it down so far. Even in this very short period the elasticity of the real demand for labour in times of depression can hardly, in this country, be numerically less than -2.

H

NOTE TO CHAPTER IX

IT may be worth while to add here a simple and direct method of proving that, if two conditions are satisfied, E_r *must* be greater than unity. The first condition is that there are no unfilled vacancies. The second and much more important condition is that, when the real rate of wage is reduced and an addition is, consequently, made to the total of wage-goods coming into existence, not more wage-goods are added to non-wage-earners' personal consumption, use in purchasing non-wage-goods abroad and so on, than the extra output of wage-goods *plus* the reduction of non-wage-earners' contribution to unemployment benefit. With this condition satisfied it is clear that E_r cannot have a value less (numerically) than the value it would have if precisely that quantity of wage-goods were added to non-wage-earners' use of them. If, therefore, we prove that then E_r is numerically > -1, we shall have proved this *a fortiori* for cases where less than that quantity of wage-goods is added to non-wage-earners' use of them.

Recalling that r signifies rate of unemployment benefit, t rate of contribution for employed workmen, and A number of would-be wage-earners, we have, from equation (i) of Part I. Chapter V. § 4, that, with a wage-rate w and K a constant, employment

$$Q_1 = \frac{K - (A - Q_1)r + Q_1 t}{w} = \frac{K - Ar}{w - t - r}.$$

In like manner, when the wage-rate has fallen to $w(1 - m)$, employment $Q_2 = \dfrac{K - Ar}{w(1 - m) - t - r}.$

Hence $\qquad \dfrac{Q_2 - Q_1}{Q_1} = \dfrac{mw}{(1 - m)w - t - r}.$

This, of course, is subject to the proviso that Q_1 and Q_2 are both less than A; but that is already implied in our assumption that there are no unfilled vacancies. The above formula enables us, on the assumptions taken, to derive, in respect of the wage-rate w,

98

the elasticity E_r of the demand (in terms of wage-good units) for the aggregate of all labour.[1] For

$$E_r = -\frac{Q_2 - Q_1}{Q_1} \div \frac{mw}{w} = -\frac{w}{w(1-m)-t-r},$$

where m approaches 0 as limit. That is to say, $E_r = -\dfrac{w}{w-t-r}$. *This is numerically greater than unity unless t and r are nil.* If $(t+r) = \frac{1}{2}w$, the formula gives $E_r = -2$. If we put $(t+r) = \frac{1}{3}w$, it gives $E_r = -\frac{3}{2}$.

The above formula implies, it will be seen, that the demand function for labour in general is neither linear nor a constant elasticity function.[2] For finite differences in wage-rate we cannot, therefore, calculate the associated differences in employment from our knowledge of the value E_r. There is no difficulty, however, in calculating them direct from the formula

$$\frac{Q_2 - Q_1}{Q_1} = \frac{mw}{w(1-m)-t-r}.$$

The percentage increase of employment associated with different wage reductions work out thus:

Wage Reduction.	Employment Increase if $(t+r) = \frac{1}{2}w$.	Employment Increase if $(t+r) = \frac{1}{3}w$.
	Per cent.	Per cent.
1% . . .	2·04	1·52
5% . . .	10·5	8·1
10% . . .	22·2	18·2

and so on.

[1] If the existence of unfilled vacancies is allowed, but it is premised that the aggregate demand function is independent at once of the aggregate number and of the distribution of unfilled vacancies, a more general formula for this elasticity is obtained, from which that given in the text can be derived. Write D_1 and D_2 for the quantities of labour demanded at the wage-rates w and $w(1-m)$ respectively, and V_1 and V_2 for the associated quantities of unfilled vacancies. Then $D_1 = (Q_1 + V_1)$ and $D_2 = (Q_2 + V_2)$. The elasticity of demand

$$E_r = -\frac{Q_2 - Q_1 + V_2 - V_1}{Q_1 + V_1} \div \frac{mw}{w}.$$

When V_1 and V_2 are both nil, this formula reduces to that given in the text.
[2] Cf. *ante*, Chap. II. § 2.

CHAPTER X

THE ELASTICITY OF DEMAND IN TERMS OF MONEY FOR LABOUR AS A WHOLE

§ 1. In a monetary economy decisions to change the real rate of wages cannot be taken in a direct way. It is money rates, and not real rates, that are the subject matter of wage bargains. Therefore it is of practical moment to know what changes in real rates of wages are implied by given changes in money rates. A little reflection shows that the fraction $\dfrac{\text{percentage change in real rate}}{\text{percentage change in money rate}}$ in any given set of conditions is not an absolute quantity, but is, in general, different for one size of percentage change from what it is for others. If we write, as heretofore, E_r for the elasticity of the real demand for labour and E_m for the elasticity of the money demand, in respect of any given quantity of labour demanded, the above fraction is given by $\dfrac{E_r}{E_m}$ for very small, but not for large, percentage changes in this quantity. For, in general, with a given percentage change in the quantity of labour demanded, E_r times this and E_m times this only give the associated percentage changes in real and money demand prices if the given percentage change of quantity is very small. In the main part of this chapter I shall concentrate attention upon that case. In the final section the analysis will be extended to the case of substantial percentage changes along the lines sketched out in Chapter II.

§ 2. It is possible to imagine a state of things in which the money wage-rate is reduced by a given percentage, and the total volume of money spent per unit of time in purchasing commodities is reduced by an exactly equal percentage, while the original output and the original volume of employment in each several occupation are both maintained. This implies that the price level, alike of wage-goods and of anything else, is altered in the same proportion as the money wage-rate, that the real wage-rate remains what it was before, and that everything goes on exactly as it used to do, save only that all transactions are conducted with counters of diminished size. It follows that, whatever change takes place in the money rate of wage, the volume of employment is unaffected: $E_m = 0$ and $\dfrac{E_r}{E_m} = \infty$. Meditation along these lines has suggested to some persons the view that in actual life reductions in the money rate of wages would simply be reflected in a proportionate fall in prices; so that no effect whatever either on the real rate of wage or on the volume of labour demanded would be produced. This suggestion, in spite of its paradoxical appearance, deserves investigation.

§ 3. If non-industrial incomes, such as those of doctors and lawyers, are left out of account, so that all income is *associated with* wage-work, though not all paid to wage-earners, and if there are no prime costs other than wages, a 1 per cent cut in money wages, *accompanied by no change in the quantity of employment*, must involve a cut of 1 per cent alike in prices and in non-wage-earners' incomes. For, quantity of employment being x and total output, as valued in wage-goods, $F(x)$, the ratio, whether in real terms or in money terms, of other peoples' real, and so money, income to wage-earners' income is fixed at $\dfrac{F(x) - xF'(x)}{xF'(x)}$. Hence wage-earners' money income cannot fall by 1 per cent without other peoples' money income also falling by 1 per cent. In that case the real rate of wages is not altered at all; and the suggestion set out in the preceding section appears to be borne out. This, however, is not really so. The conclusion we have reached is merely a hypothetical conclusion. It describes what would happen if money wage-rates were reduced *and if the quantity of employment remained unaltered*. The idea sometimes entertained that, by means of it, we can prove that the quantity of employment, and therewith the real rate of wages, *will* remain unaltered is completely fallacious. The answer is assumed before the argument has begun. A wholly different method of approach, therefore, is required.

§ 4. Let us suppose that initially the money income of non-wage-earners is Q, and of wage-earners WX. The money wage-rate is reduced from W to (W – K)—where, of course, K is less than W—and, we suppose, the quantity of employment is not affected. At the outset nothing has happened to non-wage-earners' money income: so that total money income for expenditure on an unchanged real income is reduced from (Q + WX) to $\{Q + (W – K)X\}$. It follows that the price per unit of real income, originally p, becomes $\dfrac{Q + (W – K)X}{Q + WX} \cdot p$. Therefore, if the relative values of wage-goods and other goods are unchanged, the real wage becomes $(W – K) \cdot \dfrac{Q + WX}{Q + (W – K)X}$ times what it used to be. Hence, provided that Q is not nil, *i.e.* provided that any part of the population consists of non-wage-earners, either the real wage-rate is reduced, or the value of non-wage-goods relatively to wage-goods is increased. Hence the system is not in equilibrium. Additional labour *must* be employed, and additional output be forthcoming. The suggestion that E_m is nil cannot be sustained.

§ 5. What the value of E_m actually is in relation to E_r cannot be determined without reference to the nature of the monetary system that is established in the country. A fairly general result may, however, be attained if we postulate that the system belongs to the family of systems in which the aggregate money income—call it I—that is available from time to time to set against real income is some function of the real income of the community, and so, in respect of the short period relevant to the present argument, of the quantity of labour employed. Thus write $I = \psi(x)$. Write x for the quantity of labour in the aggregate and $F(x)$ for the value, in terms of wage-goods, of the aggregate real output or income. Then the money wage-rate in equilibrium

$$=\frac{1}{F(x)}F'(x)=\frac{\psi(x)}{F(x)}F'(x).$$

Hence $E_m =\dfrac{dx}{x}\div\left\{\dfrac{d}{dx}\cdot\dfrac{\psi(x)\,.\,F'(x)}{F(x)}\div\dfrac{\psi(x)\,.\,F'(x)}{F(x)}\right\}$

$$=\frac{dx}{x}\div\left[\left\{\frac{\psi(x)F''(x)+\psi'(x)F'(x)}{F(x)}-\frac{\psi(x)\{F'(x)\}^2}{\{F(x)\}^2}\right\}\div\frac{\psi(x)F'(x)}{F(x)}\right]$$

$$=\frac{dx}{x}\div\left\{\frac{F''(x)}{F'(x)}+\frac{\psi'(x)}{\psi(x)}-\frac{F'(x)}{F(x)}\right\}.$$

$$\therefore\ \frac{1}{E_m}=\frac{xF''(x)}{F'(x)}+\frac{x\psi'(x)}{\psi(x)}-\frac{xF'(x)}{F(x)}.$$

But, we know already, $E_r =\dfrac{F'(x)}{xF''(x)}.$

$$\therefore\ \frac{1}{E_m}=\frac{1}{E_r}-\frac{xF'(x)}{F(x)}+\frac{x\psi'(x)}{\psi(x)}.$$

For the present scale of production in this country wages amount to some two-fifths of total income.

Hence we may put $\dfrac{xF'(x)}{F(x)}=\dfrac{2}{5}.$

$$\therefore\ \frac{1}{E_m}=\frac{1}{E_r}-\frac{2}{5}+\frac{x\psi'(x)}{\psi(x)}.$$

§ 6. Let us imagine a particular type of monetary system under which the aggregate quantity of money income accruing per unit of time is held constant. Under that system $\psi'(x)$ is, of course, nil, so that the element $\dfrac{x\psi'(x)}{\psi(x)}$ in the above expression for E_m disappears. Hence the above equation reduces to $\dfrac{1}{E_m}=\dfrac{1}{E_r}-\dfrac{2}{5}$: or, alternatively, to $E_m=\dfrac{5E_r}{5-2E_r}.$ From this formula, it being remembered that E_m and E_r are both negative, a table of values of E_m associated with various values of E_r can be calculated.

Thus with $E_r = 0$ $E_m = 0$

$$-\tfrac{1}{2} \qquad -\tfrac{5}{12}$$
$$-1 \qquad -\tfrac{5}{7}$$
$$-2 \qquad -\tfrac{10}{9}$$
$$-4 \qquad -\tfrac{20}{13}$$
$$-10 \qquad -2$$
$$-\infty \qquad -2\tfrac{1}{2}$$

It will be noticed that the maximum possible value (numerically) of E_m is $-2\tfrac{1}{2}$. If, in the light of what was said in Chapter IX. § 10, we reckon the value of E_r, from the standpoint of a period not shorter than the period of production of the generality of wage-goods and export goods, in times of depression to be -4, this gives, as we have seen, $E_m = \tfrac{20}{13}$. We find further that E_m is bound to be numerically > -1, so long as E_r has a value numerically greater than $-\tfrac{5}{3}$: and our previous discussion leaves us well assured that E_r is in fact substantially greater than this.

§ 7. It is conceivable in an isolated community that the monetary system should be such that the aggregate quantity of money income accruing per unit of time is smaller the larger is the real income of the community. In this case $\psi'(x)$ is negative, and, the other elements being given, $\dfrac{1}{E_m}$ has a larger negative value, and so E_m a smaller negative value, than it would have in the type of monetary system described in a preceding section. Hence, for each value of E_r the value of E_m is a smaller negative quantity than is given in the above table. Even in an isolated community, however, this type of monetary system would be something of a freak. A system in which (for short periods) the quantity of money income per unit of time grows as real income grows seems more natural and is more likely to be established. One reason for this is that, when real income grows because the real wage-rate asked for by labour is reduced, the real rate of interest on resources invested in working capital is increased; this tempts people to shift money out of passive into active balances, thus augmenting the volume of money income per unit of time, even though the stock of money is unchanged. In respect of a community that is not isolated, but is bound by a common money to the rest of the world, these considerations are strongly reinforced. For reductions in the price level there stimulate sales abroad, and so tend to promote an inflow of gold, which is likely to lead to an increase in the stock of money. It follows that the elasticity of the money demand for labour will in actual fact be numerically larger than the figure arrived at for any given value of E_r on the hypothesis of § 6; and it may be substantially larger.

§ 8. In a small country on the gold standard in a gold standard world the monetary system is of such a sort that internal changes leave the price level substantially intact; *i.e.* in my notation, $\dfrac{\psi(x)}{F(x)}$ is constant. This implies that $\dfrac{F'(x)}{F(x)} - \dfrac{\psi'(x)}{\psi(x)} = 0$. Hence the formula of § 6 reduces to $\dfrac{1}{E_m} = \dfrac{1}{E_r}$. That is to say, the elasticity of the money demand and of the real demand for labour in respect of any quantity of employment are identical. This conclusion is, of course, directly obvious to common sense. Nevertheless, it may be of some interest to have exhibited it as a particular application of a formula, in which it is included along with a number of other conclusions that are not thus obvious.

§ 9. We have now, in accordance with the promise of § 1, to take the step from elasticities to the relation between substantial finite quantities. In the limit a given percentage reduction in the money rate of wage implies a percentage reduction $\dfrac{E_m}{E_r}$ times as large in the real rate of wage. Thus, with the monetary system postulated in § 6, under which a real elasticity of -4 implies a money elasticity of $-\frac{20}{13}$, a very small percentage reduction in the money wage-rate implies a reduction $\frac{5}{13}$ as large in the real wage-rate. This relationship does not, however, in general, hold for percentage changes of substantial finite magnitude. The analysis of Chapter II. of this Part shows that it does so hold if both the demand functions in question are linear. If they are both constant elasticity functions, it can be proved from the formula

given in that chapter that a 10 per cent cut in the money
wage-rate implies, in the case here taken, a cut in the real
wage-rate, not $\frac{5}{13}$ths of this, namely, 3·84 per cent, but $\frac{3\cdot7}{100}$
of it, namely, 3·7 per cent. There is very little difference,
therefore, between the results reached on the hypothesis of
a linear and on that of a constant elasticity function.

§ 10. As was indicated towards the end of § 6, we have
seen reason in earlier parts of our discussion to believe that,
in a period of deep depression, the elasticity of the real
demand for labour in respect of the then volume of employment will, for periods longer than the period of production
of the generality of wage-goods and export goods, be
numerically not much less than – 4. With a monetary
system of the type postulated in § 6 this implies, as was
shown above, an elasticity of money demand of – $\frac{20}{13}$. In view
of what was said in that section and in § 7, we may, therefore,
not unreasonably put the elasticity of the money demand
for labour in times of deep depression at not less numerically than – 1·5. With that elasticity a 10 per cent cut in money
wage implies, if the demand function is linear, a 15 per cent,
if it is a constant elasticity function, a 17 per cent expansion
in the quantity of labour demanded. We have thus margin
enough for a fairly confident claim that, in times of deep
depression, after an interval not less than the period of
production of the generality of wage-goods and export
goods, an all-round cut of 10 per cent in money rates
of wages would lead, *other things being equal*, to a more than
10 per cent expansion in the aggregate volume of labour
demanded, and so, apart from unfilled vacancies, in the
volume of employment. The argument of § 11 of the preceding chapter combined with the calculations of § 6 of this
chapter shows that this is also probably true even for very
short periods. The phrase *other things being equal* is em-
phasised because, of course, if, at the time when the wage-
reduction was made, other influences were tending to
deepen the depression still further, the expansive effect of
the reduction would be partly or wholly masked.[1]

[1] Cf., for this chapter, the monetary analysis of Part IV.

PART III

FACTORS OTHER THAN MONEY AFFECTING THE LEVEL AND VARIATIONS IN THE LEVEL OF THE REAL DEMAND FOR LABOUR

CHAPTER I

INTRODUCTORY

THIS Part, like Part II., is preparatory. It is concerned to set out in an orderly manner certain principal factors by which the variations in the state of real demand for labour from one time to another have been brought about. Throughout the Part I postulate that the quantity of labour demanded is always and everywhere equal to the quantity of labour employed—*i.e.* that there are no unfilled vacancies. With this proviso the quantity of wage-goods paid out—the real rate of wage being given—in any industry varies with the quantity of labour demanded there. In the first eight chapters I am concerned, as in the earlier portion of Part II., with the demand for labour in particular occupations. Thereafter I pass to the aggregate demand function for labour in the sum of all occupations. In studying this I examine in Chapter IX. the reactions on the demand for labour elsewhere of disturbances in particular industries that make non-wage-goods for the home market. Chapter X. deals with the consequences of certain sorts of transfers. Chapters XI.-XIII. trace out the remoter consequences of disturbances that primarily affect wage-good industries or export industries. In Chapter XIV. I consider briefly the bearing, in various circumstances, on the aggregate real demand function for labour of excluding or restricting various sorts of imports. The final chapter deals with a quite general factor, namely, variations in the real rate of interest at which people are willing to hand over for deferred use, out of given real incomes, given quantities of resources; or, to put the same thing in other words, variations in the quantity of resources that they are willing to hand over out of given real incomes at given rates of real interest.

CHAPTER II

§ 1. In accordance with the notation of Part II. Chapter III. let us write $\phi(x)$ for the output of the service of converting raw material into finished commodity (*i.e.* processing) in any industry rendered by x labour: ψ for the demand function, in terms of wage-goods, for new output of the finished commodity produced by that industry; and, it being premised that the quantity of raw material used per unit of output is fixed independently of the quantity of output, f for the supply function, in terms of wage-goods, of this raw material. Then, as we saw in the chapter cited, under conditions of free competition, when the real wage-rate stands at w, x is given by the equation

$$\frac{d\psi\{\phi(x)\}}{dx} - \frac{df\{\phi(x)\}}{dx} = w,$$

which may, of course, be written

$$\left\{ \frac{d\psi\{\phi(x)\}}{d\phi(x)} - \frac{df\{\phi(x)\}}{d\phi(x)} \right\} \phi'(x) = w.$$

From this equation it is apparent that the quantity of labour demanded, in respect of any given real rate of wage, will be altered if alterations take place in any one of the functions ψ, ϕ and f. Our task in the present chapter is to study in detail the character and consequences of alterations in these three functions.

§ 2. There is an important preliminary difficulty. At first sight we are inclined to suppose that alterations in any of

110

these functions can be classified simply into upward and downward movements of various magnitudes in the curves that the functions represent. A moment's reflection shows, however, that, so far as *a priori* considerations go, movements may occur of a much more complex character. When the function ϕ_1 gives place to the function ϕ_2, there is nothing to prevent ϕ'_1 exceeding ϕ'_2 for some values of x and falling short of it for other values. In geometrical terms, there is nothing to prevent a part of the new curve from lying above, while another part of it lies below, the old curve. This is true of all the three functions that we have distinguished. The consequence is that the concepts, an improvement in demand for a commodity, an improvement in the supply of raw material for making it and an improvement in the productivity of the labour devoted to processing it are not, as is commonly supposed, clear-cut concepts, but, until they have been further and more precisely defined, are ambiguous.

§ 3. The way out of this difficulty is to speak, not of an improvement in respect of any of our functions in a general way, but only in respect of the particular quantities respectively of labour employed and of output that are ruling in the initial period before the change occurs. Let us write X for the quantity of labour then employed and ψ_1, ϕ_1, f_1 for the three functions. If ψ_1 becomes ψ_2 and other things remain the same, I say that there has been an improvement in the demand for new output of the commodity when

$$\frac{d\psi_2\{\phi_1(X)\}}{d\phi_1(X)} > \frac{d\psi_1\{\phi_1(X)\}}{d\phi_1(X)}.$$

If f_1 becomes f_2 and other things remain the same, I say that there has been an improvement in the supply of raw material when $\dfrac{df_2\{\phi_1(X)\}}{d\phi_1(X)} < \dfrac{df_1\{\phi_1(X)\}}{d\phi_1(X)}$. If ϕ_1 becomes ϕ_2 and other things remain the same, I say that there has been an improvement in the productivity of labour when $\phi_2(X) > \phi_1(X)$. It will be observed that, while the definitions of improvements in demand for new output of the finished commodity and in supply of raw material have the same form, the definition of an improvement of the productivity of labour in processing has a different form. What the three definitions amount to can be set out in words thus. An improvement in demand for new output of the finished commodity takes place if the price per unit (in wage-goods) that is offered for the existing rate of output is raised. An improvement in the supply of raw material takes place if the price per unit (in wage-goods) that is asked for the existing rate of supply is lowered. An improvement in productivity takes place if the aggregate output (not necessarily the marginal output) of the existing quantity of labour employed is increased.

§ 4. With these definitions it is easy to see that an improvement in demand for new output of the finished commodity necessarily implies an increase in the quantity of labour demanded at the given real wage-rate w, except in the limiting case where the quantity of commodity produced is rigidly fixed, *i.e.* where it is impossible to increase output by setting more men to work. The same proposition plainly holds of an improvement in the supply of the relevant raw material. It might be thought at first sight that we can go further and conclude also that, with a given improvement in the demand for new output or in the supply of raw material, the increase in the quantity of labour demanded at a given real wage-rate will be larger, the more elastic is the productivity function. For, the more elastic that is, the greater will be the increase in the quantity of product bought. This last statement is, of course, true, but the suggested inference does not follow; because it is also true that, the more elastic the productivity function, the smaller is the addition to the quantity of labour that is required to produce a given addition to the output. A technical investigation of this matter shows that the increase in the quantity of labour demanded depends in a complex manner on the form of the productivity function and also on that of the other functions. If after the change the demand function for the commodity over the relevant range is very elastic, this increase will, in general, be larger the more elastic is the productivity function; but, if the demand function is very inelastic, it will, in general, be smaller the more elastic is the productivity function.[1]

---

[1] The problem, ignoring raw material, can be set out geometrically thus.

§ 5. In turning to consider the effect of improvements in the productivity of labour, we must note first that such improvements *may* both increase the total output of *x* labour and at the same time diminish the marginal output. Thus we may imagine that there are introduced into an agricultural community a number of mechanical robots exactly resembling agricultural labourers. 100 men working in conjunction with the robots would obviously produce enormously more output than the 100 men working alone would do. Nevertheless the difference made to total output by the presence or absence of the 100th man—the marginal output of 100 men—may be less than before. If the robots need no human assistance whatever, this may be true even of the first man; if they need a few men, say, to wind them up, the marginal output of any number of men less than some assigned number K will be greater than before, that of any number greater than K will be less than before. Evidently K may, according to circumstances, be either greater or less than the number that were actually employed before the robots were introduced. Thus this peculiar type of improvement is clearly possible. The generality of improvements, however, whether they consist of new mechanical equipment or of new methods, are, no doubt, co-operant with labour, in sufficient measure to ensure that their presence increases the marginal productivity of all quantities of labour, or, at all events, does not reduce the marginal productivity of any quantity.

Let DD′ represent the demand for the commodity after the improvement, in such wise that PM is the price offered for a quantity OM. Let SS′ be the (short-period) supply curve of the commodity, in such wise that the total labour cost of producing OM units of it is SPMO. Since the wage-rate is supposed fixed, this is equal (with appropriate units) to the total quantity of labour employed. Let equilibrium, in respect of the demand that prevailed before the improvement, be given with an output OR and price TR. Our problem is to determine in what conditions the area TPMR will be increased by the line TP moving closer to or further from the horizontal.

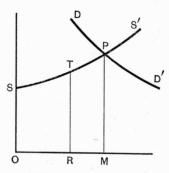

I

§ 6. It is widely supposed by popular writers that, when the elasticity of demand for labour's contribution of processing is greater than unity over the relevant range, improvements in productivity necessarily lead to increases in the quantity of labour demanded at the standing real wage-rate, and, when the elasticity of demand is less than unity, to decreases. This proposition, as a general proposition, is false. It is true only of one particular type of improvement of productivity, namely, the type that increases aggregate output and marginal output, over the relevant range of employment, *in equal proportions*. This type of improvement I shall speak of in later chapters as the normal type of improvement. Its formal definition asserts that $\dfrac{\phi'_1(x)}{\phi'_2(x)}$ is constant for all relevant values of x.[1] With improvements under which total output is increased in a smaller proportion than the marginal output of the original x men, the quantity of labour demanded at the standing real wage will be increased, not only if the elasticity of demand for the processing contributed by labour is numerically greater than unity, but also if, while falling short of unity, it does not fall short of it in more than a certain measure. With the converse type of improvement, under which total output is increased in a larger proportion than the marginal output of the original x men, the condition for an

---

[1] Thus, with F for the demand function for labour's output of processing, ϕ_1 for its productivity before the change and ϕ_2 for its productivity after the change, the demand price for x labour before the change was

$$\frac{dF\phi_1(x)}{d\phi_1(x)} \cdot \phi'_1(x).$$

After the change it is $\quad \dfrac{dF\{\phi_2(x)\}}{d\phi_2(x)} \cdot \phi'_2(x).$

But, with unitary elasticity of demand for processing,

$$\frac{dF\{\phi_1(x)\}}{d\phi_1(x)} \cdot \phi_1(x) = \frac{dF\{\phi_2(x)\}}{d\phi_2(x)} \cdot \phi_2(x).$$

∴ the demand price for labour before the change is equal to the demand price after the change if

$$\frac{\phi'_1(x)}{\phi_1(x)} = \frac{\phi'_2(x)}{\phi_2(x)}: i.e. \text{ if } \frac{\phi'_1(x)}{\phi'_2(x)} = \frac{\phi_1(x)}{\phi_2(x)}$$

for all values of x: *i.e.* if $\dfrac{\phi'_1(x)}{\phi_2(x)}$ is constant for all values of x.

increase in the quantity of labour demanded is, not merely that the elasticity of demand for labour's service shall be numerically greater than unity, but that it shall be numerically greater than unity *plus* something more. In real life improvements and additions to capital equipment are likely to be introduced in larger proportions among the firms in which labour is already specially productive than among others; so that marginal productivity is likely to benefit less than aggregate productivity. Hence, for an increase in the quantity of labour demanded to result from an improvement in productivity, we shall, in general, need an elasticity of demand for the processing contributed by labour that is more than barely in excess of unity. For all types of improvement of productivity, of course, if the demand for the industry's product is absolutely inelastic, the improvement must cause the quantity of labour demanded there at a given real rate of wage to contract.[1]

---

[1] A paradoxical result of our definition may be noticed as a *curiosum*. Improvements are possible that reduce, not only the quantity of labour employed in the industry where the improvement has been made, but also the amount of commodity produced there. We start with labour X and output of processing, and so of finished commodity, $\phi_1(X)$. After the improvement output is $\phi_2(X+h)$. Suppose, to take an extreme case, that the elasticity of the demand for labour in the industry, in terms of wage-goods, is infinite—as would be the case if there was only one sort of wage-good and our industry manufactured it. The standing wage-rate in wage-goods may be written W. Then before the improvement we have $\phi'_1(X)=W$: after it $\phi'_2(X+h)=W$. The fact that an improvement has taken place tells us, in accordance with our definition, that $\phi_2(X) > \phi_1(X)$, and it tells us nothing else. It is consistent with that proposition, not only that $(X+h)<X$, but also that $\phi_2(X+h)<\phi_1(X)$. Cases in which these things would be so are readily illustrated by diagrams of the type that Marshall employed in discussing the effect of improvements in the productivity of land (cf. *Principles of Economics*, Appendix L). Thus let PM=QN measure real wage-rate, OM the original amount of labour employed and ON the amount after the improvement. Let D_1P be the original productivity curve, and D_2Q the curve after the improvement. In the figure 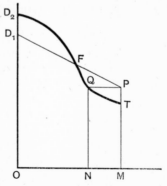 as drawn the area $D_2FD_1 >$ the area FQTP; which satisfies the condition that there has been an improvement. But the area D_2FQNO, which

§ 7. Finally we have to note that, when the demand function for the product of any industry, or the productivity of
labour, shifts in a given manner, the effect upon the quantity
of labour demanded there at a given real wage will be smaller,
the less elastic is the supply of the raw material used in it.
This proposition has an important application to practice.
From the point of view of a very short period the degree
of elasticity possessed by raw material supplies depends, in
the main, on the size of the liquid stocks on which it is possible
to draw. As an industrial depression advances, these frequently become very small indeed. Hence, on occasion, recovery may be held up, and the period of heavy unemployment prolonged, because, even though employers are now
ready to undertake increased production, they are debarred
from undertaking it in fact on account of the difficulty and
expense of obtaining raw materials for their workpeople.
Mr. Keynes lays considerable stress on this point. In his
opinion, in 1923 the stocks of raw materials had sunk so low
that the recovery of 1924 could not be helped forward by
resort to them in any appreciable measure.[1] From this point
of view a case can be made for State action to build up stocks
of materials in bad times, so that they shall be available, and
recovery shall not be held up for lack of them, when times
improve. It must be observed, however, that in the course
of the great slump of 1929–32 stocks of materials did not
contract, as they appear to have done in 1922, but, on the
contrary, steadily expanded.

represents output after the improvement, is $<$ the area D_1PMO, which
represents output before it.

[1] *A Treatise on Money*, vol. ii. p. 134.

CHAPTER III

THE PRINCIPAL FACTORS OF CHANGE IN THE REAL DEMAND FOR LABOUR IN PARTICULAR OCCUPATIONS

§ 1. As was pointed out in Chapter III. of Part II., the real demand function for new output of a commodity, that is the function ψ, is made up of the demand function of final buyers *plus* the demand function of other people desirous of adding to or reducing (in which case their demand is negative) the volume of dealers' or manufacturers' stocks. The most obvious factors of disturbance, therefore, are changes in the demand function of the final buyers. If we take the real income of these final buyers as given, shifts in their demand function result, and can only result, from shifts in their attitude of desire. Such shifts may come about through a decision on their part to adopt or abandon some purpose, for which the commodity produced by the occupation we are considering is useful. Thus, if a country decides to go to war or to make peace, the demand function for munitions is completely transformed. Shifts may also come about through people choosing in an arbitrary way some new means towards a general purpose that they continue to pursue. Thus they may seek distinction by the display of magnificent motor cars instead of magnificent jewelry. Again, shifts in the attitude of desire may occur as a consequence of changes in the age distribution of the community. Thus, if the number of young children expands relatively to the total population, the real demand for labour must grow in occupations satisfying the needs of children, while it dwindles in occupations satisfying the needs of adults. Fewer dwelling-houses, for example, and more schools per head will be wanted; more

117

nurse-maids and fewer chefs; and so on. The reader will readily develop this line of thought so far as he desires. Yet again, shifts may result from changes in the state of physical nature. People do not need so much coal or so much electric light in summer as in winter; on the other hand, they need more ice, more tennis-rackets, more bathing-suits. They tend to buy motor cars in preparation for the spring and summer, and stoves and furs in preparation for the winter. Moreover, the procession of the seasons carries with it certain shifts of desire, whose origin lies, not merely in the seasons themselves, but in social custom that has become rigidly attached to them. For example, the habit of giving large quantities of toys to children at Christmas time does not depend on the fact that the weather is cold then. Custom-induced shifts of this kind are sometimes deliberately challenged, and in part wiped out, by manufacturers' advertising campaigns concentrated on the slack seasons of the year. "An excellent example of this method is that of Hills Brothers, who pack *Dromedary Dates*. They had formerly been demanded principally in the winter, but by advertising their use in salads some demand was built up for them during the warmer months." [1]

§ 2. Shifts in people's attitude of desire are not, of course, equally liable to occur in respect of all commodities. Mr. Loveday has well observed: "The demand for goods and services satisfying secondary needs is less stable than is the demand for the necessaries of life. It roves over a wider range of choice; it is highly sensitive to changes in prospects and taste; it is optional and erratic." [2] "The surplus of income, once certain instinctive needs have been satisfied, may be spent, and may be spent by all classes of society, in a thousand different ways. The manner in which it will be spent will be determined in part by a changing conception of comfort, in part by a fickle fashion, in part by individual taste, and in part by the influence which the producer, by advertisement, can exercise on the minds of his victims." [3]

[1] Douglas and Director, *The Problem of Unemployment*, p. 86.
[2] *Britain and World Trade*, p. xi.
[3] *Ibid.* p. 93.

For, instead of merely catering for established wants, aggressive salesmanship finds profit in continually creating new ones. The high degree of wealth per head in the modern world has rendered the range of this kind of instability larger than it used to be. For it has meant that a smaller proportion of expenditure is devoted to satisfying elementary needs—to buying wheat and coarse textiles—as compared with dairy products, fruit and minor comforts.

§ 3. When everybody's attitude of desire is constant, changes in demand for particular commodities, precisely similar in character to those described above, may nevertheless take place, if purchasing power is shifted from persons who predominantly desire one sort of commodity to persons who predominantly desire another sort. If scholars became richer and sportsmen poorer, the demand for books would rise at the expense of the demand for guns. Moreover, even though everybody's scheme of desire functions were the same, a redistribution of income in favour of the poor would, nevertheless, lead to a shift of demand by rendering different groups of desires effective. Thus it would cause a reduction in the demand for expensive luxuries and, probably, for capital equipment, and an expansion in that for common comforts and *la luxe démocratique*.

§ 4. As was pointed out in Chapter III. of Part II., for commodities that are capable of being made for stock the final buyers' demand at any given real price is not necessarily equal to the total demand for new output. The relation between the two demands is of such a kind that the shock of expansions and contractions in the final buyers' demand will often be in part absorbed by stocks. Thus, when the final buyers take 10 per cent more or less than usual, the total demand for new ouptut of the product alters by less than 10 per cent. Moreover, when the cost of production for a constant output of commodity is substantially smaller than the cost of a variable output of equal aggregate amount, manufacturers themselves are stimulated to make and hold stocks in times of low consumers' demand in order to secure a fairly constant output. The existence of these reactions suggests that, other things being equal, the whole demand for new output of product is likely to undergo smaller shifts for commodities that are than for those that are not capable of being made for stock.

§ 5. Here, however, we have to bring into account a very important consideration, which points in a different direction. For commodities that are produced otherwise than by instantaneous process, that is for practically all commodities, the amount of stocks that dealers desire to hold at any time depends on the expected demand of final buyers in the future. When demand is stationary, this does not, of course, matter. But, when it varies, an expansion of the final buyers' demand now may lead dealers to anticipate still greater expansion presently. If this happens, the total demand for new output is pushed upward, not merely by the pressure of final buyers reflected through dealers, but also by the desire of dealers to increase their stocks. In like manner, when the final buyers' demand falls off, this fact may generate pessimism among dealers, and they may wish to reduce their stocks. When movements of this class are at work, total demand for new output is liable, other things being equal, to larger shifts for commodities that are than for those that are not capable of being made for stock. This is especially so when the forecasts that have to be made extend some distance into the future, as they must do for commodities that take a long time to make, and, still more, for commodities that are instruments of production, which, once made, will last and function for many years. The great complexity of modern economic structure makes it extremely difficult for any dealer to estimate correctly either the total final buyers' demand for any product a little while ahead or the extent of the preparations that other dealers are making to meet it. In lack of any real scientific ground for forecast, there is wide scope for the play of feeling and for judgements that waver between excessive optimism and excessive pessimism. In my book on *Industrial Fluctuations* I have studied these matters at length, and do not propose to repeat the study here. The reader is referred to chapters vi. and vii. of Part I. of the work named.

§ 6. There has next to be noted an important distinction between commodities that render their services in a single act or in a short time, such as articles of food and drink, and commodities which last a long time and spread their services over a number of years, such as pianos, houses and most forms of instrumental capital. When the final buyers' demand —quantity demanded at a given price—for services rendered by a commodity of the first class varies by, say, 10 per cent, this implies a variation of 10 per cent in the demand for the commodity, and so, if we neglect variations in stocks, for new output of the commodity. But, when the final buyers' demand for the services rendered by a commodity of the second class varies 10 per cent, this implies a variation in demand for new output of the commodity much greater than 10 per cent. Thus suppose that the number of units of the commodity in use is A and that, of these, nA normally need to be replaced in a year—which implies in equilibrium that the "life" of the commodity in use is $\frac{1}{n}$ years. If the quantity of the commodity's service that is demanded rises 10 per cent, this means that the quantity of new output demanded rises from nA to $\left(n\text{A} + \frac{\text{A}}{10} \right)$, namely, by $\frac{1}{n}$ times 10 per cent. Thus, if $n = \frac{1}{5}$, that is to say, if the rate of depreciation of the commodity in question is 20 per cent per annum, an increase of 10 per cent in the demand for the services rendered by that commodity implies an increase of 50 per cent in the demand for new output of it. Nor is this all. For, with commodities of this sort, when an expansion of demand for the total supply takes place in one period, this means that in the next period the stock is larger than before, so that, if the demand for the total supply then returns to its old level, the demand for new production must fall below its old level. Thus in the above illustration suppose that there is no upward trend of demand. Then in normal times the quantity of new production demanded is nA. After an expansion in one period of 10 per cent in the demand for total supply, and, consequently, of $\frac{1}{n}$-th of 10 per cent in the demand for new production, the stock stands at $\text{A}(1 + \frac{1}{10})$. The demand for total supply then reverts to what it was originally. This implies that the demand for new production falls to

$$A - A\{1 + \tfrac{1}{10}\}(1 - n) = A\{n\tfrac{1}{10} - \tfrac{1}{10}\}, \text{ that is to } \frac{11n - 1}{10n} \text{ times}$$

the normal amount. With $n = \tfrac{1}{5}$, as above, this means a contraction of new demand below the normal of 40 per cent. This line of thought goes far to explain the high variability of the demand for labour in such industries as shipbuilding. It also suggests that, when a new durable commodity, such as radios or gramophones, is invented, the demand for labour to satisfy the first *flood* of demand for it, particularly if knowledge about the commodity can be broadcast quickly by advertisement and the purchase of it facilitated by sales on the instalment system, is likely much to exceed the subsequent demand for labour for making good wastage and satisfying the *stream* of wants of new customers.

§ 7. The supply functions of different sorts of raw material, like the demand functions for different sorts of finished product, vary in different degrees. Vegetable raw materials—cotton, jute, barley and so on—are liable to disturbances in consequence of climatic irregularities leading to good and bad harvests, abnormal sowings (*e.g.* after the war) and so on, of a sort from which mineral raw materials are free. On the other hand, the supply of mineral raw materials may be altered violently by the discovery of new mines or the sudden petering out of established mines. For materials drawn from a narrow area of supply occasional severe shortages may be produced by industrial disputes or successful acts of cornering; whereas materials drawn from a wide area and many independent sources are less liable to these disturbances. When it happens, however, that the wide area of supply is in part foreign, dislocations are liable to be brought about on some occasions by political action. This happens, for example, if any source of supply, from which a material has hitherto been drawn, is cut off by war or by duties or prohibitions against exports in the exporting country, or by duties or prohibitions against imports in the importing country.

§ 8. The productivity function of labour ϕ varies in some occupations in a seasonal manner on account of variations in the amount of help or hindrance furnished by Nature. Thus a man working with given energy can dig up more ground in a given time when the soil is soft than when it is frozen. Advancing technique has, however, done a good deal to lessen the range of this type of variation in productivity. Thus the invention of cheap ways of providing artificial light out of doors has reduced the handicap of winter work as against summer work in building; steam and electricity have made unimportant the freezing, or the drying up, of sources of water power. Variations in the productivity of labour, other than seasonal variations, may also occur through inventions and technical improvements. These are more likely to be made in the manufacture of commodities that have been recently introduced than in old-established industries. But recent developments in agricultural technique show that even the most ancient of industries is not exempt from them.

CHAPTER IV

STATE STIMULATION OF EMPLOYMENT IN PARTICULAR OCCUPATIONS

§ 1. THE analysis of Chapter II. is readily extended to cover various sorts of State stimulation to the demand for labour in particular occupations. A number of methods of stimulation are available, which, for the same effect on the quantity of labour demanded, involve very different expenditures by the State. Thus, let us suppose that its action is concentrated upon a particular type of occupation, in which initially A men are employed. The State may (1) give a subsidy to all wages paid there, (2) give a subsidy to the wages of additional men (in excess of A) employed there, (3) give a subsidy to all output there, (4) give a subsidy to additional output (in excess of that due to A men), (5) give guarantees of interest. When the subsidy methods are employed, it is immaterial for the present purpose whether the subsidy is paid by the State to private entrepreneurs or whether, the State acting as its own entrepreneur, the subsidy is paid, so to speak, to itself.

§ 2. Plainly, the method that is cheapest for the State at the moment is that of guarantees of interest; for at the moment these involve no outgoings whatever, but, on the contrary, yield savings to the State equal to the addition to net employment multiplied by the rate of unemployment benefit *plus* the rate of employed workpeople's contribution. Write E_d for the number of men directly brought into employment and E_k for the number indirectly driven out of employment in other industries. Then the cost to the State is $-(r+t)(E_d - E_k)$. This cost *must* be negative.

124

§ 3. The next cheapest method is that of a bounty on wages, or on output, confined to the new workpeople who are called into employment in the industry affected, and not extended to the wages, or output, of those who are employed there already. Let the rate of bounty required to produce the same effect on employment as above be s per wage-earner. Then obviously the total cost to the State is $s . E_d - (r + t)(E_d - E_k)$. This cost *may* be negative.

§ 4. For practical reasons it is exceedingly difficult to devise any scheme of bounties under which the bounty payments are confined to the wages or output of the additional men called into employment in the industry affected. If these payments are made in respect of all the men in employment, old as well as new, the expense to the State obviously exceeds what it would be in the case just contemplated by an amount As. It is equal to $s(A + E_d) - (r + t)(E_d - E_k)$. Even this cost may be negative; but it is much less likely to be so than the cost under the preceding plan.

§ 5. When the State employs extra men itself in public works, it has to pay, not merely a bounty on their wages, but the whole of their wages. In this case the total cost to it— I ignore the incidental payment to associated non-wage-earners—is $E_d w - (r + t)(E_d - E_k)$. If $(r + t)$ is $< w$, this cost obviously cannot be negative in any circumstances. In one special set of conditions the cost to the State in this case is the same as in that of a general subsidy on all wages. The condition is that the demand schedule in terms of wage-goods—and so here also in terms of money—for labour in the relevant occupation has the form of a rectangular hyperbola, *i.e.* has an elasticity throughout the relevant range equal to -1. For on that condition $Aw = (A + E_d)(w - s)$; which implies that $(A + E_d)s = E_d w$.

§ 6. From our present standpoint these distinctions are of secondary importance. It is fairly plain that all sorts of State stimulation to employment in particular industries can be equated, so far as their effect on the demand for labour there is concerned, to general subsidies on wages there. Hence, when the effect of these has been analysed, the effect of all other sorts of State stimulation have been analysed also. The required analysis can be set out thus. The quantity of labour demanded in any occupation in the absence of any subsidy is given—for simplicity I ignore raw material costs—by the equation $\dfrac{d\psi\{\phi(x)\}}{d\phi(x)} \cdot \phi'(x) = w$. If a subsidy is paid in respect of wages, we have $\dfrac{d\psi\{\phi(x)\}}{d\phi(x)} \phi'(x)$ $= w - s$. It is required to determine the consequences to the quantity of labour demanded in the industry affected of this subsidy. Obviously the effect is the same as would follow from a reduction in the wage-rate stipulated for by an amount equivalent to the rate of subsidy per wage-earner. In the special case where the demand for the product is perfectly elastic, both these effects are the same as would follow from a lifting of the productivity curve by the same constant amount throughout its length, in such wise that $\phi'_2(x) = \{\phi'_1(x) + s\}$ for all values of x. It is obvious that in all circumstances, save only when the demand for the product is perfectly inelastic, the quantity of labour demanded must be increased in consequence of this type of subsidy.

CHAPTER V

THE INTERDEPENDENCE OF DEMAND CHANGES IN RESPECT
OF SUBSTITUTES AND COMPLEMENTS

§ 1. A SHIFT in desire, and so in demand, for one of two commodities that are substitutes for one another is often the part effect of a more general change that carries with it a shift *in the opposite direction* in the desire for the other commodity. In like manner a shift in desire for one of two complements is often the part effect of a more general change that carries with it a shift in *the same direction* in the desire for the other commodity. But a shift in the desire for one of two correlated commodities, though it may, in this way, be accompanied by, does not itself generate, any shift in the desire for the other. Hence it does not generate any (appreciable) shift in the demand, in terms of wage-goods, for the other. Nor, obviously, does it generate any shift in the productivity function of the other. Hence shifts of the function ψ, in respect of one commodity, do not react in any way to produce variations in the quantity of labour demanded in making substitutes or complements for that commodity. So far, therefore, nothing needs to be added to the analysis of the preceding chapters. When, however, the demand function for labour is altered in one of two occupations that make either substitutes or complements in consequence either (1) of the grant of a State subsidy or (2) of a change in productivity, the position is different. Secondary reactions of an important kind now do take place. In the following paragraphs I shall study these two cases in turn.

§ 2. Let us consider first State action. When any form of

State encouragement is given to the making of a commodity
for which another commodity is a substitute, the increase in
the quantity of labour demanded in the industry making the
subsidised (or otherwise stimulated) commodity is necessarily
offset in some measure by a contraction in the quantity demanded in the industry that makes the substitute. The
subsidy, or whatever the stimulus applied may be, because
it directly expands production in the subsidised industry,
through that very fact indirectly contracts it in the rival
industry. Its effect on the quantity of labour demanded in
the two industries together is, therefore, in general, less than
its effect on the quantity demanded in the subsidised industry. Thus, if a wage subsidy is given to some coal mines
and, as a consequence, their output expands, the desire to
employ men in other coal mines is adversely affected; if
house-building by municipalities is stimulated by cheap loans,
employment among private house builders falls off. In the
simple case of two centres producing perfect substitutes, *i.e.*
identical goods, it is easy to see, without resort to symbols,
that, given the expansion of employment in the stimulated
centre, the contraction in the other centre will more and
more nearly cancel it: (1) the less elastic, in terms of wage-
goods, is the demand for the commodity that the two centres
produce; (2) the larger is the unstimulated centre relatively
to the other; (3) the more elastic is production in the stimulated centre; and (4) the less elastic is production in the unstimulated centre. When the demand is absolutely inelastic,
the contraction of output in the unstimulated centre must
completely offset the expansion in the other. Thus, if a
municipality builds a gas-works to meet a rigidly limited
demand, which otherwise would have been met by private
industry, there will be no net gain to the output of gas, and
the quantity of labour demanded in the aggregate will be
approximately unchanged. By similar reasoning it is easy to
see that, if the State encourages, by subsidy or otherwise, the
production of a commodity, to which some other commodity
is a complement, its action will indirectly cause the demand
for this other commodity to expand, and, therefore, the
effect on the quantity of labour demanded in the aggregate

will be larger than the effect on the quantity demanded in the subsidised industry.

§ 3. We may now turn to the effect, in respect of substitutes and complements, of improvements in the productivity of labour. Suppose that the productivity function is improved in an industry that makes something for which another industry makes a substitute. It is plain that the quantity of labour demanded will be affected in the second industry as well as in the first. But the problem is more complicated with an improvement in productivity than it is with a subsidy, because, while, with a subsidy, the quantity of labour demanded both in the subsidised industry and, in a lesser degree, in both industries together, must in all circumstances be increased, with an improvement this need not be so. The matter may be set out thus—it being premised that the improvement which has occurred is of the "normal" type.[1] Let us again confine ourselves to the simplest case of perfect substitutes, so that, in effect, the improvement takes place in one of two centres that produce the same thing. The demand function for the output of the improved centre is derived from the demand function for the output of both centres together by subtracting from this the supply function of the non-improved centre. The elasticity of the resultant demand for the output of the improved centre is determined as follows. Write for this elasticity E_s, for the elasticity of demand for the product as a whole η, for the elasticity of supply of the product from the unimproved centre e, for the original output of the improved centre A, of the other B.

Then $E_s = \dfrac{(A + B)\eta - eB}{A}$. Since e, from a short-period standpoint, is positive, it follows that E_s is numerically larger than η. That is to say, the demand for the output of the improved centre is more elastic than the demand for output as a whole. Even therefore, when the demand for output as a whole has an elasticity numerically less than unity, the demand for the output of the improved centre may have an elasticity greater than unity. In conditions where it has an

---

[1] Cf. *ante*, Chap. II. § 6.

elasticity less than unity the quantity of labour demanded
in the improved centre after the improvement will be less
than before: the quantity demanded in the other centre will
also be less than before. Hence the quantity of labour demanded as a whole will be less than before; the aggregate
contraction, moreover, exceeding the contraction in the improved centre. In conditions where the elasticity E_s is greater
than unity, the quantity of labour demanded in the improved
centre after the improvement will be greater than before,
while the quantity demanded in the other centre will again
be less than before. The quantity demanded in the aggregate
may, therefore, according to circumstances, be either greater
or less than before. It is more likely to be greater than before,
the more elastic is the demand for the product as a whole.
The only universally valid rule is that the quantity demanded
in the aggregate will be affected less favourably than the
quantity demanded in the improved centre. So far we have
been considering substitutes. There remain complements.
When an improvement of productivity takes place in respect
of one of two complements, the quantity of labour demanded
in the industry where the improvement is made may be
either diminished or increased, but the quantity demanded
in the complementary industry is necessarily increased. Thus
in this case the quantity of labour demanded in the aggregate
is affected more favourably than the quantity demanded in
the improved industry.

CHAPTER VI

THE STATISTICAL DETERMINATION OF MOVEMENTS OF THE DEMAND FUNCTIONS IN PARTICULAR OCCUPATIONS

§ 1. In Chapter III. of Part II. inquiry was made into the feasibility of determining from statistical data the elasticity of the short-period real demand functions for labour in particular occupations. A like inquiry has now to be made about the movements of short-period real demand functions. The relevant data are money values of output per head, money wage-rates, the index of the money value of wage-goods and statistics of unemployment and of unfilled vacancies. The problem is to determine whether, and in what conditions, a manipulation of these data will enable us to ascertain how the real demand function for labour in a given occupation has moved between two dates.

§ 2. Let us represent the quantities of labour demanded at the two dates to be compared by X and (X + R): the real wage-rates obtained by dividing the price of a wage-goods unit into the rate of money wages, by W and (W + h): and the real values of output per head, obtained by dividing the price of a wage-goods unit into the money value of output per head, by P and (P + Q). Write F(x) for the demand function at the first date and $\psi(x)$ for that of the second date. It is obvious that our data are inadequate by themselves to determine the relation between ψ and F, and that, in order that any inferences may be drawn, certain postulates about the nature of these functions must be made.

§ 3. Let us consider first what can be deduced if we postulate simply that both functions are linear. We then have the following equations:

(1) $F(X) = W.$ $\qquad$ (3) $\dfrac{F(o) + F(X)}{2} = P.$

(2) $\psi(X + R) = (W + h).$ $\qquad$ (4) $\dfrac{\psi(o) + \psi(X + R)}{2} = P + Q.$

From (1) and (2), $\psi(X) - F(X) = h - R\psi'.$

From (3) and (4), $\psi(X) - F(X) + \psi(o) - F(o) = 2Q - R\psi'.$

$\qquad \therefore \ \psi(o) - F(o) = (2Q - h).$

That is to say, the vertical distance of the initial position (*i.e.* the position corresponding to nil employment) of the second demand curve above the first can be calculated. It is equal to twice the excess of the second real value of output per head above the first *minus* the excess of the second real wage-rate above the first. If no further postulate beyond that of linearity is made, this is all that we are able to infer.

§ 4. Obviously, however, if we hold ourselves free also to make postulates about the slope of the curves, we can determine how far, in respect of any quantity of employment, the second curve lies above the first. Thus we may suppose that the second curve is set above the first at the same *absolute* distance throughout. It follows that $(2Q - h)$ measures this constant distance. The relation between the functions ψ and F is thus completely known. Again, we may suppose that the second curve is set above the first at the same *proportionate* distance throughout, *i.e.* that $\psi(X) = mF(X)$ for all values of X. This condition implies that, in respect of each quantity of labour demanded, the elasticity of demand is equal for both curves. If it is satisfied, we may proceed as follows:

We have $\qquad \dfrac{\psi(o) + W + h}{2} = P + Q..\qquad . \quad . \quad .$ (1)

And $\qquad \dfrac{F(o) + W}{2} = P.\qquad . \quad . \quad . \quad .$ (2)

Hence $\qquad \dfrac{\psi(o)}{F(o)} = \dfrac{2(P + Q) - (W + h)}{2P - W}.$

But $\qquad \dfrac{\psi(X)}{F(X)} = \dfrac{\psi(o)}{F(o)}.$

$$\therefore \frac{\psi(X)}{F(X)} = \frac{2(P+Q) - (W+h)}{2P - W}.$$

Hence $\psi(X) - F(X) = \dfrac{W\{2Q - h\}}{2P - W}.$

Thus the vertical distance of the second demand curve above the first, in respect of the quantity X of labour demanded, is determined in terms of our data: and similar determinations can be made, if desired, for other points on the curves. Again, therefore, the relation between the functions ψ and F is completely known. A number of other postulates might be adopted, on the basis of which our data would enable similar computations as to the relation between the two demand curves to be made. But no other postulate has any *prima facie* plausibility.

§ 5. In real life we are seldom warranted in laying down *a priori* either of the two postulates employed in the preceding section. In these circumstances our statistical data are not sufficient to enable us to infer the nature or extent of the movement which has taken place in the demand function between the dates to which they refer.

CHAPTER VII

TRANSITIONS FROM COMPETITIVE TO MONOPOLISTIC ACTION
BY EMPLOYERS AGAINST THEIR CUSTOMERS, AND *VICE VERSA*

§ 1. Up to this point we have tacitly postulated conditions
of free competition. The present chapter follows upon the
analysis of monopolistic restrictions upon output given in
Part II. Chapter IV. For simplicity I suppose that we are
concerned with an independent commodity, for which there
are neither substitutes nor complements. Since the object of
restriction in any occupation is to enable the employers there
to sell their product on better terms against the output of
other occupations, this policy is not one that can be applied
with success all round. If one industry cuts its output 10 per
cent, it may thereby secure a larger real income: but, if all
industries do this, they necessarily secure a smaller real income. Hence, if all industries were under a single control, and
there was nobody outside industry, the policy of restricting
output along monopolistic lines would never be adopted anywhere. Since, however, different industries are in truth con-
trolled by different people, the fact that restriction is futile
as a universal policy does not prevent it from being effective
as an individual one. Since, by refraining from restriction, A
will not secure that B, C and D shall also refrain, A would
lose, and not gain, by refraining himself. Consequently, restriction all round, though injurious to all, is, nevertheless,
in a sense, beneficial to each; and, when agreement within
industries proves feasible, is likely to be undertaken. In fact,
as experience shows, it is often undertaken. In some industries
monopolistic policy rules regularly and continuously. This
case does not concern us. It frequently happens, however,

that monopolistic policy on the part of employers in particular industries is practised, not continuously, but in some periods and not in others, or, at all events, in a more marked degree in some periods than in others.

§ 2. If, in any industry, monopolistic policy, whether in the guise of formal agreement, or of tacit understanding or of a general refusal, without any understanding, to sell down to prime cost, were introduced in periods when the demand for the product of that industry was expanded and removed in periods when it was contracted, the real demand function for labour there might be rendered more stable than it would have been had either free competition or monopoly ruled throughout. If shifts between competitive and monopolistic policy took place in a random manner, neither policy being more likely to occur in times of low than in times of high demand, these shifts, though they might on some occasions make for stability, would, on the whole, promote oscillations in the real demand function for labour in the occupations affected. If shifts towards monopoly took place predominantly in times of low demand for the commodity (or high supply price of the raw materials used in making it) and shifts towards competition predominantly in good times, the tendency to promote oscillations would be still more marked.

§ 3. There can be little doubt that the third of these situations is the one actually realised. In bad times employers find that they are getting a much smaller return on their investment than they had anticipated. If they have borrowed on debentures to make the investment, they may find themselves unable to provide the interest on their borrowings out of their business earnings. More or less concerted restriction of output, through some form of monopolistic procedure, presents itself to them as a main means of salvation, and is undertaken—*e.g.* organised short time in the Lancashire cotton industry—to palliate the evils of depression. Thus there occur shifts from competitive to monopolistic policy. In good times the pressure is relaxed and competitive practices return. It follows that, even though the introduction of monopolistic policy had the same proportionate restrictive effect on labour demand when introduced in bad times as when introduced in good, the transitions that actually take place between monopoly and competition would have a substantial effect in causing this demand to vary.

§ 4. This, however, is not all. In any industry the proportionate extent to which the introduction of monopolistic policy on the part of employers towards their customers affects the real demand function for labour (in the sense of the quantity of labour demanded in respect of any given real rate of wage) is not the same in all circumstances. Thus write y for the quantity of product, $F(y)$ for the quantity of labour required to produce y, and, therefore, $WF(y)$ for the short-period cost, in wage-goods, to employers of producing y when the stipulated real wage-rate is W. The marginal supply price (in wage-goods) per unit of product when y units are being produced is then obviously equal to $WF'(y)$, and the average supply price to $\dfrac{WF(y)}{y}$.[1] If $\phi(y)$ be written for the demand price of the commodity, the output under competition will be given by the root of the equation $\phi(y) = WF'(y)$, say, Y. The output under monopoly will be given by the root of $\dfrac{d}{dy} \cdot \{y\phi(y) - F(y)\} = 0$, say, Y'. It is obvious that the ratio $\dfrac{Y'}{Y}$, and, therefore, the ratio $\dfrac{F'(Y')}{F(Y)}$, depends on the form of the relevant functions and on the way in which the curves they represent are related to one another.

§ 5. There is reason to believe that in the short period, as the quantity of labour moves upward from nil, marginal output will at first increase, then be fairly steady, then decrease slowly, and finally decrease rapidly; since after a point, with a given equipment, even an infinite addition to the supply of labour would add nothing to output.[2] This implies that the curve of marginal supply prices, $i.e.$ the (short-period)

---

[1] For long-period competitive equilibrium, as is well known, the marginal supply price and the average supply price of the equilibrium firm must coincide. This is not necessary, however, for short-period competitive equilibrium. For that the marginal supply price must, but the average supply price need not, be equal to the demand price.

[2] Cf. Part II. Chap. III. p. 51.

supply curve, will, in the first part of its course, be descending, then for some time horizontal, then slightly ascending, then steeply ascending, until finally it becomes a vertical straight line. It is evident in a general way that, if, under competitive conditions, the demand curve is cutting the curve of marginal supply prices in the part of it that is horizontal or only slightly ascending, the introduction of monopoly will involve a large proportionate reduction alike in output and in quantity of labour employed; but, if the demand curve is standing so high that its intersection with the curve of marginal supply prices takes place far up on the vertical part of that curve, output and the quantity of labour employed need not be reduced at all. Thus, *prima facie*, the proportionate restrictive effect of monopolisation upon the quantity of labour demanded at a given real wage seems likely to be larger if monopoly is introduced when the demand for the commodity is small (*i.e.* in bad times) than if it is introduced when that demand is large (*i.e.* in good times).

§ 6. It is possible to construct a highly simplified model, in respect of which this matter can be treated with exactitude. Suppose that the demand curve for the commodity in which we are interested is a straight line; that the supply curve is a horizontal line standing at a distance p above the base-line till output r is attained, and thereupon becoming a vertical line—*i.e.* when further output is impossible. Let the demand be such that, at price p, purchasers would be willing to take s units. Then, obviously, under monopoly output will be $\frac{1}{2}s$. If the demand curve lies so low that $s < r$, output under competition $= s$. Therefore the shift to monopoly halves output and, in the case supposed, also halves the quantity of labour demanded and employed. If, however, $s = > r$, output under competition $= r$. Therefore the transition to monopoly contracts output and employment from r to $\frac{1}{2}s$. The matter can be put thus. Write $r = ms$. Then the proportionate contraction of output, and so of employment, due to this shift $= \dfrac{m - \frac{1}{2}}{m} = \dfrac{2m - 1}{2m}$ when $2m > 1$: and nil when $2m < 1$. For example, if $r = \frac{3}{4}s$, the proportionate contraction is $\frac{1}{3}$; if $r = \frac{4}{5}s$ it is $\frac{3}{8}$. More generally, there is a certain critical

position (1) of the demand curve for the commodity, in respect of which, and of all higher positions, the passage from
competitive to monopolistic policy makes no difference to
output or to the quantity of labour demanded. There is a
second lower critical position (2), for which, and for all positions below which, output and the quantity of labour demanded under monopoly will be one-half what it is under
competition. Over the range of positions lying between (1)
and (2) the ratio of the quantity of labour demanded under
monopoly to that demanded under competition will fall
gradually from equality to one-half as we pass down the
series of positions lying between position (1) and position (2).
It follows from this that, the state of equipment being given,
a passage from competitive to monopolistic policy is likely
to bring about a larger proportionate contraction in the quantity of labour demanded if it is made in bad times, when
demand is low, than if it is made in good times.

§ 7. The foregoing analysis, it will have been noticed, has
proceeded on the assumption that the market is perfect or,
more properly, that whatever frictions and imperfections may
exist will not seriously affect the result. If slight imperfections in the market are postulated, so that the several producing firms are, within limits, each possessed of monopolistic
power in their private markets, conclusions substantially
similar to the above follow. Thus Mr. Kahn has shown that
the presence of imperfections in the market and the monopoly
power conferred by them do not make output appreciably
different from what it would have been in conditions of pure
competition, so long as in the generality of firms concerned
$\frac{1}{2}s$ is not less than r. When, however, in consequence of the
demand curve standing at an abnormally low level, $\frac{1}{2}s$ is
much less than r, the presence of monopoly makes itself felt
and employment contracts accordingly. On this method of
analysis, instead of saying that monopolistic action is introduced in bad times and causes employment to fall, we may
say that monopolistic action, which has been present in em-
bryo all the time, *makes itself felt* in bad times and causes
employment to fall. The two methods of analysis thus lead
to identical results.

§ 8. The conditions of real life are, of course, much more complicated than those postulated in the artificially simplified case considered in the two preceding sections. Our model analysis warrants us, I think, in concluding that monopolisation will have a larger proportionate effect on the quantity of labour demanded if it is introduced in times of deep depression than if it is introduced when the demand for the commodity is *very high indeed* relatively to the capacity of the industry. But the issue is not so clear when bad times are contrasted with moderately good times. For it must be remembered that, in the region where the curve of marginal supply prices is inclined steeply but is not vertical, a given proportionate contraction of output means a substantially larger proportionate contraction in the quantity of labour at work. Thus the results reached in §§ 5-6 can only be applied to actual conditions with doubt and caution. In so far, however, as we do venture to apply them, the general conclusion reached in § 3 is confirmed and strengthened.

CHAPTER VIII

A SPECIAL POINT CONCERNING CHANGES IN RELATIVE
DEMANDS

§ 1. BEFORE we pass to wider issues it is convenient to introduce here a brief note on a special point. At first sight it is natural to suppose that, though in actual life relative movements of demand in different occupations occur, yet, so long as real income per head of people of working age does not alter, there is no inherent necessity for their occurring, and it is possible, without incoherence, to conceive of a state of things in which they do not occur. This is, of course, true of a community in which the number of people of working age is constant. For a community in which the population of working age is expanding it is not, however, true in general. The reason is that, if the real income per head of the working population is to remain constant, the stock of capital equipment must expand in the same proportion as the working population; and it is only in certain conditions that this can happen, and *also* that the number of work-people demanded (and employed) in the industries which construct capital equipment can expand in the same proportion as the number demanded (and employed) in other occupations. We have to determine what these conditions are and what happens when they are not satisfied.

§ 2. Let us first make the assumption that capital-goods, once made, last for ever. Let $f(t)$, a function of time, represent the stock of these things. This stock is required to increase at the same (geometrical) rate as the flow of immediately consumable goods; both these rates being equal to the rate of expansion of the working population. In order, therefore, that there may be no movement of relative demand, as between wage-earners engaged in making capital-goods and wage-earners engaged in making immediately consumable goods, the *change in the stock* of capital-goods, that is, the new production of them, must expand at the same proportionate rate as the *aggregate stock* of them. The condition for this is that $\dfrac{f'(t)}{f(t)} = \dfrac{f''(t)}{f'(t)}$. This condition is satisfied if $\dfrac{f'(t)}{f(t)}$ is constant; that is, if the proportionate (geometrical) rate, at which new production in the industries making capital-goods (and so also in those making consumable goods) changes, is constant; that is if, in the conditions here supposed, the proportionate (geometrical) rate of increase in the population of working age is constant. If $\dfrac{f'(t)}{f(t)}$ is not constant but increasing, $\dfrac{f''(t)}{f'(t)} > \dfrac{f'(t)}{f(t)}$. That is to say, in order that parallelism may be maintained between the expansion in the stock of capital-goods and in the flow of immediately consumable goods, the annual production of capital-goods must expand faster than the annual production of immediately consumable goods. This implies that the demand for labour in the occupations making the former class of goods must continually expand relatively to the demand for labour in occupations making the latter sort. If $\dfrac{f'(t)}{f(t)}$ is not constant but decreasing, the converse is true. When the assumption that capital-goods last for ever is abandoned, let us suppose that they last for k years. Then the capital stock at any time $= f(t) - f(t-k)$, and the rate of increase in it $= f'(t) - f'(t-k)$. If the proportionate (geometrical) rate of change in the stock is constant, we have

$$\frac{f'(t) - f'(t-k)}{f(t) - f(t-k)} = \frac{f''(t) - f''(t-k)}{f'(t) - f'(t-k)};$$

so that $\dfrac{f''(t) - f''(t-k)}{f'(t) - f'(t-k)}$ is also constant. This implies that $\dfrac{f''(t)}{f'(t)}$ is constant. Hence the conclusions reached above do not need to be modified when the assumption that capital-goods last for ever is removed.

§ 3. It follows that, with constant real income per head, which implies constant capital equipment per head, the demand for labour in the industries that make capital-goods and consumption-goods respectively will be constant relatively to one another if the population of working age is expanding at a constant geometrical rate. With working population expanding at an accelerating geometrical rate, however, the proportion of men demanded in the capital-making industries must grow: with working population expanding at a decelerating geometrical rate—of which a constant arithmetic rate is a particular case—the proportion so demanded must decline. These conclusions depend, of course, on the tacit assumption that, if the quantity of output per head alters at all, it alters in the same direction and to the same extent in both groups of industries.

CHAPTER IX

CHANGES IN PARTICULAR NON-WAGE-GOOD AND NON-EXPORT
INDUSTRIES IN RELATION TO THE REAL DEMAND FOR
LABOUR IN THE AGGREGATE

§ 1. WHEN the real rate of wage stipulated for is given, the
quantity of labour demanded in the aggregate of all industries
varies, and can only vary, in precise proportion to the quantity
of wage-goods available for, and devoted to the payment of,
wages. In a particular occupation a disturbing cause may
bring about changes in the quantity of labour demanded
there, that are operated through wage-goods being *transferred*
from wage-earners in other occupations, without the total
quantity of wage-goods devoted to wage payments being
altered at all: and, if the occupation only employs a small
part of the total labour force, the change effected by a given
disturbing cause in the quantity of labour demanded there will
be substantially the same whether the aggregate quantity of
wage-goods available for wage-payments is readily expanded
or is rigidly fixed. Plainly, however, nothing of this kind can
be said of the quantity of labour demanded in the aggregate
of all industries. If the wage-fund, as we may call it, is rigidly
fixed, an expansion (or contraction) in the quantity of labour
demanded at a given real rate of wage in one occupation is
necessarily offset, on the assumption that there are no unfilled vacancies, by an exactly equal contraction (or expansion) in the quantity demanded in other occupations; so that
the quantity of labour demanded in the aggregate is left unchanged. It is only in so far as the aggregate wage-fund is able
to expand or contract that a decision to engage more or less
labour in one occupation can be satisfied without an equiva-

lent offset in the quantity of labour demanded elsewhere. In the present chapter, in accordance with the programme sketched in the Introductory Chapter to this Part, I suppose that there has taken place, in a non-wage-good industry or group of non-wage-good industries, working for the home market, some event that has raised the real demand function for labour there. This event may have been an enhancement of non-wage-earners' desire for the products of the industry or group of industries, or an improvement in productivity in confrontation with an elastic demand, or some form of State stimulation. Our problem is to determine how far the addition to employment in the industry or group of industries that has expanded is net, and how far it is at the expense of withdrawing wage-goods from financing employment in other industries.

§ 2. When, for any reason, the people controlling a particular occupation or group of occupations elect to engage more workpeople there, they do not, of course, rely, for the wage-goods needed for that purpose, solely on wage-goods in their own personal control. They attempt, in general, to supplement their private resources by borrowing from other people, either directly through an issue of ordinary shares or, if need be, of debentures at fixed interest, or indirectly by means of a loan from bankers. These borrowings are, of course, in form money loans, but in substance they are loans of the wage-goods on which the borrowed money, after being paid out in wages, is spent. If the expectations of the general public as to the prospects of the particular industry, as well as the expectations of the persons directly controlling it, have improved, the general public will be ready to come in at their own risk; but, even if the general public's attitude is unchanged, the controllers of the industry can still draw on them by offering a tempting rate of fixed interest backed by a sufficient appearance of security. Whatever the precise process adopted, pressure is set up for wage-goods to be passed to the controllers of the industry in question. These must be drawn either wholly from employing wage-earners in other home non-wage-good industries, in which case the aggregate quantity of labour demanded in industry as a whole

is left as it was before; or from one or other of the sources
indicated by the letters C, S, M and $\{(A - E)r - Et\}$ in
the formula of Part I. Chapter V.; or partly from one of
these sets of sources and partly from the other.[1] It is the
distinction between drafts on other home non-wage-good industries and drafts on the aforesaid other sources that alone
has relevance to our problem. The effect on the aggregate
quantity of labour demanded is precisely the same if new
employment is financed out of wage-goods that non-wage-
earners would have added to stocks—and so turned into
capital—as if it is financed out of wage-goods that they would
have consumed. It is also exactly the same—in this case nil
—whether it is financed at the expense of the construction
of new capital instruments or at the expense of the construction of non-wage-goods intended for consumption.

§ 3. This last point is not always clearly understood. Thus,
in recent discussions of the so-called "Treasury view" as to the
effect of additional road-making upon aggregate employment, all the disputants believed the issue to turn on how
far the road-making was to be financed at the expense of
non-wage-earners' consumption and of capital construction respectively. This is an error. Just as there is no net
addition to the aggregate demand for labour, and so to
employment, if wage-goods are shifted to road-making
from machine-making, so also there is no net addition if they
are shifted to it from the making of luxury motor cars or silk
dressing-gowns or other articles of consumption too costly to
enter into wage-goods. It would not, indeed, be true to say
that ultimately and on the whole it makes no difference
whether the wage-goods for road-making are taken away
from machines or from silk dressing-gowns. In the former
event the stock of capital equipment for the future is *pro tanto*
diminished, whereas in the latter event it is left intact; and,
of course, other things being equal, the bigger the stock of

---

[1] It is sometimes thought that a further source is available in extra
output from the wage-good industries, due to "secondary" employment
stimulated there. Provided, however, that the real wage-rate is maintained,
the quantity of labour demanded and employed in the wage-good industries cannot have been increased. On the contrary, since the rate of interest
must have risen, it will be slightly diminished. Cf. *ante*, Part II. Chap. VII. § 4.

capital equipment, the larger is the real demand for labour. So far, however, as immediate effects are concerned—and these alone are relevant here—the aggregate quantity of labour demanded is affected in exactly the same way if the wage-goods to finance new road-making are taken from any one kind of non-wage-good and non-export industry as if they are taken from any other kind.

§ 4. The extent to which wage-goods to finance the new employees are obtained respectively by cutting down employment elsewhere and by expanding the wages fund depends on the tendency of demand for labour elsewhere to contract under the influence of rising rates of interest, balanced against the readiness of non-wage-earners to surrender, under that influence, wage-goods from the three uses represented by my letters C, S and M and the reactions set up in respect of unemployment benefit. With sufficient knowledge it would be possible, in any particular case, to determine this issue quantitatively. In actual fact we cannot, of course, do this. We can only set out in a general way the kind of influences upon which the probable responsiveness of the wages fund to a given stimulus depends. To this end I proceed to consider in turn C, S and M, namely, (1) personal consumption of wage-goods by non-wage-earners, (2) storage of wage-goods, (3) the purchase by non-wage-earners of non-wage-goods (including securities) from abroad; discussion of the remaining element $\{(A - E)r - Et\}$ being postponed to § 9.

§ 5. Non-wage-earners constitute only a small part of the population. Moreover, since wage-goods are, in the main, elementary articles of prime necessity, for which everyone's requirements are strictly limited, the chief part of the real incomes of those persons whose incomes are large is not likely to be devoted to these things. Hence in normal times only a small proportion of the country's total consumption of wage-goods is likely to attach to non-wage-earners. Therefore even a considerable percentage change in their consumption would only enable the quantity of wage-goods available for other uses to be increased or diminished by a small percentage. Nor is this all. Non-wage-earners are very unlikely voluntarily to undertake other than small percentage changes

in their consumption of wage-goods, even though their desire
to use them as a means of hiring labour alters largely, since
their desire to consume them is presumably inelastic. It
follows that my item C—personal consumption of wage-
goods by non-wage-earners—is highly stable. No substantial
variations in the "wage-fund" available to pay labour are
likely to come about through direct reactions on the consumption of wage-goods by non-wage-earners.

§ 6. Consider next the item S. If the rate of interest,
measuring the prospects of investment elsewhere, improves,
holders of stocks of wage-goods can obtain a better return
for lending them—or, what comes to the same thing, for
lending money and then selling them for money—to would-
be borrowers than they normally get. Hence it will pay them
to allow their stocks to run down; that is to say, the item S
will expand. For a short time this reaction may well be
important. If the whole domestic consumption of wage-goods
were by wage-earners, a reduction in stocks of these goods to
the extent of one week's consumption would finance an addition to aggregate employment of nearly 2 per cent for one
year: and, if non-wage-earners' consumption of wage-goods
be put at one-quarter of the whole, the corresponding figure
is $2\frac{2}{3}$ per cent. Plainly, however, this source of supply being
a fund and not a flow, it cannot be drawn upon for long
without becoming exhausted. Moreover, it is known that the
normal stocks of wage-goods are small relatively to annual
consumption—perhaps, on a rough average, two months'
consumption [1]—so that, if we start from normal times, their
exuding capacity, so to speak, is narrowly restricted: very
little can be got out of them without trenching on working
capital that is essential for operating the machine of distribution. Owing to the high cost and the risks of loss involved
in holding large stocks, their absorbing capacity is also narrowly restricted. Hence reactions on S, like reactions on C,
are not, in general, important. There is, however, a difference
between the case of an expanding and that of a contracting
demand for labour. In expansions there is an absolute limit
to the draft that can be made on stocks to finance the ex-

---

[1] Cf. Keynes, *A Treatise on Money*, vol. ii. p. 134.

pansion, since it is impossible for them to fall below zero. In contractions there is no such absolute limit. It is physically possible for drafts *into* stocks to continue indefinitely.

§ 7. The third source, distinguished in § 4, under the letter M, would not be available at all to an isolated country or to the world as a whole regarded as a unity. But for a single country, in the face of fluctuations confined to that country, it may be extremely important. Thus, when the desire for home non-wage-goods expands, we may bring in from abroad less non-wage-goods, including less purchases of foreign securities, and, instead, more wage-goods, not for consumption by non-wage-earners, but for setting labour to work in making the home non-wage-goods. The contraction in our purchases of foreign non-wage-goods may be proportionately very large, since our desire for these goods (including foreign securities) is probably elastic. Moreover, the volume of these purchases in normal times is known, for this country, to be large absolutely. Hence provision may be available along this route for financing considerable proportionate fluctuations in the aggregate quantity of labour demanded. It must be borne in mind, however, that booms and slumps are largely international in character, so that the whole world, rather than a single country, is the proper object of study. For the whole world, however, the item M is, as we have seen, nil.

§ 8. So far we have tacitly assumed that the particular home non-wage-good industry in which the quantity of labour demanded has increased does not make use of imported raw material. Let us now consider an industry which does make use of such material. Suppose, as in Chapter II. § 1, that the quantity of material employed per unit of product is constant. Then, if the quantity of labour demanded in the finishing industry is increased, the quantity of imported raw material that is used must also be increased. If the quantity of labour demanded there is diminished on account of a falling off in desire for the product, the quantity of raw material used must be diminished. If the quantity of labour demanded there falls off on account of an improvement in productivity in the face of an inelastic demand for the product—the improvement being of the normal type distinguished in Chapter II. § 6, the quantity of imported raw material used will be increased. Apart, then, from this last case, an expansion in the quantity of labour demanded in one group of industries causes an expansion in the element M—wage-good claims devoted to buying imports of non-wage-goods; and a contraction a contraction. The wage-fund is thus, *pro tanto*, rendered, so to speak, inversely responsive. If this were the only factor at work, an expansion in the quantity of labour demanded in the particular industry would be offset, not merely by an equivalent, but by more than an equivalent, contraction in the quantity demanded elsewhere; and a contraction in the particular industry would, in like manner, be offset by a more than equivalent expansion elsewhere—always assuming that there exist elsewhere industries that do not make use, per workman employed, of an equal value of imported raw material.[1] In real life, of course, the factor here described is never the only factor at work; and it is highly improbable that these extreme consequences will follow. None the less, if the particular industry or group of industries, in which we are supposing the quantity of labour demanded to expand (or contract), is one that uses imported raw material, the associated contraction (or expansion) elsewhere is likely to be larger, and so the expansion (or contraction) in the aggregate quantity of labour demanded smaller, than it would be in similar conditions if the particular industry or group of industries did not use imported raw material.

§ 9. It remains to consider the last relevant element that was distinguished in § 4, namely $\{(A - E)r - Et\}$. This expression represents the flow of wage-goods devoted to paying unemployment benefit to unemployed wage-earners *minus* the contribution towards this handed over by employed wage-earners. Some study of this element has already been made in Part II. Chapter IX. It will be understood that what has to

---

[1] In the case of a contraction in the quantity of labour demanded in a particular industry, due to an improvement of normal type in the face of inelastic demand for the industry's product, a relation opposite in character to that just described is, of course, present.

be said is relevant, not merely to unemployment benefit as
organised under the insurance laws, but to all payments,
whether from the State by insurance and by Poor Law, or
by private charity, or by loans from shopkeepers, which are
made to unemployed persons as such, and which would cease
if the recipients became employed. Here, it would seem,
there is a further independent source capable of being drawn
on to finance new employment with wage-goods. Thus advo-
cates of Government enterprise as a means of creating such
employment in bad times sometimes appeal to the fact that
real funds are already passing through the Government's
hands for providing unemployment benefit. These funds, it
is argued, are there and available. Since they are there, the
plea that Government can only secure the employment of
new workpeople by causing real funds to be diverted from
paying wages to workpeople who are employed already, is, it
is urged, on the face of it, false. This reasoning is, however,
fallacious. If the system of unemployment insurance were
to be abolished, the wage-goods now used to operate it would,
indeed, be available for other purposes, including the purpose
of engaging more wage-earners. But nothing of that kind is
here in question. The existing system of unemployment insurance is conceived to be retained, but *nevertheless* the unemployment fund is thought of as available to finance additional
employment. Now the real rate of unemployment pay together
with the contribution per employed workman, namely $(r + t)$,
is always in practice less than the real rate of wage w.
Therefore it is impossible for any new man to be set to
work by means of wage-goods drawn from the unemployment fund, *unless at the same time some wage-goods for that
purpose are being obtained from somewhere else.*[1] Hence the un-

---

[1] This, it may be noted, would not be so if the rate of unemployment
pay were equal to the rate of wage *minus* the workers' contribution towards
unemployment benefit, *i.e.* if w were equal to $(r + t)$. In this case, provided
that the funds to provide unemployment pay were collected by methods
that involve their withdrawal from hiring labour, there would be a position
of unstable, or, rather, of neutral equilibrium. If employers in a particular
industry engaged 100 new men, the issue whether the wage-goods to pay
them—in the absence of other sources—would be got by the dismissal of
men in other occupations or by an equivalent reduction in unemployment,
is indeterminate.

employment fund is not an independent source, from which wage-goods for financing unemployment can be drawn, on a par with my elements C, S and M. It is like an explosive that, if left to itself, remains inert, but, when something is added to it from outside, can become exceedingly active. Thus suppose that 1000 new men are taken into employment in a particular non-wage-good industry. If nothing can be got to pay their wages out of the elements C, S and M, the whole of the wage-goods for these wages must be withdrawn from employing other men in other non-wage-good industries. The unemployment fund helps not at all: the aggregate quantity of unemployment is not reduced. If, however, the elements C, S and M are prevailed upon to make a contribution, thereupon automatically the unemployment fund makes a contribution also. France has become reasonable; the United States forthwith lends a hand. For an employment-making policy that, if the unemployment fund does not help, will fail, that fund contributes nothing: but for a policy that, without its help, would succeed in some measure, it will provide the means of enlarging that success.

§ 10. This broad statement can be worked out ·in detail thus. Let us suppose that the quantity of labour demanded in our particular industry or group of industries is expanded by Q. The wage-goods needed to pay these men amount to Qw. There is at the same time a reduction in the quantity of unemployment pay provided for unemployed men equal to Qr and an addition to workpeople's contribution towards that of Qt. Therefore the Government has to raise $Q(r + t)$ less than before for purposes of unemployment pay. Therefore the total extra amount that has to be provided is, not Qw, but $Q(w - r - t)$. Suppose that, as a consequence of this provision, the quantity of labour demanded elsewhere is reduced by V, so that the total addition to the quantity of labour demanded is $(Q - V)$. This implies that the fund raised from the sources C, S and M amounts to $(Q - V)(w - r - t)$. The fund raised from savings on unemployment benefit is obviously $(Q - V)(r - t)$. Hence the sum of wage-goods raised *via* unemployment benefit is equal to $\dfrac{r + t}{w - r - t}$ times the sum raised from the sources C, S and M.

For this country $(r + t)$, when we conceive of unemployment pay in the wide sense of § 9, may probably be put at not much less than one-half of w. With this figure, for any given contribution made out of the three sources the unemployment fund adds an equal contribution.[1]

§ 11. Throughout this analysis, it will have been observed, no account has been taken of the fact that, when the number of wage-earners called into employment is increased, in general some additional non-wage-earners are called into employment also, and that, even if this does not happen, the remuneration accruing to existing non-wage-earners for their services and the use of their equipment is fairly certain to be increased. In so far as any part of the extra remuneration of non-wage-earners is taken out in the form of wage-goods, whether for personal consumption, storage, or sale abroad, the draft made on these goods is, of course, correspondingly increased. Suppose that, over the relevant range, the payment of w wage-goods to each additional wage-earner implies an associated payment of wage-goods for these purposes to non-wage-earners measured by kw. The sum of wage-goods made available *via* unemployment pay for hiring new labour is then, not $\dfrac{r + t}{w - r - t}$ times the sum raised from the three sources, but $\dfrac{r + t}{w(1 + k) - r - t}$ times that sum. Now, if it were only wage-goods added to the personal consumption and storage of non-wage-earners that concerned us, k would probably be very small; but, since claims to wage-goods used to buy foreign non-wage-goods and securities are also relevant, it may well be a substantial figure. Let us guess that $k = \frac{1}{3}$. Then the conclusion of the preceding section is modified in such wise

---

[1] It may possibly be objected to the foregoing analysis that, since a man does not cease receiving unemployment benefit until *after* he has been taken into wage-work, it is impossible, in the nature of things, for resources saved from unemployment benefit to be used in financing the wage payments through which the need for unemployment pay is diminished. The answer is that any finite unit of time can be split up into an indefinitely large number of parts. If the parts are made small enough relatively to the unit, the amount of unemployment pay saved in a unit of time through unemployed men being engaged for wages can be made to approach without limit towards the amount of resources set free towards paying these wages.

that, with $(r + t) = \frac{1}{2}w$, the contribution added from the un-employment fund is $\frac{2}{3}$ths of that made from the three sources C, S and M.

§ 12. From another angle further light may be thrown on our problem thus. Let the total amount of wage-goods that is drawn out of the three sources, under the pressure of an increased demand for labour in particular groups of occupations, be R. Then the addition to the quantity of labour demanded in the aggregate is obviously $\dfrac{R}{w(1 + k) - r - t}$. This, with $k = 0$ and $(r + t) = \frac{1}{2}w$, is equal to $2\dfrac{R}{w}$: with $k = \frac{1}{3}$ and $(r + t) = \frac{1}{2}w$, to $\frac{6}{5}\dfrac{R}{w}$.

§ 13. A word must be added of the special case where the impulse to additional demand for labour consists of State stimulation applied to this demand in some particular occupation or group of occupations. When the stimulation takes the form of guarantees of interest, that may be called upon in the future but involve no expense to the State at present, what has already been said exhausts the problem. But, when recourse is had to a State subsidy, there has further to be taken into account the reaction set up by the collection of the funds for that subsidy. It may be that these funds will be drawn from employing labour elsewhere and from the alternative sources described above in the same proportion as funds raised voluntarily by employers would have been. In this case, again, there is nothing further to be said. The proportion in which the funds are drawn from the different sources will, however, be different according as the necessary taxes are imposed on rich people or on poor; so that it would be an accident if it worked out the same as the proportion for voluntary borrowings. If it does not work out the same, the difference made to the final result, when the stimulus to expansion is State action, will be larger or smaller according as the method of stimulation chosen involves greater or less expense to the State. The discussion of the several forms of stimulation in Chapter IV. is, therefore, relevant here.

CHAPTER X

§ 1. We have seen in the earlier part of our discussion that a fundamental factor determining the aggregate quantity of labour, which is demanded at a given real wage-rate, is the proportion in which people use their claims to wage-goods, on the one hand, in personally consuming these goods, storing them and buying with them imported non-wage-goods and securities, and, on the other hand, in setting labour to work to make home non-wage-goods. Since people do not all act in this matter in the same way, if command over wage-goods is transferred from one set of people to another, the fact of transfer may produce important effects on the aggregate quantity of labour demanded at a given real rate of wages. It will be convenient to consider separately transfers between one set of non-wage-earners and another set and transfers between non-wage-earners and wage-earners.

§ 2. If one set of non-wage-earners are accustomed to a certain real income and have established a standard manner of using it, and a part of this real income is transferred to another set of non-wage-earners, it may happen that the other set are for a time at a loss how to use it. Consumption and new capital-goods attractive to them may not be immediately available. They may, in short, suffer from Mr. Robertson's temporary "gluttability of wants"; and it may come about that wage-goods, which, had no transfer occurred, would have been used by the original possessors in setting men to work at making one or another sort of non-wage-goods, come

154

instead to be piled up by the transferees in idle stores or used by them in buying foreign securities. If this happens, the aggregate real demand function for labour in the country affected may be seriously depressed. From the standpoint of the world as a whole the same sort of effect may be produced by transfers of real income between nations. For the world as a whole, indeed, wage-goods are not used up, as they are from the standpoint of a particular country, when they are devoted to the purchase of foreign securities. Hence, apart from additional personal consumption by non-wage-earners, such using up as takes place can only assume the form of an accumulation of stocks. Such accumulation of stocks, however, in view of the high costs and heavy risks, is likely soon to reach a limit. Hence, if the output of wage-goods is held at its original level, which it must be *unless the real rate of wage is surreptitiously raised through monetary processes*, transfers of this type, though they may reduce the real demand for labour in particular countries in a large degree, cannot reduce it much over the world as a whole. This conclusion is not inconsistent with the view that in recent times such transfers have played a predominant part in contracting employment in a disastrous manner in nearly all countries: because, as will be shown in Part V. Chapter IX., the condition italicised above has not in fact been satisfied.

§ 3. I now turn to transfers between non-wage-earners and wage-earners. We have premised, it will be remembered, that wage-earners take out the whole of their income in the personal consumption of wage-goods. Non-wage-earners, *per contra*, take out a substantial proportion of their income in home non-wage-goods. It is certain, therefore, that, in so far as purchasing power is transferred from non-wage-earners as a body to wage-earners as a body, these transfers, other things being equal, render the aggregate quantity of labour demanded at a given real rate of wage smaller than it would have been had no such transfers taken place. All gratuitous payments to poor people and all social services, in so far as they are financed at the expense of the richer non-wage-earning classes, whatever benefit they confer on the community in other respects, of necessity reduce *pro tanto* the quantity of labour demanded at a given real wage-rate. It follows incidentally that, by withdrawing pensions and other gifts that they have been accustomed to make to poor people—who may be presumed to spend them chiefly on wage-goods—and spending what they have thus "saved" on home luxuries or on home investment, rich men will, in the short period, increase the aggregate quantity of labour demanded at a given real rate of wage. By contracting pensions and unemployment pay and remitting equivalent taxation on the well-to-do—apart from possible effects in forcing reductions in real wage-rates—the State will accomplish a like result.[1]

§ 4. To these conclusions the reader, even if he has assented to the successive stages of the argument by which they have been reached, will probably feel an instinctive resistance. For it is a commonplace of the textbooks that transfers from rich to poor, apart from momentary incidents of the process of transition, while they modify the direction of employment, leave its total volume unchanged. There is, however, no real incompatibility between the intention of that thesis and what has been set out here. I am concerned with the state of the demand function for labour—the quantity of labour that is demanded at each several rate of wage in terms of wage-good units. The thesis of the textbooks is concerned with the total quantity of labour demanded on the tacit assumption that, after a transfer from rich to poor, the rate of wage will be adjusted in such wise as to permit of the same amount of employment, namely full employment, as was supposed to

---

[1] Transfers that take money from one set of wage-earners for the purpose of making payments to other—or the same—wage-earners plainly have no relevance here. No effect, for example, from our present standpoint is produced when contributions are raised from workpeople and used to finance pensions, sickness pay and unemployment benefit for other wage-earners. In like manner, no effect is produced when taxes are collected from non-wage-earners and the proceeds paid over to other non-wage-earners of similar wealth in the form of interest on war loan or gratuities to retired generals. It may be that the whole complex of transfers from non-wage-earners in their capacity of income-tax payers to non-wage-earners in their capacity of holders of war loan alters the distribution of spendable income among that class in such a way that some effect, from our present standpoint, is produced. On the basis of our present knowledge, however, we cannot tell what that effect is—whether it is on the whole favourable or adverse to employment. Nothing further, therefore, need be said concerning it.

prevail before. If the thesis had asserted that, after the transfer, full employment would be maintained *at the original rate of real wage*, it would, indeed, have been inconsistent with my argument. But it does not assert this. There is no inconsistency: and, therefore, there is here no basis for resistance to the conclusions of the last section.

§ 5. What has been said so far is independent of the methods by which transfers are effected. With some methods, *e.g.* lump-sum levies from the rich and lump-sum gifts to the poor, the *process* of transfer is neutral, and the discussion of the preceding sections exhausts the subject. Plainly, however, the collection of the funds from transferors and the handing of them to transferees may be conducted by methods that react on the quantity of labour demanded at a given real rate of wage. Now the transferees, whether recipients of war loan interest or beneficiaries of social services or of unemployment insurance, are paid on such a plan that the amount received is not sensibly dependent upon, or capable of being modified by, voluntary action on their part. The associated levy on transferors is, however, in the main made by means of taxes that are assessed on income or property or on dealings in certain commodities. This type of taxation may be expected, through its "announcement" effects,[1] to reduce somewhat the accumulation of capital equipment, and so indirectly, in the long run, the productivity of labour in respect of wage-goods. Transfers accomplished by these means, then, besides exercising the immediate and direct adverse influence on the real demand for labour described above, also probably exercise a further adverse effect that is slow-working and cumulative.

[1] Cf. *A Study in Public Finance*, Part II. chap. iv. § 1.

CHAPTER XI

§ 1. So long as attention is confined to non-wage-good industries that work for the home market it is plain that any increase in the quantity of labour demanded in one of them has to be financed, so to speak, with wage-goods obtained from somewhere else, and, in like manner, that any decrease in the quantity of labour demanded there sets free for use somewhere else the wage-goods that are released from paying labour there. With wage-good industries, since their output itself contributes towards financing employment in them, the matter is not so simple. To clarify ideas, I shall, in this chapter, imagine that there exists only a single sort of wage-good, and shall inquire in what way the effect of disturbances set up in the industry that makes that good differ from those that follow from similar disturbances in a non-wage-good industry.

§ 2. At the outset we may rule out one sort of disturbance altogether. Shifts in the desire of non-wage-earners in respect of the products of a non-wage-good industry carry with them shifts in the demand for labour in that industry. Such shifts were, therefore, included among the movements whose consequences were investigated in Chapter IX. Such shifts in desire on the part of non-wage-earners, however, when they are directed towards wage-goods as a whole, or, in the simple case here taken, towards wage-goods assumed to be of one kind only, are, so far as our present purpose is concerned, completely sterile of effect. They cannot, from a short-period point of view, increase either the quantity of labour demanded at a given real wage in the industry producing them or the quantity of wage-goods produced.[1] From a long-period point of view indeed, this is by no means true. For, if non-wage-earners come to desire wage-goods more keenly, they will do more work in co-operation with wage-earners in making these goods, and more capital equipment will be built up for that purpose. Hence the marginal productivity of any assigned number of wage-earners engaged in providing these goods will be increased, and so, at a given rate of real wages, more employment will be available. For the short period, however, changes in capital equipment are irrelevant. Moreover, for a rough approximation, we may fairly ignore, as of secondary importance, changes in the amount of effort put out by non-wage-earners. In these circumstances, increases in non-wage-earners' desire for wage-goods in general cannot have any effect on the quantity of labour anywhere demanded. For, apart from monopoly action, the quantity of labour that it pays employers to engage in any occupation is necessarily that quantity which makes the (discounted) value of the marginal net product of the labour there—as defined in Part II. Chapter III. § 1—in terms of wage-goods equal to the real wage-rate: and changes of desire of the type here contemplated cannot alter this.

§ 3. We may turn then to the second main kind of disturbance, namely, improvements in productivity. As hitherto, I shall leave aside complex types of improvement and consider only that type, here called the normal type,[2] in respect of which $\dfrac{\phi'_2(x)}{\phi'_1(x)}$ is constant for all relevant values of x. When

---

[1] If non-wage-earners come to desire wage-goods more relatively to other things, their withdrawal of demand for labour in non-wage-good industries will tend to lower the real rate of wages there, and so also in the wage-good industries. When it has done this, it will, of course, lead to an increased output of wage-goods. This, however, is outside the subject matter of the present Part.

[2] Cf. *ante*, Part III. Chap. II. § 6. It should be noted that the abnormal robot type of improvement described in the chapter cited cannot diminish the aggregate quantity of labour demanded at a given real wage so much as it diminishes the quantity demanded in the wage-good industries: but there is no certitude that it does not diminish it to some extent.

there is only one sort of wage-good, the demand function, in terms of wage-goods, for labour in the industry making it is plainly, apart from discounting for delayed production, identical with the productivity function. Hence—I neglect the cost of raw material—the general equation $w = \dfrac{d\psi\{\phi(x)\}}{dx}$, set out in Chapter II., degrades to $w = \phi'(x)$. If, then, there is an improvement in productivity of the type defined above, it necessarily follows that the quantity of labour demanded in the wage-good industry is increased. It also necessarily follows that the amount of the surplus of wage-goods over and above what is used up in paying wages in the wage-good industry is increased. The part of the increase which is connected with the work of the original number of wage-earners makes its appearance immediately, the part connected with the work of the new wage-earners after an interval measured by one period of production. Of this additional surplus, while some part is likely to be devoted to increasing non-wage-earners' consumption of wage-goods, to adding to stocks and, in a more important measure, to off-setting extra purchases of non-wage-goods from abroad, some part will also be devoted to employing more labour in home non-wage-good industries. This would be so even though no part of the non-wage-good industries was devoted to making instruments for use in wage-good industries. Since in fact a large part is so devoted, the argument is *a fortiori*. Not only are the *means* for employing men in non-wage-good industries increased, but also the profitableness of so employing them. Other things being equal, therefore, an improvement (of normal type) in the home wage-good industry, which affects the quantity of labour demanded and the volume of output there in the same way as an analogous improvement in a home non-wage-good industry would do, has a direct tendency, not present in the analogous improvement, to increase the quantity of labour demanded elsewhere. It must be remembered, more-over, that, as was shown in Chapter IX., the extra gain to employment is not limited to the number of new men set to work in the wage-good industry *plus* the number of the new men in non-wage-good industries whose wages are provided out of the new surplus. It includes also men in the non-wage-good industries whose wages are paid out of savings on unemployment pay.

§ 4. There remains the third main kind of disturbance, namely, State stimulation of output by any of the forms of subsidy distinguished in Chapter IV. In consequence of such stimulation it will pay employers to engage more workpeople in the wage-good industry. If an equal quantity of extra employment were evoked by this means in a non-wage-good industry, all the wage-goods needed to pay the new men would have to be taken from an outside source. When the industry affected makes wage-goods, the new men provide by their work a part of the wage-goods needed for their own wages— except in the practically impossible case of a bounty on wages substantially larger than the rate of wages. There is, therefore, less tendency than there is with State stimulation of non-wage-good industries for the quantity of labour demanded to be cut down elsewhere. Indeed, up to a point, if new men are called into employment in the wage-good industry by State action, the output of the new employees, when combined with the saving on unemployment benefit in respect of them, will exceed the wage-goods paid to them as wages: so that wage-goods are actually released from the industry, and there is a tendency for the quantity of labour demanded elsewhere to be increased.

§ 5. The analysis of the preceding paragraph, in the special case where the productivity function is linear, can be expressed in exact terms as follows. I shall consider a subsidy in respect of wages and paid to new and old wage-earners alike, leaving it to the reader to adjust the argument to other forms of subsidy. Let A be the quantity of labour engaged in the wage-good industry in the absence of a subsidy. Then we have $w = \phi'(A)$. Let a subsidy s be given per wage-earner: and let r be the rate of unemployment benefit and t the rate of employed workpeople's contribution to this. Write h for the addition to employment in the wage-good

industry due to the presence of the subsidy s. Then $h = - \dfrac{s}{\phi''}$.

The output of the new h workers is $\{h\phi' + \tfrac{1}{2}h^2\phi''\} = \tfrac{1}{2}\{2w - s\}h$.

M

Therefore what has to be provided towards their wages in excess of this output $= \frac{1}{2}sh$. The saving in unemployment benefit is $(r+t)h$. Therefore, if a rate of subsidy is provided equal to twice the rate of unemployment pay *plus* employee's contribution, no wage-goods have to be taken from elsewhere to provide the subsidy, and nothing is available to be handed elsewhere.

When this critical condition is satisfied, since $s = 2(r+t)$, $h = -\dfrac{2(r+t)}{\phi''}$. It we put η for the elasticity of the productivity function in respect of A employment, this may be written $h = -\dfrac{2(r+t)}{w}\eta A$. If $(r+t) = \frac{1}{3}w$, this $= \frac{2}{3}(-\eta)A$: if $(r+t) = \frac{1}{2}w$, it $= -\eta A$. Obviously, if η is numerically much greater than unity, h will be large relatively to A.

If the subsidy is at a lower rate than $2(r+t)$, more is saved on unemployment pay than is required to fill the gap between the output and the wages of the new workers in the wage-good industry; so that there is a surplus, some of which is likely to be used in increasing employment in the non-wage-good industries. In the converse case there is a deficit: wage-goods in excess of the savings on unemployment pay are needed to fill the gap, and some of them are likely to be withdrawn from employing labour in non-wage-good industries.[1]

[1] A more general view may be obtained thus. Suppose that a sum K taken from outside, together with the total savings on unemployment pay, is devoted to filling the gap between output and wage of new men called into employment in the wage-good industry. Let the productivity function of labour in the wage-good industry be ϕ; and let the addition to employment, consequent on the new arrangement, in the wage-good industry and other industries together be h. As before, let the original number of men engaged in the wage-good industry be A.

First, suppose that the whole of K is taken from employing men in non-wage-good industries. Then we have:

$$\frac{K + h(r+t) + \phi\left\{A + h + \dfrac{K}{w}\right\} - \phi(A)}{w} - \frac{K}{w} = h.$$

Hence
$$h = \frac{r+t}{-\phi''} - \frac{K}{w} + \sqrt{\left\{\frac{r+t}{-\phi''}\right\}^2 + \frac{w-r-t}{w}\cdot\frac{2K}{-\phi''}}.$$

This may be written:

$$h = \frac{r+t}{w}\eta A - \frac{K}{w} + \sqrt{\left\{\frac{r+t}{w}\eta A\right\}^2 + \frac{w-r-t}{w}\cdot\frac{2K\eta A}{w}}.$$

§ 6. If the funds out of which the subsidy is paid are collected by a tax which penalises the production of wage-goods, *e.g.* by a tax assessed on the output of wage-goods or on the output of industries that make instruments used in providing wage-goods, an indirect check will be put on the production of wage-goods, which must, of course, be set against the expansion due to the subsidy. This check will be more important the higher are the rates of tax needed to finance the subsidy. The net benefit to employment is thus larger with subsidies on additional labour or additional output, which cost the State relatively little, and so necessitate only low rates of taxation, than with subsidies on all labour or all output, which cost it much more.

When $K = 0$, this, of course, reduces to $\dfrac{2(r+t)}{w}\eta A$; the value given in the text.

Secondly, let K be taken, not from employing men in non-wage-good industries, but from the use of wage-goods by non-wage-earners for other purposes. The resultant addition to employment is

$$\frac{(r+t)}{w}\frac{\eta}{A} + \sqrt{\left\{\frac{r+t}{w}\eta A\right\}^2 + \frac{2K\eta A}{w}}.$$

It will be noticed that this expression differs from the preceding expression, not only in that the element $-\dfrac{K}{w}$ is absent, but also in that the element $\dfrac{w}{w-r-t}$ inside the square root is absent. This is accounted for by the fact that the non-withdrawal of employment from non-wage-good industries means that there is less unemployment benefit needed there. This expression also, of course, reduces, when $K = 0$, to $\dfrac{2(r+t)}{w}\eta A$. Obviously, when K is drawn from any source other than the payment of wage-earners in non-wage-good industries, increases in K must always increase aggregate employment so long as there are any unemployed men available.

CHAPTER XII

§ 1. As we saw at the beginning of the preceding chapter, if there were only one sort of wage-good, changes in non-wage-earners' desire for it could not, in the short period, affect the demand in terms of wage-goods for labour in the industry making it, or on the output of that industry. When, however, as in real life, there are a number of different sorts of wage-goods, changes in non-wage-earners' desires—and the same thing is, of course, true of changes in the distribution of income among non-wage-earners with different desires—are not thus sterile. In this chapter, therefore, where we are concerned with disturbances set up in particular wage-good industries, there are not only two kinds of disturbances, but three; namely, (1) these changes, (2) improvements in productivity, and (3) State stimulation.

§ 2. If the desire of non-wage-earners for a particular sort of wage-good alters, the relative values of different sorts of wage-goods will alter, and, therefore, the absolute values of each sort in terms of wage-good units, as defined in Part I. Chapter IV. § 6. These variations are liable to affect the quantity of labour demanded at a given real wage-rate in the sum of all wage-good industries. An expansion in demand in terms of wage-good units for one wage-good item *implies* a contraction in demand in these terms for other wage-good items. The quantity of labour demanded in the industry making the item for which demand has expanded increases; the quantity demanded in the other industries diminishes. Our first problem is to determine in what con-

164

ditions the quantity demanded in all wage-good industries together will be increased, and in what conditions diminished.

§ 3. Let us suppose that there are only two items of wage-goods, A and B, and that a units of A *plus* b units of B make up a unit of wage-goods. Let us start with a state of relative demands such that in equilibrium, *i.e.* when output is appropriately adjusted, the money price of a unit of A is p_a and of a unit of B is p_b; and let us write $\dfrac{p_a}{p_b} = r$. Then one wage-good unit is worth $\left(a + \dfrac{b}{r} \right)$ units of A: and is also worth $(ar + b)$ units of B. We have to conceive of variations in comparative demands bringing about, after output has been adjusted, variations in the relative price of A and B; that is, of $\dfrac{p_a}{p_b}$; that is, of r. Our problem then reduces to that of determining the way in which variations in r, brought about by variations in comparative demands, are related (when the supply schedules are given) to variations in the sum of employment in the A industry and the B industry together.

§ 4. Choose units in such a way that a wage-good unit consists of one unit of A *plus* one unit of B: that is, so that $a = b = 1$. Write $f_a(y)$ for the quantity of labour in industry A whose marginal output is y: and $f_b(y)$ for the quantity in industry B whose marginal output is y. It follows that the total quantity of labour employed in industries A and B together, when the rate of real wage is what it is, namely, one wage-good unit, $= f_a\left(1 + \dfrac{1}{r} \right) + f_b(r + 1)$. The first differential of this to r is

$$-\frac{1}{r^2} \cdot \frac{df_a\left(1 + \dfrac{1}{r} \right)}{d\left(1 + \dfrac{1}{r} \right)} + \frac{df_b(r + 1)}{d(r + 1)}.$$

In the general case, when nothing is known about the form of the functions f_a and f_b, not much can be got out of this. But let us suppose, for the purposes of an approximation, that these functions are linear, so that f_a' and f_b' are constant. Then the above expression reduces to

$$f_a' \left\{ \frac{f_b'}{f_a'} - \frac{1}{r^2} \right\}.$$

We may fairly assume, from a short-period standpoint, that f_a' and f_b' are both positive. It is then obvious that the above expression is positive so long as r has a value greater than a certain critical value, and negative so long as it has a value less than this critical value. A value for r such that $r^2 = \frac{f_a'}{f_b'}$ makes the quantity of labour demanded in industries A and B together a minimum. As r moves away from this critical value in either direction, the quantity of labour so demanded is increased.

§ 5. These results may be translated into other terms thus. Write A for the quantity of labour demanded in industry A for a given value of r, and E_a for the elasticity of demand for labour in respect of this quantity: and write B and E_b with a like significance for industry B. The above condition $r^2 = \frac{f_a'}{f_b'}$ then translates into the condition $r = \frac{E_a A}{E_b B}$. That is to say, the quantity of labour demanded in the two industries A and B together is a minimum when the comparative demands of non-wage-earners for the two wage-good items are such that their prices per unit are proportionate to the quantities of labour multiplied by the elasticities of demand for labour employed in making them. The more the actual conditions of comparative demand for the two wage-good items diverge from the conditions thus specified, the larger will be the quantity of labour demanded in the sum of these two wage-good industries. This result can be generalised for the case in which there are, not merely two, but a large number of, wage-good items.

§ 6. It thus appears that, if the desire of non-wage-earners for a particular item that enters into wage-goods is expanded, the effect on the quantity of labour demanded in the sum of all wage-good industries may, according to circumstances, be either favourable or unfavourable. In any event, however, it is plain that the quantity of wage-good units left available for use outside the regions immediately affected must be diminished. *Pro tanto*, therefore, the quantity of labour demanded in non-wage-good industries will be affected unfavourably. The net effect upon the aggregate quantity of labour demanded everywhere must, therefore, be unfavourable where the effect upon the quantity demanded in the sum of all wage-good industries is unfavourable: in the converse case it *may* be favourable.

§ 7. We have next to consider the effects of an improvement in productivity—of normal type—in a particular wage-good industry. If the demand in terms of wage-good units for the product of that industry has, over the relevant range, an elasticity greater than unity, an improvement in productivity will increase the quantity of labour demanded in the industry, and will also increase the output of this particular wage-good item. This item consequently becomes cheaper in terms of other wage-good items. That fact, since it implies an increase in the value of every other wage-good item in terms of wage-good units, will make it worth while for employers, at a given real wage-rate, to engage more men in other wage-good industries. The quantity of labour demanded there will, therefore, increase. Moreover, there being a larger total of wage-good units in being, and, therefore, a larger surplus available to non-wage-earners, these persons will, in general, devote more wage-goods than before to setting labour to work in non-wage-good industries. In fact the same type, though not, of course, the same degree of reaction takes place in other industries as would have taken place if there were only a single type of commodity included among wage-goods.

§ 8. It is possible, however, that non-wage-earners' attitude towards the particular item of wage-goods is such that the demand for it in terms of wage-good units has an elasticity less than unity. In this case the quantity of labour employed upon it will decrease in consequence of an improvement of normal type. None the less, however, the output of the commodity must be increased. Hence, by the same process as before, a tendency is set up for the quantity of labour demanded in industries making other wage-good items and in non-wage-good industries to increase. It is not certain, however, that this increase will exceed the decrease in the industry primarily affected.

§ 9. There remains State stimulation. If the factor of disturbance is not an improvement in productivity, but, say, a State subsidy in respect of wages, the same conclusions in regard to reactions on other industries hold good. With a subsidy, however, it is not possible, as we have just seen that it is possible with an improvement, for the quantity of labour demanded in the industry primarily affected to be diminished. This quantity must in all circumstances—apart from the limiting case of a perfectly inelastic demand for the product—be increased. Hence the aggregate quantity of labour demanded must be increased.

§ 10. The following rider on our discussion may be added. If in any industry the rate of wage stipulated for by wage-earners is reduced from w to $(w - s)$, the effect on the quantity of labour demanded there is, as was shown in Chapter IV. § 6, the same as would be produced by the grant of a State subsidy to wages at the rate s, the wage-rate remaining unchanged: for employers in each case find themselves able to hire labour at a cost to them of $(w - s)$ units. If, however, the industry affected is a wage-good industry, the effect on the aggregate quantity of labour demanded in the sum of all industries is not the same. For, when the wage-rate in wage-good industries is reduced by s, the surplus available to employ labour in non-wage-good industries is always affected more favourably than when a subsidy on wages is paid at that rate. This general result can be set out exactly in the special case where there is supposed to be only a single sort of wage-good, the productivity function of which is linear. Then, A being the number of men employed initially in the wage-good industry, with a wage reduction s, the addition to the surplus is $s(A + \frac{1}{2}h) + rh$: with a subsidy s it is $(rh - \frac{1}{2}sh)$. Thus, whether the latter quantity is positive or negative, it always falls short of the former quantity by $s(A + h)$.

CHAPTER XIII

§ 1. EXPORT industries are here conceived as industries that "produce" claims on imports of wage-goods. Improvements in productivity in a wide sense may, therefore, occur in either of two ways, namely, (1) through an improvement (or the reverse) in the actual physical productivity of the labour engaged in making the export industries' output, or (2) through an enhancement, in terms of wage-goods, in foreigners' demand for this output.

§ 2. Let us suppose, as before, that the only improvements of physical productivity that arise are improvements of the normal type, *i.e.* such that $\dfrac{\phi'_2(x)}{\phi'_1(x)}$ is constant for all values of x. It follows that the quantity of labour demanded in our export industries at a given real rate of wage is expanded or contracted by improvements in productivity according as, over the relevant range, the demand of foreigners, in terms of wage-goods, for our exports has an elasticity greater or less than unity.

§ 3. Now of the state of foreign demand for our exports *in terms of foreign goods in general* we can form a fairly confident opinion. Though, no doubt, there are a few special articles of British export for which the foreign demand is inelastic, articles of this type are very rare. For the whole world, when confronting a single country, which is necessarily a small part of itself, has, in general, a large number of other sources alternative to that country, from which it can supply itself at need with the things that that country makes. This is especially so as regards this country in view of the non-specialised character of our principal exports. Hence, we may conclude, it is probable that the foreign demand both for British exports as a whole and for any ordinary individual export, in terms of foreign goods in general, is substantially greater than unity. This does not necessarily imply that the foreign demand in terms of wage-goods has an elasticity greater than unity: for the latter demand must be less elastic than the former. I suggest, however, that, in the special case of this country in confrontation with the world, the difference between these two elasticities is not likely to be very large: so that in fact the foreign demand for our exports in terms of wage-goods is also greater than unity.

§ 4. If this be so, it follows that an improvement of physical productivity in respect of any ordinary British export will involve an increase in the quantity of labour demanded in the industry that makes it.[1] Moreover, it is probable that, when, in consequence of improvements in our export industries, foreigners pay to us more claims on wage-goods, the addition to imports will, in large measure, consist of actual wage-goods. Hence, a further factor making for expansion in the aggregate quantity of labour demanded is present. The total flow of wage-goods being enlarged, a part of the extra flow will, in general, be employed in engaging additional workpeople in the home non-wage-good industries. It may be added—the analysis may be left to the reader—that the presence among our imports of a large volume of raw materials also makes the expansion of demand for labour in the aggregate larger than it would have been if the place of these materials had been occupied by finished non-wage-goods or securities.

§ 5. There remain improvements in the productivity of our export industries in a wide sense, consequent on an im-

---

[1] A failure to perceive this has led popular writers into a curiously confused argument. It is frequently said that rationalisation, in the sense of improvement in the technique of production, in industries that compete with foreigners, is likely to throw men out of work for a time, but is nevertheless essential, lest the competition of the foreigners should overwhelm us. In industries that compete seriously with foreigners it is practically certain that the demand for the output from our national centres will, for that very reason, be elastic, and not inelastic. Hence in the case contemplated rationalisation will *not* throw men out of work.

provement in foreign demand, in terms of wage-good units, for our exports—an improvement such as will come about if foreigners' taste for our exports is enhanced, or if supplies rival to ours are cut off, or if the efficiency of foreigners in producing wage-goods is increased. In this case the quantity of labour demanded in our export industries at a given real rate of wages must increase; and a secondary expansion in other industries of the kind described in the preceding section must also take place. It should be noticed, however, that an enhancement of foreign demand in terms of particular wage-good items is compatible with a contraction in terms of wage-good units. What has been said, therefore, is not inconsistent with the widely held belief that the recent fall in the value of imported wheat, for which our demand is inelastic, has injured British export industries.

CHAPTER XIV

THE EFFECT ON THE REAL DEMAND FOR LABOUR AT HOME OF EXCLUDING IMPORTS OF GOODS OR SECURITIES

§ 1. In this chapter I leave aside two lines of approach that are familiar to students of international trade. It is well known that in certain circumstances the temporary exclusion of particular foreign imports, by enabling productive technique to be developed in infant industries well suited to a country, or by preventing productive technique from being destroyed in developed industries well suited to a country that are being attacked by foreign monopolists, will cause the real demand function for labour there to be raised ultimately above the level which it would attain otherwise. It is also well known that in conceivable circumstances the permanent exclusion of particular foreign imports may modify the scheme of production there in such a way as to increase the amount of real income that constitutes demand for labour, even though aggregate real income is diminished. These matters, which are in the nature of long-period reactions, I set on one side, and concentrate attention on certain short-period issues, at once less familiar and more relevant to the problem of this book.

§ 2. Let us imagine a country in which wage-goods and nothing else are made. The wage-earners in the wage-good industries consume their share of the output; the non-wage-earners export a part of their share in exchange for foreign non-wage-goods and securities. At the same time the real rate of wage established in the country is such that a number of would-be wage-earners, capable at need of making non-wage-goods, are out of work. If in such a country the importation of foreign non-wage-goods and (or) securities is

172

estopped or restricted, the non-wage-earners' export of wage-goods is also restricted. They are not at all likely personally to consume the whole of the balance. On the contrary, it is practically certain that they will devote a substantial part of it to setting labour at home to work in making the non-wage-goods that they are now prevented from obtaining from abroad, or some substitute for them. Thus it is practically certain that the aggregate quantity of labour demanded at a given real wage, and so the aggregate volume of employment, will be substantially enlarged. At the same time non-wage-earners, on the one hand, will find their wants less well satisfied than before—for, unless the new method of obtaining non-wage-goods were less effective than the earlier method it would have been used already—and, on the other hand, will make a saving in respect of unemployment pay. The conditions here postulated are, however, plainly not realised in England.

§ 3. Let us turn, therefore, to a country in which many sorts of goods are made and in which wage-goods are not exported, but are imported along with other things. Clearly, if the importation of wage-goods, but of nothing else, is estopped or restricted, the aggregate quantity of labour demanded at a given real wage must be contracted. If, however, the importation of foreign non-wage-goods, but of nothing else, is estopped or restricted, the situation is complicated, and it is necessary to distinguish three principal cases. In the first of these the estopped or restricted non-wage-good imports consist of further consumption-goods which do not compete directly with any home product, i.e. which cannot in any ordinary circumstances be made at home. Obviously foreign securities fall under this head as well as, for England, such things as champagne and caviare. In the second case the estopped or restricted imports are directly competitive with home-made articles. In the third they consist of materials, half-manufactured goods and machinery, that are used in the conduct of British industry.

§ 4. In the first case the English non-wage-earners, who have hitherto engaged men to produce these estopped things for them *via* exports, will no longer do this. Up to a point the effect will be exactly the same as would follow from the imposition of a legal ban on the direct home production of some non-wage-good. The quantity of labour demanded in the industries immediately affected will be contracted. Since, thereupon, wage-goods are released in proportion to the fall of employment in these industries, a portion of them will be devoted to making other sorts of non-wage-goods; but this offset will not cancel, it will only mitigate, the contraction in aggregate labour demand. When, however, it is importation, not home manufacture, of a non-wage-good that is restricted or estopped, further reactions have to be taken into account. For, unless the foreign demand for British exports is perfectly elastic, the estoppel or restriction of one import, or group of imports, must cause other imports to be offered to us on better terms. Hence Englishmen will be encouraged to make more exports than before for the purchase of non-estopped imports. Unless the foreign demand for our exports is absolutely inelastic, this reaction cannot prevent the quantity of labour demanded here in the export industries from contracting in some measure; though it will mitigate the contraction. If, therefore, the imports, that are thus indirectly stimulated, are all non-wage-goods, it cannot prevent the aggregate quantity of labour demanded here from being contracted. But the imports indirectly stimulated will be in part wage-goods. So far as this is so, a new factor is introduced making for an increase in the quantity of labour demanded here at a given real rate of wage. This *may* be so large that the net effect on the aggregate quantity of labour demanded here is favourable, not unfavourable. That result is certain if the foreign demand for our exports is absolutely inelastic: impossible if that demand is absolutely elastic. In fact, as was argued in Chapter XIII., the rest of the world's demand for the exports of this country is likely in ordinary circumstances to be highly elastic. Hence, though it is *possible* that the estoppel or restriction of imports of non-wage-goods and (or) securities, that do not compete directly with home products, may lead to a net increase in the aggregate quantity of labour demanded here at a given real wage, it is *likely*, on the whole, to lead to a net decrease.

§ 5. In our second case we suppose the estopped or restricted imports to consist of goods that are directly competitive with home-made articles—such things, for example,
as motor cars. The situation here is different from that
treated in the preceding section, because the non-wage-
earners, who are prevented from using their command over
wage-goods to hire men to produce motor cars for them by
importation, are not left in the air, but have a direct inducement to hire men to produce home motor cars in place of the
estopped imported ones. If their demand for motor cars has
an elasticity greater than unity, they will direct a less total
of wage-goods to obtaining motor cars by the new process
than by the old. In this case it is more probable than it is in
the case discussed in the preceding section that the aggregate
quantity of labour demanded here will be increased ; but it is
not certain. If, however, our non-wage-earners' demand for
motor cars has an elasticity less than unity, the estoppel or
restriction of imported cars will make an addition to labour
demand in the home industry greater than the contraction in
the relevant part of the export industry: and it is certain
that the aggregate quantity of labour demanded at a given
real wage here will be increased; just as this result would be
certain if a dis-improvement, so to speak, occurred in the
productivity of labour devoted to making at home some
non-wage-good of inelastic demand.

§ 6. It is sometimes urged that, in the case of competing
imports, there is also set up a further process favourable to an
expansion in the aggregate demand for labour in the country
affected. Suppose that there is an industry in England
equipped for making motor cars, and that there are attached
to this industry a large number of men in excess of the number for whom, at the ruling rate of real wages, employment can
be found. The importation of motor cars from abroad is
estopped or checked. Consequently, unless the home demand
for motor cars is perfectly elastic, some more motor cars will
be built at home and some of the hitherto unemployed motor
car makers brought into work. Even if the contraction of
motor imports is wholly offset by a contraction in English
exports, so that no addition is made to imports of wage-

goods, may there not be an addition to the quantity of wage-goods made at home, and so not only a new means of paying wages to labour, but also a direct addition to the quantity of labour demanded in our wage-good industries? Will there not, in short, be a direct inducement for some of the men driven out of our export industries to make wage-goods for our new motor-makers instead of export goods for foreign motor-makers? In considering this matter we need not trouble our-selves with questions as to the mobility of labour. In certain conditions it would, no doubt, be relevant to observe that people accustomed to mine coal and build ships for export cannot readily turn instead to making clothes and growing food. I do not wish, however, to take that point; for in a state of general depression it may well be that there are a number of men trained to making wage-goods who are out of work and available for employment if there is a demand for them; so that immobility on the part of men in the export industries, though it would prevent *their* finding employment in wage-good industries, would not prevent an equivalent number of other men from finding it. There is, however, in the way of this a fundamental obstacle. When the conditions of pro-ductivity in the wage-good industries are given, the number of men that it pays to employ there is determined, as was shown in Chapter VII. § 4 of Part II., by the rate of real wage that rules there in conjunction with the rate of interest. Restriction on the importation of foreign motor cars cannot affect favourably either of these things. Hence it cannot lead to any addition to employment in home wage-good industries. There is nothing, therefore, to be added under this head to what was said in the preceding section. There is no further scope than was there indicated for aug-menting employment by restricting imports.

§ 7. There remains the third case distinguished in § 3, where the estopped or restricted imports consist of raw material, half-finished goods or machinery. When the supply of these things available to us is reduced, our labour and capital equip-ment is subjected to a handicap and cannot yield the output of service of which it would otherwise be capable. If, for in-stance, our supplies of raw cotton are cut off, nobody will want to engage cotton operatives. Hence, in general, restrictions on the importation of raw material, half-finished goods and machinery will cause the demand in terms of our export goods for imports of wage-goods (with which to pay the wages of workpeople), to contract. Hence the readiness of foreigners to offer wage-goods to us on better terms does not imply that they will necessarily send more of these goods to us. They may, on the contrary, easily send less of them; and the aggregate real demand for labour here may easily be contracted and not expanded. This class of consideration is in practice very important. It shows that, for a country situated as England is, there is only a very small group of commodity imports (as distinguished from security imports), the estoppel or restriction of which can be expected with any confidence to exercise even a small favourable effect on the real demand for labour at home. It will, of course, be understood that in this chapter I am concerned solely with the real demand for labour, that is, the quantity of labour demanded at each several rate of real wage. I am not considering possible effects of import restrictions on the price level, and so indirectly, in so far as money wages are rigid, on the rate of real wage for which workpeople stipulate.

N

CHAPTER XV

THE SIGNIFICANCE OF CHANGES IN THE RATE OF INTEREST

§ 1. In this final chapter of the present Part we have to study a quite general factor that is relevant to the real demand function for labour in the aggregate. This factor is the real rate of interest (*i.e.* the rate in terms of wage-goods), or, rather, the schedule of rates, in return for which people are ready to hand over to a deferred use given quantities of present resources. Changes in this schedule may come about in any one of four ways. First, they may result from changes in the productivity of the factors of production in respect of wage-goods. Obviously, other things being equal, the larger the annual output of wage-goods, the smaller will be the rate of interest associated with the withdrawal of a given quantity from consumption. Secondly, they may result from changes in non-wage-earners' desire for certain non-wage-goods, any addition to the output of which involves the prior building up of a structure of either fixed capital or working capital. Thus, if non-wage-earners, expecting a good return, elect, over any given period, to invest more per annum than they have done hitherto in railways or in electric plant, without cutting down correspondingly their rate of investment in other things, the rate of interest in wage-goods—and, in general, in money also—will rise. Again, if their desire function for some sort of non-wage-good, which serves the purposes of consumption, is raised from one level to another level, at which it thereafter stands, during the period of production before work devoted to making the consumption-good yields its fruit, the rate of

178

interest will stand higher than it did before: though, afterwards, since no further working capital is being created, it
will relapse to its original level.[1] Thirdly, changes in the rate
of interest may result from changes in people's attitude
towards the future or from shifts in the distribution of
income from people with one sort of attitude to people with
another. Fourthly, from the standpoint of a single country,

---

[1] In the text nothing has been said of the effects on the rate of interest
of an expansion of non-wage-earners' desire for non-wage-goods which have
a nil period of production, such as the direct personal services of chauffeurs.
Prima facie it would seem that such an expansion of desire, since it involves no building up of new capital, but merely a shift from one kind of
consumption to another, cannot affect the rate of interest at all. This,
however, is not so. A distinction must be drawn between the case in which
the change of taste is recognised as temporary and that in which it is
expected to be permanent. Plainly, if it is recognised as temporary, *e.g.* if
soldiers' services are wanted for a war, the rate of interest in respect of any
given volume of new capital construction will go up; because the devotion
of a given quantum of wage-goods to present uses satisfies a more urgent
desire than it used to do, while its devotion to future uses does not. If,
however, the change of taste is expected to be permanent, the issue is less
clear. Suppose that $f(x)$ is the marginal utility from the consumption of x
units of wage-goods, or their fruits, by non-wage-earners—conceived, for
simplicity, as all alike—both this year and next year; and also that, this
year and next year alike, their income of wage-goods (apart from the fruit
of this year's investment) is X. Write i for the rate of interest for one year
and A for the amount of wage-goods that it would pay to invest (*i.e.* post-
pone consumption of) for one year for the sake of $(1+i)$A wage-goods at the
end of it. Suppose, for an approximation, that the marginal utility function
for wage-goods is linear and that constant returns prevail, so that the yield
of A wage-goods invested for a year is $(1+i)$A for all values of A. Then in
equilibrium

$$f(\text{X}-\text{A})=(1+i)\{f[\text{X}+(1+i)\text{A}]\}.$$

Hence
$$\text{A}=-\text{X}\left\{\frac{i}{1+(1+i)^2}\cdot\frac{f(\text{X})}{\text{X}\cdot f'(\text{X})}\right\}.$$

Now $\dfrac{f(\text{X})}{\text{X}f'(\text{X})}$ is the elasticity of the utility function in respect of the consumption of X wage-goods. Hence $\text{A}=-\dfrac{i}{1+(1+i)^2}\eta\text{X}=$approximately
$-\dfrac{i}{2(1+i)}\eta\text{X}$, subject to the condition that A is not $>$ X. If $i=\cdot05$ (that is, if
interest is at 5 per cent), this gives $\text{A}=-\frac{1}{42}\eta\text{X}$. Hence a larger or a smaller
rate of investment will be performed at a given rate of interest, *i.e.* with a
given rate of investment the rate of interest will be smaller or larger, than
before, according as the effect of the change of taste is to render the utility
function of non-wage-earners' consumption of wage-goods more or less
elastic in respect of their original rate of consumption. There seems no
general reason to expect that this elasticity will be appreciably affected in
either sense, and, therefore, no reason to anticipate any appreciable shift in
the rate of interest.

they may result from any of the above types of change initiated outside that country. Changes of the first type are not to be regarded from our present standpoint as causal factors determining shifts in the aggregate real demand function for labour. They are, rather, reflections and accompaniments of these shifts, the joint effect with them of the developments or retrogressions in productive technique and so on, that have made the magnitude of real incomes alter. Changes of the second type are, in like manner, not causal factors in respect of the particular industry in which changes in demand or supply conditions have come about, but they are causal factors in respect of all other industries. Changes of the third and fourth types are causal factors in respect of all industries. We have to show in what way, when they are causal factors, changes in the real rate of interest produce their effect.

§ 2. In Chapter V. of Part II. it was shown that the demand price of any rth unit of labour under conditions of free competition is only equal to the actual value of the marginal net product of r units provided that the fruit of the labour emerges on the market instantaneously—a state of things that prevails over only a very small part of the industrial field. If it does not prevail, the demand price is equal to the discounted value of the marginal net product. This depends in part on the length of the production process and in part on the ruling rate of interest in terms of wage-goods. It is easy to see that, when the schedule of real interest rates confronting any set of industries changes, the demand function for labour in those of them whose fruit is not yielded instantaneously must also change, expanding if the interest rate falls and contracting if it rises. The purpose of the present chapter is to develop this general statement in detail. In the calculations that follow I suppose that labour costs are all the costs that there are and neglect costs of materials and so on. There would be no difficulty, if the facts were known, in bringing these things into account.

§ 3. All labour ultimately produces services to consumers. It produces these things after an interval either (1) directly in a single lump, or (2), *via* some durable object, in a series spread through time. The second of these divisions represents what happens in occupations manufacturing machines, which yield a product during their life, and in occupations manufacturing durable pieces of consumption capital, which afterwards yield a series of services.

§ 4. Consider, first, occupations which produce final commodities consumed at once—not spread through time—after a certain interval or period of production. Write r for the period of production in years; period of production being interpreted to mean the interval between the *average* worker's effort and the results produced. Then, if all the work is done to-day and the product emerges a year hence, $r = 1$: but, if the work is begun to-day and carried on for a year by a constant staff of men, $r = \frac{1}{2}$. Write p_1 for the original rate of interest per cent in terms of wage-goods: p_2 for the rate after it has changed. It follows from the analysis of Part II. Chapter V. that a fall in the rate of interest from p_1 to p_2 involves a rise throughout its range in the demand function for labour in the centres affected in the proportion $\left(\dfrac{100 + p_1}{100 + p_2}\right)^r$. Thus a fall in the rate of interest from 5 per cent to 4 per cent raises the demand function throughout its length by approximately $\frac{1}{2}$ per cent for labour whose period of production is six months; for labour with a period of one year by 1 per cent; for labour with a period of two years by approximately 2 per cent; for labour with a period of five years by approximately 5 per cent. In like manner, a fall in the rate from 5 per cent to 3 per cent raises the demand function for labour with the above several periods by approximately 1 per cent, 2 per cent, 4 per cent and 11 per cent respectively.

§ 5. Consider, secondly, occupations in which the final commodity is yielded, not once for all, but in a series spread—let us suppose evenly—over an interval of n years: as when a machine, whose period of production is r years, yields its product over a life of n years. When the rate of interest falls from p_1 to p_2, this involves a rise in the demand function for labour throughout its range in the proportion

$$\frac{p_1}{p_2}\left\{\frac{100+p_1}{100+p_2}\right\}^r \cdot \left\{1 - \frac{100}{100+p_2}\right\}^n \div \left\{1 - \frac{100}{100+p_1}\right\}^n.$$

It is easy to see that, r being given, the maximum possible value of this expression is attained when $n = \infty$: that is to say, when the commodity produced by our industry, after being produced, goes on yielding its services for ever. When $r = 0$ the maximum possible value is $\frac{p_1}{p_2}$. That is to say, a reduction in the rate of interest from 5 per cent to 4 per cent involves a rise in the demand function, as above defined, throughout its range of 20 per cent. The corresponding implications for other conditions are readily worked out. For example, with houses taking, say, two years to build and lasting forty years, the rise in the demand function for labour throughout its range (*i.e.* in the demand price for each several quantity of labour), due to a reduction in the rate of interest from 5 to 4 per cent, is $16\frac{1}{2}$ per cent.

§ 6. In the light of what has been said it is easy to see that the extent to which a given shift in the real rate of interest, or, more strictly, in the schedule of real interest rates, will affect the real demand function for labour in any group of industries depends on the proportionate parts played in the group by industries whose final fruits are yielded after periods of different lengths. Hence a given change in the rate of interest produces a larger effect on the aggregate demand function for labour in a country a large part of whose labour is devoted to distant ends than in one a small part of whose labour is so devoted. In all circumstances, however, a fall in the rate of interest causes some expansion, and a rise some contraction, in the aggregate real demand function for labour.

PART IV

MONETARY FACTORS AFFECTING VARIA-
TIONS IN THE LEVEL OF THE REAL
DEMAND FUNCTION FOR LABOUR

CHAPTER I

§ 1. IN the preceding Parts we have not, except in one chapter, made any reference to the mechanism of money and credit, with the aid of which the main part of the economic activities of the modern world are conducted. This does not mean that our analysis has assumed the monetary mechanism to be non-existent, and so relevant, not to the actual world, but only to an abstract and unreal simulacrum of it. On the contrary, everything that has been said is relevant to the actual world. All the influences of which an account has been given play their part there in the way that has been described. We have, in short, not assumed that there is no money, but simply postponed our discussion of its rôle.

§ 2. From this prelude it would seem that the task of the present Part must be to determine in what way the "monetary factor" causes the average amount of, and the fluctuations in, employment to be different from what they would otherwise have been. This sounds definite and clear-cut. In fact, however, the word "otherwise" conceals a serious ambiguity. For it is not in the least plain what the alternative is with which situations containing the monetary factor are supposed to be contrasted. Money in the modern world performs, as is well known, four functions. It serves as a common measure of value, a medium of exchange, a standard in terms of which the main body of deferred payments are contracted for, and a store of value. *Prima facie* the alternative, to be set over against actual money economies, may be either an economy in which the functions now performed

185

by money are not performed at all or an economy from
which the specialised money that now performs these several
functions is withdrawn. Let us consider these two alternatives
in turn.

§ 3. It is easy to imagine an economy of the same general
type as actual economies, in which the first three of the functions of money distinguished above are not performed at all.
There might be no common measure of value; no generally
accepted medium of exchange might be used, but all
"prompt" transactions might be carried through by direct
barter; no single standard of deferred payments might be used,
but every loan, being made in some specific quantity of a particular thing, might carry a provision for repayment and payment of interest in terms of that particular thing. If, however,
the function of store of value, as now performed by money,
were not performed at all, the essential feature of a modern
economic community—the fact of trade—would have to be
cut out. In any economy in which that feature remains people
are bound to hold some sort of store of value to serve the
purpose to which the store they actually hold in money is
devoted. They are bound, that is to say, to hold some real
balances—control over a certain modicum of resources in
immediately available form. They must do this partly to
facilitate everyday purchases and sales, since their incoming
claims do not always exactly offset their outgoing obligations;
and partly as a means of insuring themselves against difficulty in the event of expected incomings not materialising or
unexpected outgoings becoming necessary. If, therefore, they
do not hold a store of money and bankers' promises to provide money, they will need, in order that trade may continue,
a store of something else to serve the same purpose. To
think away this function of money is thus to think ourselves
into a state of things so remote from reality that a comparison between it and our actual state is altogether without
interest.

§ 4. The other alternative seems at first sight more promis-
ing. We have simply to imagine the specialised money, by
which the functions of money are now performed, abolished.
This leaves it possible for the function of providing a store of

value—real balances—as set out in the preceding section to be performed by something else, and so allows our imaginary community to carry on trade. Reflection, however, shows that this alternative, viewed as a whole, is no better than its rival. If the specialised money were done away with, there is no single clear-cut situation that would necessarily confront us. Any number of different situations are possible. The first three functions of money distinguished above might not be performed at all; or they might all be performed, some by one thing, some by another; or one of them might be performed and another might not; and so on endlessly. There is no reason for postulating any one of these situations rather than any other. The "otherwise", which we have to imagine in contrast with actual conditions, is either hopelessly ambiguous or the product of arbitrary choice. Nothing of value can emerge from an investigation conducted along these lines.

§ 5. In deference to these considerations we shall do well to surrender any ambition we may have felt to determine what "difference" is made to unemployment and its fluctuations by the presence, as contrasted with the hypothetical absence, of the monetary factor. We must take it for granted that the monetary factor in some form exists and that the economic cosmos is lubricated by its agency. This does not mean, however, that the problem of unemployment can be satisfactorily discussed without any discussion at all of monetary machinery. There are a number of different ways in which this machinery can be constructed and operated. The employment situation will be materially affected by the choice that is made among these ways. Some comparison between different types of monetary system is thus essential to my purpose. This might be carried through on several plans. Here, the plan proposed is as follows. I set up on the one side a certain imaginary monetary system, which I call the standard system, and on the other side systems of the general type of those that actually rule in the modern world. A study of these contrasted systems will be found to have significance for the problems examined in this book.

§ 6. What precise system shall be set up as standard is a

matter of more or less arbitrary choice. There is no suggestion, it must be clearly understood, that a system can be found— or should be sought—under which economic life will proceed as it would do if there were no money at all; no suggestion that our standard monetary system provides a neutral money in that sense.[1] Moreover, it is immaterial to our purpose whether the monetary system to be labelled standard is a "good" system, or a "better" system than others. Yet again, it is immaterial whether it is one which it would be feasible to operate with the existing banking organisation. Our object-ive, in short, is not a social ideal, but a reference model, by help of which the functioning of actual monetary systems may be conveniently studied. For this purpose the standard system must be reasonably simple. It follows that it must be in some sense stable. This, however, does not take us far, for there are many different kinds of stability. Thus there is stability of total money income, stability of the price level, in any one of the many senses in which the term price level may be used, and stability of money income per unit of the factors of production at work. I am not concerned to discuss the comparative social effects of these various kinds of stability. The kind that is postulated in my standard monetary system will be described in detail in Chapter V.

§ 7. It will be shown in Part V. that the real rate of wages for which workpeople stipulate tends to be adjusted to the real demand for labour in such wise that the *average* level at which this demand stands over a long period—and, therefore, the factors which govern that average level—have little rele-vance to the problem of unemployment. The factors which have relevance are those determining the *fluctuations*, on the one hand in real wage-rates, on the other hand in the real demand function for labour. Of the part which monetary

---

[1] The conception of a neutral money, which shall allow everything to proceed as it would do if there were no money at all is parallel to that of a "neutral" lubricant, whose presence shall make no difference to anything. The only lubricant which "makes no difference" is a non-existent lubricant. A perfect lubricant generates no frictions and is thus, in a sense, passive. But nobody imagines that the search for a perfect lubricant will lead to the discovery of a "neutral" one!

arrangements play in regard to the former set of fluctuations something will be said in Chapter IX. of Part V. In the present Part attention is concentrated on the part which they play in promoting fluctuations in the real demand function for labour.

CHAPTER II

THE RELATION BETWEEN REAL OUTPUT, REAL INCOME AND MONEY INCOME

§ 1. I DEFINE economic services as services for which money payments are made. They include the services of factors of production that members of a community own abroad, whether directly or by way of sleeping partnership through debenture holdings, or otherwise. The net fruit of these services, as rendered by all the factors of production appertaining to a community, that emerge in a unit of time, I call the *real output* of that unit of time. By net fruit is meant what is left over after the depreciation of existing capital associated with the work performed on it has been made good. The real output thus defined comprises (1) the inflow of consumption-goods and (2) the net new creation (which may be negative) of fixed, working and liquid capital. These two parts of real output I call respectively A and B and the total O. Thus O = (A + B).

§ 2. A portion of the services of factors of production is devoted, neither to making consumption-goods nor to adding to capital stock, but to replacing wear and tear of capital stock, in such wise as to maintain it intact. The factors, whose services are devoted to this purpose, plainly receive payment just as the other factors do. They do not, however, produce real output. Hence, it seems *prima facie* that those factors which do produce real output are somehow mulcted, in the interest of the others, of a part of what they produce. It is difficult to see how this can happen: and a paradox results. The explanation is, however, simple. The factors that are engaged in producing real output in that act destroy part

of the existing capital equipment. Their net product, therefore, is not the total flow of consumption-goods and creation
of new capital, but this flow *minus* the associated destruction
of existing capital. They hand over to the other factors
such part of their product as is required to pay for these
factors' work in making good this destruction. What is left
to them is the whole of their net product when this negative
element is, as, of course, it should be, taken into account.
They are thus not mulcted of any part of it. The real output
of the whole community is the flow of consumption-goods
and additions to capital *minus* the consequential capital destruction *plus* a replacement of this destruction. These two
latter elements cancel out and leave the results set out in
the preceding section intact.

§ 3. Real income is customarily defined as everything that
is produced *minus* capital depreciation. If, therefore, capital
depreciation were equal to the destruction of capital by
work done upon it, as defined in the preceding section, real
income would be the same thing as real output. In fact,
however, capital depreciation, though it is not usually taken
to include damage inflicted on capital by act of God or the
King's enemies, is always so defined as to include loss of
value consequent upon obsolescence. It follows that real
income falls short of real output by whatever portion of the
latter is required to offset obsolescence. In modern conditions,
where machinery often becomes obsolete very quickly, this
difference may be substantial. For rough approximations it
may, however, be safely ignored; and in the discussion that
follows the terms real output and real income will be treated
as synonyms.

§ 4. The money income of the community in any unit of
time I define as the sum of money received by factors of production (including, of course, entrepreneurs) in payment for
services. From it, therefore, are excluded all money receipts
other than those made against these services. Thus there are
excluded those receipts of business men that are, in effect,
repayments of expenses incurred by them. Debenture interest,
mortgage interest, and war loan interest are included only
on condition that equivalent amounts are excluded as ex-

penses from the money incomes of the payers. Moreover, there are excluded all receipts that are gratuities against no services—as widows' pensions, unemployment benefit and so on. Hence, if a man, hitherto unemployed and receiving £1 a week benefit, accepts work at a wage of £3 a week, aggregate money income is increased, not by £2, but by the whole £3. No doubt there may be difficult cases in which what is nominally wage payment is really in part charitable donation, but for our present purpose it is not practicable to enter into niceties of that kind. Finally, there are excluded all receipts that result from sales of property—existing houses, securities and so on.[1]

§ 5. We thus have, for any unit of time, a real output—or income—O, representing the net fruit of the services rendered by factors of production that emerge in that unit of time, and a money income I, representing the money paid over to those factors of production in that unit of time for services rendered. If it were the custom to pay for the services of factors of production on the instant that their fruit emerges, this would imply that in any unit of time I is the money income received by the factors of production in payment for the services (whenever performed) that are embodied in the real output of that unit of time. Thus, if we write O_t for the real output of any instant t, e_t for the money payment for the service of producing a unit of O_t, and I_t for the corresponding money income, we should have $I_t = e_t O_t$. In fact, however, the services rendered by factors of production at instant I_t are not, in general, paid for at the instant when their fruits emerge, but at various other instants. Thus wage-earners are usually paid at the end of the week for all the work done during the week, and salaried workers are paid at the end of monthly or quarterly periods of service. Both these

---

[1] These points are well put by Professor Wagener in his distinction between primary and derivative income. "Receipts not based on the rendering of economic service—for example, charitable donations, allowances paid to students and presents—" are derivative income. "All receipts, however, which are obtained as hire for labour power or capital are primary income, and are, therefore, essential elements in our reckoning. The total primary income accordingly reflects the total production of the national economic system, provided that the distinction drawn above is maintained." *Economic Rhythm*, pp. 32-3.

sets of payments in large part precede the sale of the particular units of commodity in which they are embodied. The shareholders of companies, on the other hand, receive payment for the services of the equipment which they own *after* the commodities embodying these services have been sold; and so also do retailers. If there were a uniform period of delay between the emergence of embodied services on the market and the associated money payment made to the factors of production providing them, measured by c, the relevant equation for instant t would be, not $I_t = e_t O_t$, but $I_t = e_{t-c} O_{t-c}$. For the non-uniform time intervals of real life, some negative and some positive, no short and simple formula is available.

§ 6. What has just been said leads naturally to another point of like character. In a community where the whole of people's money income is spent regularly on consumption-goods and additions to capital stock, that is to say, where the rate of money income and the rate of expenditure on these things in each unit of time are equal, it is natural to speak as though the money that is spent in purchasing the real output of any time unit is the money income *of* that time unit. On our definition, however, that is not right. It would, indeed, be right if the money income accruing in each unit of time were expended instantaneously in making purchases. But money income is not in fact expended the instant that it is received. Thus consider £100 paid over to A as A's money income on January 1 of a given year. All of this money will be held by him for some finite time. Moreover, the intervals between receipt and payment will be different for different parts of it, some being paid away almost at once, others after a considerable time. Hence, I_t being, as before, the money income of time unit t, if we write E_t for the money expended by income receivers in that time unit, E_t, even when it is numerically equal to I_t, will not have the same content. It will be made up of bits of I belonging to a number of antecedent time units. It is not the money income of (*i.e.* accruing in) that time unit.

CHAPTER III

THE RELATION BETWEEN MONEY INCOME AND THE STOCK OF MONEY

§ 1. THE total stock of money in the country I define as the quantity of currency in the hands of the public (*i.e.* not in bank tills) *plus* the bank balances held by the public (including the Government's balances, but excluding the balances held by one bank in another) *plus* the sum of unused overdraft facilities. Since each unit of currency in the Central Bank carries on its back many units of bank money, this complex character of the stock implies that shifts in the distribution of *currency* between people's pockets and the Central Bank are accompanied by changes in the total stock of money. This consideration, however, lies outside the present argument. What concerns us here is the relation between the stock of money and the stream of money income as described in the preceding chapter.

§ 2. When the stock of money and the stream of money income per unit of time (*e.g.* per month or year) are given, there is necessarily some determinate arithmetical relation between them. Thus, if I represents annual income and M the total stock of money, we may write $I = Mv$. With this notation it is customary to name v the income velocity in the period under review of the total money stock. If we prefer it, however, we are equally entitled to separate off a part of the total stock, say M′, to call this the *relevant* or active stock and to write $I = M'v'$. Here v' is, of course, the income velocity per unit of time of the relevant or active part of the money stock. Obviously, so far as mere algebra goes, the two formulae come to the same thing, and there is nothing to choose between them. Obviously also, if we write k for the proportion of real income per unit of time that people choose to hold in money and k' for the proportion that they choose to hold in active money, $\dfrac{1}{k} = v$ and $\dfrac{1}{k'} = v'$.

§ 3. There is, however, something more than this to be said. With the formula $I = Mv$, v is a mere arithmetic ratio without any physical significance. It is *defined* by the formula in which it figures. That formula asserts simply that the income I per unit of time is v times the total stock of money. With the formula $I = M'v'$, however, this is not so. When we call M' the relevant stock of money, we must mean, if we are to mean anything, that each unit of M' becomes income at least once during the period under review. With this understanding let us conceive a period, for the duration of which rates of money income and rates of expenditure on consumption - goods *plus* additions to all sorts of capital are at once constant and equal to one another. In respect of such a period suppose that the relevant stock of money is also constant. Then for that period v' has a physical significance. It measures, in any unit of time (say a year) within our period, the frequency with which a representative unit of the relevant stock of money enters into income. £100 of money income is received by A on January 1. Some of it, as we saw above, is expended at once, other parts on a succession of later dates. Of what is expended on any date the part that is paid for direct personal services enters at once into somebody else's money income. But the rest of it only so enters by degrees. For example, suppose that, on a given day, £10 is spent on buying something in a shop. Only that part of the £10 which represents the retailer's profit enters into income immediately. The remainder enters into it at later moments, as the retailer makes payment to the wholesaler and the wholesaler to the manufacturer. The intervals between the receipt and the spending of money by A and the various intervals described above are determined by social custom, business practice and so on. These are objective facts. The v', to which they give rise, is a genuine physical magnitude.

§ 4. If the money stock consisted of physically distinguish-able pieces separated into two groups, the members of one of which never appeared in the income stream during our period, while all the members of the other did so appear at least once, the magnitude of M′ could be found by direct observation. Since, in fact, the money stock does not, in the main, consist of physically distinguishable pieces, this can-not be done. It is open to us, however, to evaluate a *cer-tain proportion* of the total stock which is passive and so irrelevant to the stream of money income. Thus we may conceive that, in a given period, out of the total stock one part is held as savings; a second part as a basis of financing capital transactions on the stock exchange and the real estate market; a third part as a means of financing move-ments of partially finished commodities inside the structure of industry; and a fourth part as a basis of the ordinary income transactions of consumers. Of these several parts of the total stock all except the part held as savings are relevant in the above sense. Hence, if we write M′ for the relevant stock, (M – M′) is savings, and, if we know what this amount and also what the amount of the whole stock is, we are in a position to infer the magnitude of M′. Unfortunately, how-ever, at all events in this country, we have no proper figure for money held as savings. For the figures recorded as time deposits represent these in a very imperfect way. Neverthe-less, it is possible to make a guess. Mr. Keynes has suggested that for Great Britain in 1926–8 the money held as savings, including the savings deposits in the Post Office and Trustee Savings Banks, amounted to about 1000 millions; and that the remainder of the stock of money amounted to some 1075 millions of bank deposits, *plus* some 250 million notes not held by the banks—in all, 1325 millions.[1] If, then, we put total money income at about 4000 millions, this implies that v' is equal approximately to 3: or, in other words, that the average period that intervenes between the successive ap-pearances of a representative £ of active money as income has in recent time for this country been about four months.

§ 5. Mr. Keynes has set out further figures, which can be

---

[1] *A Treatise on Money*, vol. ii. pp. 28-9.

used to split this period of four months into two parts, namely,
(1) the average period between the receipt of money income
and its expenditure, and (2) the average period between the
expenditure of money income and its reappearance as somebody else's income. His guess is that there are held as a
basis for income-transactions 275 millions of bank deposits,
plus 225 millions of notes, and as a basis for business, finance
and so on, 800 millions of bank deposits, *plus* 25 millions
of notes.[1] If these figures are roughly right, $\frac{5}{13}$ths of our four
months, *i.e.* about seven weeks, on the average is the interval
between the receipt and the expenditure of a £ of income,
and about 10 weeks the interval between the expenditure
of a £ and its subsequent reincarnation as new income. If,
the stock of active money being unchanged, everyone paid
out again every unit of money income the instant it was
received, aggregate money incomes would become $\frac{17}{10}$ths of
what they are; if every unit of expenditure was reborn as
income instantly, they would become $\frac{17}{7}$ths of what they are;
if, *per impossibile*, both these changes were accomplished,
they would become infinite!

§ 6. The foregoing analysis should suffice to prevent a serious
misconception. It is sometimes thought that, if the total stock
of money M is increased by the creation of new bank credits,
a consequent increase in the magnitude of I must take place.
This, however, is not so. If we use the formula $Mv = I$, the
inference is only valid provided that v has not diminished. If
we use the formula $M'v' = I$, it is only valid provided that, in
consequence of the credit creation, M', and not merely M, is
increased. If I withdraw from the income-expenditure circuit
£100,000, whether to hoard it as a savings deposit or for any
other purpose, my action diminishes I, in such wise that,
in order for it to be kept at its old level, the banks must
create £100,000 of credit for another man, who turns it into
the income-expenditure circuit. This action on the part of the
banks merely offsets my action; and there is no net increase
in I. We may not, therefore, infer that I must increase merely
because we see that the sum-total of bank balances is mount-
ing up, even though we know that the whole of the new

[1] *Loc. cit.* p. 28.

balances are turned into the income-expenditure circuit. Since, however, bank records indicate in a general way when increases in the total stock of money are being made, while decreases in v—or in M'—are only very imperfectly traceable in statistics of time deposits, the possibility of increases in the stock of money serving, not as a disturber, but as a stabiliser of money income and expenditure is liable to be overlooked. Mr. Robertson's work has made it plain that, if that is done, very serious error results.

CHAPTER IV

A MECHANICAL MODEL

§ 1. SOME readers may find their ideas on the relation between money stock and money income clarified by contemplating a mechanical model. Let us imagine a number of thick
tubes bent round in a circle and closed. Each tube is of a
length in inches equal to the number of days that it takes for
the money inside it to pass from being income once to being
income a second time. In every tube there is fitted a series of
metal cylinders, each of them one inch long and capacious
enough to hold the maximum quantity of money ever put into
it, and all of them together occupying the whole tube. These
cylinders move round the tubes at a constant speed of one
inch per day. Every tube is open on one side, so that it is
possible at any point in it to insert money into the cylinder
opposite the point, or to take money out of it. The tubes are
suspended vertically in a line in such wise that an imaginary
horizontal plane one inch thick intersects all of them. Where the
plane intersects any tube, the money, if any, in the cylinder
there embraced is income. Thus the total income of any day is
equal to the quantity of money in all the tubes that is standing
in the plane on that day. The total stock of money on the day
is equal to the quantity of money standing in the whole of all
the tubes, and not merely in those parts of them that are in
the plane. Thus, if l_r inches be the length of any rth tube and
a_r the amount of money in it, the total income, not, indeed, on
each day, but on an average day, is $\Sigma \dfrac{a_r}{l_r}$, and the total stock
of money is Σa_r. In like manner the (weighted) average period

of circulation in days of active, or relevant, money is $\dfrac{\Sigma l_r a_r}{\Sigma a_r}$: and
the reciprocal of this multiplied by 365 is the average annual
velocity of active money—the v' of the preceding chapter.
There are, unfortunately, no statistical data from which the
proportionate distribution of money among tubes of various
lengths can be obtained.

§ 2. With this model it is possible to represent many of the
characteristics of monetary events. All the money that is
in the tubes is properly to be regarded as active. Each piece
of it only appears as income on certain days, but on the
other days, whilst it is sealed up in industrial processes or in
financial processes or in the pockets or balances of private
persons, it is always *advancing towards* its next income appearance. Money that is not doing this, but is hoarded as savings
deposits or in stockings, is outside the tubes altogether. Our
model enables us to picture what will happen when money,
either newly created for the purpose or taken out of hoards,
is inserted at any point into one of the tubes; or when money
is removed from one of the tubes and either destroyed or turned
into hoards. We can also study the effect of transfers of money
from one tube to another, whether the transfer is made in the
income plane or elsewhere: and the effect of a lengthening or
shortening of any of the routes which money follows between
successive appearances as income. In the sections that follow
the more important of these movements are investigated.

§ 3. If on a given day money is inserted from outside into
a cylinder, standing in the income plane, that belongs to a
tube l inches long, this new money revolves and appears
as income on every lth day, so long as it remains in the
tube. Suppose then that on zero day Q new money is inserted in this way into this tube: and that r days afterwards
an equal amount is removed from the cylinder in it that then
stands in the income plane. We must postulate, of course, that
there is enough money in the cylinder on that day to allow of
this. Write $r = (pl + k)$, where p is either nil or a positive integer
and $k < l$. Obviously the income of the rth day receives an
increment Q, and the income of the $(r + l)$th day suffers a
decrement Q. Thus income is transferred from the $(r + l)$th

to the rth day. This *must* happen. But, over and above this, something else, much more important, namely, a modification in aggregated money income accruing, in respect of this tube, over the whole of time, *may* happen. This aggregated income is increased by pQ. If $r < l$, that is to say, if the interval between the insertion of Q and the later withdrawal of it is less than the period of circulation of money in the tube, so that p, and, therefore, $pQ = 0$, aggregated income is not affected at all. If $r > l$, aggregated income is increased by Q multiplied by the number of times that the period of circulation is contained in the interval. That is to say, there is a net creation of that amount of income. If the withdrawal of the money takes place first and the insertion subsequently, the above result holds good with sign reversed. There is a net destruction of a precisely equal amount of income.

§ 4. A more complicated case is as follows. Suppose that on a given day Q money is inserted, not into one, but into all the tubes, in proportions equal to the proportions of money already there. All these insertions are made into cylinders standing on the income plane. Subsequently, after r days have elapsed, an equal sum is withdrawn in the same manner from the cylinders then standing in the income plane. The total insertions into the several tubes were then $Q\dfrac{a_1}{\Sigma a}$; $Q\dfrac{a_2}{\Sigma a}$; and so on. Write $p_1, p_2, \ldots$ for the number of times that the length of each tube divides completely into r, so that p_1, p_2, and so on, are either nil or positive integers. Then the aggregate creation of money income over the whole of time in respect of all the tubes together, consequent upon the insertion and subsequent withdrawal of the Q money, is equal to $\dfrac{Q}{\Sigma a}\{p_1 a_1 + p_1 a_2 + p_3 a_3 \ldots\}$. All the terms in respect of which the value $p = 0$, of course, disappear. Thus, if r contains fewer days than the shortest of all the tubes, *i.e.* of all the periods of circulation, no net creation of income takes place, only ante-dating. But, if r contains more days than the shortest tube, there must be some net creation. There may be regions over which an increase of r does not imply an increase in any p. Hence we are not entitled to say without qualification that, provided r exceeds the length of the shortest circulation period, *every* increase in r involves an increase in the quantity of aggregate income that is created. Subject, however, to possible discontinuities—which can in no event last longer than the shortest circulation period,—it is true that, the larger r is, the greater is the aggregate volume of income created. As in the simpler case considered in the preceding section, so also here, if the withdrawal of Q money takes place first and its insertion subsequently, the result reached holds good with sign reversed. The figure obtained above for net creation of income becomes a figure for net destruction of it.

§ 5. If, on a day when a cylinder containing money in a tube l_1 inches long is standing in the income plane, Q units of money are taken from it and transferred to a cylinder, also in the income plane, belonging to another tube l_2 inches long, on every l_1th day during which the new arrangement lasts money income is less by Q than it used to be, and on every l_2th day is greater by Q. How is aggregated income affected over a period of r days? Let r as before be equal to $(pl_1 + k)$, where p is an integer and $k < l_1$. Let it also be equal to $(ql_2 + h)$, where q is an integer and $h < l_2$. Then the excess of aggregate income during the r days over what it would normally have been is $(p - q)Q = \left\{ \dfrac{r-k}{l_1} - \dfrac{r-h}{l_2} \right\} Q$. If h and k are both nil, this $= rQ\left\{ \dfrac{1}{l_1} - \dfrac{1}{l_2} \right\}$. Since, if $l_1 = l_2$, h must be equal to k, when the two tubes affected are of equal length the effect on aggregated income must in all circumstances be nil.

§ 6. Finally, suppose that one of the tubes, previously of length l, is elongated to $(l + w)$ inches, the extra w inches being added to the part of it adjoining the income plane on the side of outflow at the moment when a cylinder containing all the tube's money is standing in the income plane. Let the amount of money in the tube be a. The effect of the change is that henceforward a becomes income on every $(l + w)$th day instead of on every lth day. To determine the effect on the aggregated income accruing during a period r, write, with the same implications as before, $r = (pl + h) = \{q(l + w) + k\}$. When the tube is elongated in the manner described, the aggregated money income of the following r days becomes qa instead of pa. That is to say, it is diminished in the proportion $\frac{q}{p}$. This contraction is obviously the same as would have resulted if the length of the tube had not been changed, but instead, on the same day, money had been withdrawn from the cylinder standing in the income plane, in such wise that the quantity in it fell in the proportion $\frac{q}{p}$. Provided that $h = k = 0$, that is to say, that r is an exact multiple both of l and of $(l + w)$, $\frac{q}{p}$ is obviously equal to $\frac{l}{l + w}$. When, therefore, that condition is satisfied, a given proportionate increase in the length of any tube, *i.e.* in the period of circulation of money through it, has exactly the same effect on aggregated money income as an inverse proportionate decrease in the quantity of money contained in it.

CHAPTER V

THE STANDARD MONETARY SYSTEM

§ 1. Suppose that non-wage-earners' desire for home-made non-wage-goods in the aggregate becomes keener, while at the same time their desire to use their claims on wage-goods in their own personal consumption of wage-goods and in making purchases of foreign non-wage-goods becomes less keen in precisely equal measure. There will then take place a certain transfer of wage-goods from the latter class of use to the former, while the rate of interest, in terms of wage-goods—and everything else of relevance—remains unaltered. In these conditions under monetary systems of the current type, the money concomitants of the real movement work themselves out as follows. Non-wage-earners in the aggregate, who we suppose, have decided to devote so much extra wage-goods to hiring labour, instead of consuming these wage-goods or surrendering claims on them for imported non-wage-goods, pay out to new wage-earners an amount of money, withdrawn from purchasing wage-goods and imported non-wage-goods, sufficient to enable them to buy the wage-goods that represent their real wages; money wage-rates and prices remaining the same as before. If W is the real rate of wage, K the number of additional workers employed and P the money price per unit of wage-goods, the amount of money thus withdrawn and handed over —I ignore the changed income of extra associated non-wage-earners—is obviously KWP. There is no motive for the non-wage-earners to hand over any money other than what they have withdrawn from their own expenditure on wage-goods and imported non-wage-goods. The action of non-wage-

earners who engage labour at the expense of cutting their
purchases of home non-wage-goods is, of course, without effect
on money income. Hence the aggregate money income of the
community is increased by KWP. What happens is readily
expressed in the language of the so-called quantity theory of
money. Nothing has occurred to alter the size of the total
stock of money M. Therefore, since income per unit of time
has increased from I to $\{I + KWP\}$, and since, by definition, the income in any time unit is equal to Mv, it follows
that v, the former income velocity of the total money stock,
has increased to v_2, where $v_2 = \dfrac{I + KWP}{I} v$.

§ 2. Now in actual life the kind of real movement described in the preceding section seldom happens. From time
to time the desire of non-wage-earners to secure certain sorts
of home non-wage-goods becomes keener; but this extra keenness is not offset by diminished keenness in their desire for
claims on wage-goods for either of the purposes set out in the
last section. Again, their desire for labour to make home
non-wage-goods is increased on account of an improvement
in productivity: with no corresponding offset. Yet again, the
quantity of labour they wish to employ is expanded because
the real rate of wage asked for has been reduced; still with
no corresponding offset. Finally, through some happening on
the side of money, the rate of interest at which money loans
are offered is reduced, so that the profit obtainable from invest-
ing borrowed money in hiring labour is enhanced. In all these
cases under actual monetary systems the extra money handed
to wage-earners is not balanced against an equal contraction
in the expenditure of non-wage-earners upon wage-goods for
their personal consumption or upon imported non-wage-goods.
On the contrary, in general the contraction of expenditure in
these directions is substantially less than the expansion of expenditure on hiring wage-earners. Consequently in general,
when there is an upward movement, total money income is
increased by substantially more than KWP; and, when there
is a downward movement, it is decreased by substantially more
than this. *I define the standard monetary system as one so constructed that, for all sorts of movements in the real demand function*

for labour or in real rates of wages, whether they last for a long time or a short, the aggregate money income is increased or diminished by precisely the difference made to the number of workpeople (or other factors of production) at work multiplied by the original rate of money wages.

§ 3. A standard monetary system so defined has certain important implications. The first of these has to do with the active stock of money as defined in Chapter III. § 2. If wage-earners spent the whole of their earnings instantly on receipt of them, alterations in the money income of wage-earners would not necessitate any alteration in this stock. For no stock at all would be required to underpin wage-earners' incomes; or, in other words, so far as these incomes are concerned, the income velocity of active money would be infinite. In real life, however, wage-earners do not expend the whole of their incomes instantly on receipt of them, but hold, on the average, a certain balance of real value in money form. When the number of wage-earners is increased, and the new wage-earners handle as wages perhaps twice as much money as they have been handling hitherto in the form of unemployment benefit, they will, we may presume, in a little while build up for themselves real balances more or less equivalent to those held by existing wage-earners. The income velocity of active money for them will, that is to say, soon come to be much what it is for other wage-earners. In order that this may happen, it is necessary that the stock of active money shall be, in some measure, increased. In like manner, if the number of wage-earners at work is contracted, this stock must be, in some measure, decreased. Thus the successful establishment of a standard monetary system implies some expansion of the stock of active money when the volume of employment is enlarged and some contraction when it is diminished. These variations may be brought about either by variations in the total stock of money or by variations in the part of the total stock that is active. Over short periods it may be presumed that both sorts of variation will play a part: while for long-period changes, unless some outside factor intervenes, the proportion between active and non-active money may be expected to be constant, so that what is required will have to be accomplished by way of the total stock.

§ 4. A second implication of the standard monetary system has to do with the price level. Before this can be discussed usefully the sense to be given to the term price level must be defined. Here there are two difficulties. The first has to do with the nature of the items whose prices are to be regarded as relevant. *Prima facie* it seems proper to take account of all goods that enter into real income as defined in Chapter II. § 3. The real income of any time interval includes, however, any additions that are made during it to working capital; and there are no units in which these additions can be measured. Hence they must be omitted; and, if they are omitted, it seems logical to omit additions to fixed capital also. If this is done, paradoxes, of course, arise; *e.g.* we have to include motor cars bought by private persons, while excluding precisely similar cars bought by garages; and so on. Provided, however, that we do not change our dividing line in the middle of an argument, it does not greatly matter that this line is a dubious one. With this understanding we may agree to exclude that part of real income which consists of additions to either working or fixed capital, and to mean by price level the price level of consumption-goods. This, however, does not exhaust the matter. Our second difficulty remains. There is no such thing as a price level of consumption-goods until the quantities of the several sorts of consumption-goods to be taken into account have been settled; in other words, until the structure of the composite commodity by which consumption-goods are to be represented has been determined. Now, if the consumption-goods on which the part of money income not devoted to additions to capital is spent were always grouped together in the same proportions, the proper composite commodity to choose would obviously be a microcosm of this collection of things. In real life, however, different items are included at different times in what money income buys, and, even of those items that are always included, the proportions vary. There is no reason why, as between two periods to be compared, our composite commodity should be a microcosm of the purchases of one period rather than of the other, nor can any compromise commodity be set up as the "right" one in any absolute sense. Several different definitions of the price level are thus equally legitimate: and it is evident that the behaviour of the price level in given circumstances will be different according to the way in which our— necessarily arbitrary—choice of a definition falls.[1]

§ 5. For the present purpose, however, it is not necessary to enter into these niceties. We may rest content with two broad conclusions, that hold good independently of the precise way in which changes in price level are defined. The first of these concerns a state of things in which the general technical efficiency of the factors of production, conceived as grouped together in given proportions, is held constant. Even so, it is unlikely that, after conditions have changed in such wise as to alter the volume of employment, the price level will be exactly the same as before. For this change in conditions will probably have altered the proportions in which the factors of production are distributed among different activities. Unless conditions of constant return prevail everywhere, this will involve a change in the *relative* prices of the several items embodied in the composite commodity, whose price level is being measured; and, apart from an accident, this is bound to mean *some* variation in the price of that composite commodity. Provided, however, that the general technical efficiency of the factors of production is not altered, the price level, on any plausible definition, is not likely to vary much. The second broad conclusion, really implied in the first, is that, in so far as inventions and so on expand the general technical efficiency of the factors of production, the price level will tend to fall in some rough proportion to the average improvement in productive efficiency. Hence, without defining in a precise manner the relevant composite commodity, we may conclude that, under a standard monetary system, the price level will be, not indeed absolutely, but fairly stable, so long as no marked improvements in productive efficiency occur; if such improvements occur, it will fall in a proportion not far from the inverse of that in which the improvements have caused output to increase.

---

[1] Cf. *ante*, Part I. Chap. IV.

§ 6. To this conclusion some readers may perhaps object as follows. When a number of new men are taken into employment, they do not yield their final product of commodities immediately. For the first k days, say, six months, the whole of their service will exhaust itself in building up a stock of working capital, or goods in process. For this period the output of commodities will be unchanged; but, when the period is over, if the new and higher rate of employment continues, the services rendered by all of the extra workpeople will be offset by a corresponding extra outflow of commodities. In these circumstances during the preliminary period, when the stock of working capital is being built up, the price level will rise—for there is more money income than before but the same quantity of commodities for sale—and, afterwards, when the new flow of commodities for sale begins, it will fall back to what it was originally. This, however, is an illusion. In the two periods money income is the same. The difference between the two periods is that in the former some of this money income is generated by investment in additions to working capital and some by expenditure on consumable goods, whereas in the latter no investment is being made in additions to working capital, and the whole—so long as no investment in additions to fixed capital is taking place—is generated by expenditure on consumption-goods. Thus expenditure on consumption-goods is larger in the second period in roughly the same proportion in which the flow of consumption-goods is larger. The same thing may be expressed from another angle by saying that in both periods the newly employed workpeople, like other workpeople, spend their money incomes on consumption-goods: in the former these men are building up working capital and not producing consumption-goods, so that payments to them are made direct and not *via* the purchase of consumption-goods; in the latter they have been shifted over from making additions to working capital to making consumption-goods, and payments are made to them *via* the purchase of consumption-goods.

§ 7. From this discussion it is apparent that the establishment of a standard monetary system by no means implies that the real demand function for labour in the aggregate

P

will remain stable. What it does imply is that, *if* the real demand function varies, money income will vary with it in a certain specified way, and not otherwise. With monetary systems not of standard type money income does vary otherwise than in this specified way. In consequence, as will be argued in later chapters, disturbances of the real demand function for labour take place that would not take place with a standard monetary system, and disturbances, which would have taken place in any event, though in certain circumstances they may be damped down, are, in general, aggravated.

CHAPTER VI

THE STANDARD MONETARY SYSTEM AND THE MONEY RATE OF INTEREST

§ 1. To establish and maintain the standard monetary system, in other words to prevent money income from varying otherwise than in that precise manner which, as explained in Chapter V., the standard monetary system requires, some controlling mechanism is needed. The principal weapon available for this purpose is, it is generally agreed, the money rate of interest charged by the banks to their customers, this in turn being governed by the discount policy of the Central Bank, supplemented at need by the sale and purchase of securities on its behalf. The rate of bank interest which at any time conforms to the requirements of the standard monetary system may, for convenience and without any ethical implication, be called the *proper* rate.

§ 2. It is sometimes thought that this rate can be defined in a clear-cut objective manner. In order that money income shall vary in correct accord—as defined in Chapter V. § 2—with variations in the quantity of factors of production at work, industrialists in times of boom must only obtain money for engaging more labour to the extent that they and the people from whom they borrow abstain from spending money upon wage-goods and imported non-wage-goods; and in like manner in times of depression, in so far as industrialists invest less money in hiring labour, they or other people must spend correspondingly more money upon wage-goods and imported non-wage-goods.[1] Hence, we are tempted

---

[1] It is not, of course, necessary that the immediate correspondent of the industrialist should make this kind of cut in expenditure. He may, for instance, sell a security. But somebody, *e.g.* the person who buys the security, must make this kind of cut.

to say, the *proper* rate of money interest—the rate that is needed to maintain a standard monetary system at any time —is such rate that no difference is made from the money side to the degree in which industrialists' needs for real resources are satisfied. Since the degree to which these needs are satisfied obviously affects the rate of interest in terms of wage-goods (or of any other specified composite commodity) that rules in the community at large, we may paraphrase this by saying that the *proper* rate of bank interest is that rate which makes no difference to the—or more correctly to *any*—real rate of interest;[1] *i.e.* that the real rate is the same as it would otherwise have been. In saying this, or in saying what comes to the same thing, that the *proper* rate of bank interest is that rate which leaves the "natural rate" of interest unaffected, we seem to be making a statement that has significance. But there is much peril in the terms "make no difference to", "leaves unaffected" and "would otherwise have been". Unless "otherwise" means "if there had been no monetary system", it means nothing at all. Already, however, in the first chapter of this Part, we have seen that "otherwise" cannot mean "if there had been no monetary system". It is illegitimate to abstract money away and leave everything else the same, for the reason that, in the absence of money, everything else would necessarily not be the same. The abstraction proposed is of the same type as would be involved in thinking away oxygen from the earth and supposing that human life continues to exist. It is an improper application of the method of difference to imagine a cause to be removed but its effect, nevertheless, to remain. Hence the verbal manœuvres we have been attempting lead to nothing. The proper rate of bank interest is that rate which maintains the standard monetary system, as defined in Chapter V. § 2. Nothing further can, or need, be said.

§ 3. The question whether the establishment or maintenance of the standard monetary system is practicable is thus identical with the question whether the actual rate of bank interest can be made to coincide with the *proper* rate. This question falls into two parts: first, can the banking system

[1] Cf. *ante*, Part II. Chap. V. § 4.

always so adjust the actual rate of bank interest that it conforms to the existing *proper* rate; secondly, if the banking system cannot do this of its own motion, can State policy so modify the *proper* rate of bank interest as to enable it to do this? In principle, it is clear that there are no limits to possible upward movements in the actual rate of bank interest. Hence, no matter how intense the real factors making for an expansion in aggregate money income may be, the banks have always at their command a weapon adequate to counter them. But, when factors on the real side are making for a contraction in aggregate money income, this is not so. Since money can be stored at practically nil cost, any bank, or banking system, that offered to lend at a negative rate of interest would not only be acting in direct opposition to its own interest, but would be confronted with an unlimited demand for accommodation. It would pay *everybody* to borrow £100 on condition of paying back £99 at the end of the year. Hence the actual rate of bank interest cannot fall below nil. The weapon available to the banks for cancelling real factors that make for *contractions* in aggregate money income has thus a restricted scope. If the real factors are sufficiently powerful, it may not be adequate to cancel them. It is, indeed, always possible for the Central Bank, by open market operations, to force out money into balances held by the public. But in times of deep depression, when industrialists see no hope anywhere, there may be *no* positive rate of money interest that will avail to get this money used. The *proper* money rate, *i.e.* the rate which would maintain the standard monetary system, may, in short, be a negative rate, and, therefore, one which it is impossible to introduce. In these circumstances attempts to uphold the standard monetary system, so long as reliance is placed on purely monetary defences, are bound to fail. If, however, at the same time that the banking system keeps money cheap the Government adopts a policy of public works, the risk of failure is greatly reduced. For this policy, providing, as it does, new openings for real investment, pushes up the *proper* rate of bank interest above what it would otherwise have been. Thus it may turn a negative *proper* rate, to which it is impossible for any actual rate to conform, into a positive one.[1] The position is still more secure, for a gold standard country, if the combined policy of credit expansion and public works is adopted, not by that country alone, but by the general body of gold standard countries acting in unison: for in that case low actual rates of bank interest can be maintained without setting up foreign drains of gold—drains, which, if they occur, must sooner or later force a reversal of the cheap money policy.

[1] It is sometimes supposed in a confused way that the *suppression* of public works and other forms of general expenditure, because it leads to low actual bank rate, promotes real demand for labour. Such a view neglects the fact that this action directly contracts to real demand for labour and the further fact that forced levies, with whatever expansion of demand they imply, result, not from the actual rate being low, but from it being lower than the *proper* rate.

CHAPTER VII

THE TWO MAIN TYPES OF DISTURBANCE UNDER ACTUAL MONETARY SYSTEMS

§ 1. THE fundamental characteristic of the standard monetary system is, as we have seen, such regulation of the rate of money interest charged by the banks that variations in the money required by industrialists to pay for labour are always balanced by equal and opposite variations in the expenditure of themselves and the people from whom they borrow upon wage-goods or imported non-wage-goods. This, of course, implies that, when the requirements of industrialists do not vary, these expenditures also do not vary. Under actual monetary systems these adjustments are liable to fail in two separate ways. On the one hand, when the requirements of industrialists expand, the money rate of interest charged by the banks is not pushed up far enough to bring the adjustment about, and, when the requirements of industrialists contract, it is not pushed down far enough. On the other hand, the state of industrialists' requirements being given, the money rate of interest charged by the banks is liable to be pushed up or down by influences, initiated in money supply, that have nothing to do with these requirements. In this chapter I shall inquire how these two sorts of maladjustments come about and how they are interrelated. In accordance with the language of Chapter VI. § 1, I shall, in what follows, speak of that rate of money interest charged by the banks which satisfies the needs of the standard monetary system as the *proper* rate of bank interest.

§ 2. The type of disturbance on the real side which here chiefly interests us is a shift in the desire of non-wage-

215

earners for some form of home-made non-wage-good, not offset by a corresponding shift in the opposite direction in their desire either for other forms of home-made non-wage-goods or for claims on wage-goods for their personal use or for exchange against foreign non-wage-goods. When such a shift occurs—let us suppose that it is an upward shift—industrialists, in general, find profit in turning more wage-goods per unit of time to hiring labour to build up fixed or working capital than they have done hitherto. To obtain the extra wage-goods for this purpose they—or the people from whom they borrow—are not obliged to dispense with an equivalent amount of them in personal consumption and use for making purchases abroad. It is open to them to obtain part of what they need from other people by increasing, on the one hand, the income velocity of existing balances, and, on the other hand, by borrowing from banks additional balances. Unless the banking system puts up the actual rate of bank interest to what I have called the *proper* rate, it pays them to make use of this opening. But the banking system, so long as it acts on current principles and does not follow a deliberate policy of stabilisation, will not push up the actual rate of bank interest so high as this. For it is to its interest to lend more than usual when borrowers are offering better terms than usual. Hence, in the face of an upward movement in the demand for labour initiated on the real side, banking systems, as currently operated, always allow the actual rate of bank interest to rise less than the *proper* rate. In like manner, in the face of a downward movement, the banking system always allows the actual rate of bank interest to fall less than the *proper* rate.

§ 3. I now turn to disturbances initiated on the side of money. In an isolated community the separation of these disturbances from those initiated on the real side is quite clear-cut. Monetary disturbances fall into two divisions, according as they operate on (1) the quantity of legal money in a country's banking system and (2) the proportion maintained between this legal money and the superstructure of bank money. These two divisions are not, however, rigidly separate.

For an increase in the supply of legal money may lead to a decision on the part of the banking system to reduce the ratio of bank money to legal money; a decision on its part to increase that ratio may, with full-value bullion standards, bring about an outflow of legal money to non-monetary uses. This, however, is a secondary matter. It does not threaten in any way our concept of what disturbances initiated on the side of money are.

§ 4. In a community which is linked up with an outside world the supply of money to it is liable to be affected by outside happenings. If it is operating a gold standard, or gold exchange standard, its aggregate money supply is altered by anything that alters the value of gold relatively to commodities in other countries. If it is not on a gold basis but has an independent paper money, *prima facie* it cannot be affected by external events of this character. It must be borne in mind, however, that, even when there is no formal acknowledgement of dependence of one money upon another, nevertheless management may in fact be conducted in some measure with an eye on foreign exchange rates. After the abandonment of the gold standard by Great Britain in September 1931, the Bank of England, in determining its discount policy, was undoubtedly influenced in some degree by a desire to prevent the foreign exchanges from depreciating unduly.

§ 5. Of disturbances that originate in the outside world some are monetary disturbances from all points of view. The discovery or petering out of foreign gold mines, and the absorption or release of gold abroad, in consequence of some foreign country's deciding to change its monetary standard or to modify its law about bank reserves, clearly fall into this class. But, when one country's money is tied to the money of other countries, the supply of it to that country may also be altered by changes for the demand for it elsewhere, that have a real, and not a monetary, origin. If the United States, for example, undertook to double the track of its railways, the supply of money in all gold standard and gold exchange standard countries would be contracted. Such changes, from the standpoint of the countries, so to speak, of primary impact, do not originate in money; but, from the standpoint of countries of secondary impact, they do so originate. This point is elementary and obvious. Nevertheless, failure to grasp it has led to much confusion in popular diagnosis of the present world situation. The maldistribution of gold—the heavy accumulation of that metal in France and the United States—is regarded by many as *the* cause of the economic collapse: money gone mad is the villain of the piece. From the standpoint of certain particular countries, whose economy has been upset by foreign drains of gold, this is a legitimate point of view. But from the standpoint of the world as a whole the maldistribution of gold is an effect of State policies about reparations and tariffs, of business policies about foreign lending, and so on. It is responsible, indeed, for secondary reactions of a very disastrous kind.[1] But no one endeavouring to take a general view of the great depression can possibly regard it as a prime mover.

§ 6. There are, for a country linked up by a common monetary system with the outside world, disturbances of yet another type, which it is necessary to distinguish. These disturbances do not arise out of the factors behind the real demand for labour, nor yet are they strictly monetary in origin. Thus the people of this or any other country have annually a certain foreign balance made up of the excess of their claims on foreigners on account of exports, shipping services, interest due on past loans, and so on, over their debts to foreigners on account of imports. The magnitude of this foreign balance is determined, in the first line, by the comparative levels of costs of production in terms of the common money here and abroad. We (any country) also lend annually a certain net sum to foreigners through net purchases of new and old securities. The magnitude of this sum is determined in the first line by the comparative rates of interest obtainable from investments at home and abroad. Thus the amount of a country's foreign balance and the amount of its real foreign lending are determined in the first line by different sets of

---

[1] These reactions have, no doubt, been aggravated by the fact that in France, to which a large part of the world's gold has recently moved, little use is made of cheques, so that the superstructure of money built on a given quantity of gold is smaller than it is, *e.g.*, in this country. Cf. Salter, *Recovery*, p. 67.

considerations. Gaps between them may, therefore, from time
to time be threatened either by the decision of financiers to
make a loan abroad or by an enhancement of imports, in consequence, say, of a bad harvest at home. When gaps of this
kind occur, the direct reaction, which, for a country with
an independent money, is a fall in the rate of exchange,[1] for

[1] This general statement needs, for accurate analysis, to be qualified.
When a country possesses an independent money, threatened failures of
its claims on foreigners to balance its obligations abroad cannot, in all
circumstances, be filled up by movements in the rate of exchange. Clearly,
they could not be so filled up at a given moment if all contracts between
one country and others falling due for payment at that moment were in
terms *either* of that country's money *or* of the other country's money. In
that event, so far as international relations are concerned, the several
countries would, in effect, be on a common money basis. Nor could a
threatened gap be estopped if the major part of the debit contracts were
in foreign and the major part of the credit contracts in domestic money.
This matter can be set out more exactly thus. Let c_i and c_e be a country's
credits for immediate payment due in its internal money and external
money respectively, and d_i and d_e its corresponding debits. Let r be the
rate of exchange, *i.e.* the number of units of external money that a unit
of internal money will buy. In order that our mechanism may be available there must be some value of r which will make $rc_i + c_e = rd_i + d_e$:
that is, which will make $r(c_i - d_i) = (d_e - c_e)$. This condition implies that
$(c_i - d_i)$ and $(d_e - c_e)$ are both negative or both positive (neither of them
being nil). That is to say, *either* the country's credits in internal money
must fall short of its debits in internal money *and* its debits in external
money must fall short of its credits in external money; or its credits in
internal money must exceed its debits in internal money *and* its debits in
external money must exceed its credits in external money. Moreover, the
second of these conditions is not really sufficient to make the mechanism
available. For, if an adverse gap threatens to appear, this reduces r, the
quantity of foreign money that a unit of our country's money will buy,
and so makes matters worse. There is thus, in truth, only one condition
that allows the mechanism to work, namely, that that country's relations
with the rest of the world are so organised that it has at all relevant
moments a net debit in internal money and a net credit in external money.
It may be added parenthetically that, when a given gap is threatened, the
extent of the shift in the rate of exchange that is needed to prevent it
emerging is intimately associated with the relative magnitudes of c_i, d_i,
c_e and d_e. With a given total trading position in normal times, in order to
obviate a threatened gap (measured in either money at the normal rate of
exchange) of given magnitude, the rate of exchange must shift more
largely (1) the larger is the proportion of the country's credits that are
in domestic money, and (2) the smaller is the proportion of its debits that
are in foreign money. Thus the fact that a large part of Great Britain's
credits consists of sterling interest makes it necessary, when we are off the
gold standard, for larger swings in the rate of exchange to occur to obviate
given gaps than would be needed if the credits were all in dollars. When,
owing to a country's debt being predominantly in foreign currency, as in
the post-war difficulties of Germany, a fall in the exchange fails to close,
but rather widens, threatened gaps, the only means to avoid default may

one tied to an international gold standard is an outflow of gold.

§ 7. Disturbances on the money side do not in themselves affect real conditions, and therefore, when they happen, the *proper* rate of bank interest is not altered. These disturbances do, however, bring about changes in the actual rate of bank interest. For banking systems, in a given environment of law and tradition, will not allow substantial alterations in their reserves to occur without taking steps, by raising or lowering this rate of interest, to alter their liabilities in a similar sense. On the one hand, when an influx of gold occurs, the Central Bank, not wishing to hold a larger proportion of its assets in a barren form than custom requires, puts the discount rate down. On the other hand, when outside happenings threaten to bring about a foreign drain of gold, the Central Bank sooner or later forces up the discount rate, with the immediate purpose of attracting foreign balances and so estopping the drain. Hence, divergences between the actual rate and the *proper* rate of bank interest are created.

§ 8. Actual monetary systems differ from one another considerably in respect of what may be called their elasticity. This is larger, the smaller is the reaction in the rate of bank interest stipulated for by bankers that results from a given absolute shift in the amount either of their liabilities or of the ultimate currency reserve. The main factors by which it is determined are the rules and customs governing the relation between variations in bank deposits and the cash reserves of the Central Bank, and the principles in accordance with which the fiduciary note issue is permitted to vary. The larger the Central Bank's normal reserve of cash against given liabilities and the more free the fiduciary issue, the greater is the elasticity of the monetary system. In this country, if it were customary for the clearing banks to allow the volume of the deposits that they hold on a given basis of cash and balances at the Bank of England to vary, the result, for elasticity, would be the same as that of an enlargement in the

be to export domestic money to foreign speculators. If this happens, the country's monetary system is, of course, acted on in a manner no less direct than that of a gold standard country called on to export gold.

normal cash reserve of the Central Bank.[1] All this is tolerably familiar, and need not be discussed in detail. The point of importance for our present purpose is that high elasticity in the monetary system has opposite consequences as against disturbances introduced from the real side and from the money side respectively. The greater the elasticity of the monetary system, the smaller is the shift in the actual rate of bank interest brought about by a disturbance initiated on either side. But, since disturbances on the real side imply movements in the *proper* rate of bank interest, while disturbances on the money side do not, anything that restricts movements in the actual rate of bank interest promotes, for the first sort of disturbance large, for the second sort small, divergences between the actual rate and the *proper* rate. Hence, when disturbances on the real side take place, *e.g.* when the desire of non-wage-earners to invest in the services of labour is enhanced or contracted, the reactions of actual monetary systems are less like that of the standard system, the more elastic they are: when disturbances on the money side, *e.g.* influxes or effluxes of gold, take place, the reactions are more like that of the standard system, the more elastic they are.

§ 9. It is conceivable that, for some country with a monetary system of non-standard type, events should so shape themselves that disturbances initiated on the side of money supply always exactly offset disturbances initiated on the real side, so that at every moment the *proper* rate of bank interest

---

[1] Cf. *The Macmillan Report*, p. 159. In this connection it is a matter of some importance that wage-earners do not as a rule have banking accounts, and that wage payments are made, not in transfers of bank money, but in actual currency. A given issue of currency obviously lowers the proportion of reserves to deposits held in the banking system more than an equal issue of new credit would do, and so evokes stronger protective reactions. The degree of difference for this country may be indicated as follows. The joint-stock banks are accustomed to hold their deposit liabilities, some 2000 millions, at about nine times their cash (probably about 150 millions) and their balances at the Bank of England (about 60 millions); and the Bank of England holds in the banking department currency about equal, as it happens, to the bankers' holdings of balances at the Bank of England. In these circumstances the same strain is placed on the banking system in finding one additional £ for engaging new labour as would be involved in finding nine additional £s for a purpose for which bank balances, and not actual currency, would serve.

was actually established. In such a case a monetary system not standard in intention would be standard by accident. Plainly, however, nothing of this kind is in the least likely to happen in the actual world. Disturbances of monetary and of non-monetary origin will on practically no occasion exactly cancel out. In so far as they are independent, they are likely to be complementary about as often as they are contradictory to one another. In so far as what we have called disturbances on the monetary side are not strictly of monetary origin, but arise out of the circumstances of international trade, they are not independent of the other class of disturbance. They are then more likely to be complementary than to be contradictory to them.

CHAPTER VIII

ACTUAL MONETARY SYSTEMS IN RELATION TO MONEY INCOME AND THE PRICE LEVEL

§ 1. THE fundamental characteristic of the standard monetary system is, as we have seen, that aggregate money income is only varied in correspondence with variations in the quantity of the several factors of production at work. Under actual systems it invariably happens that (short-period) additions to the quantity of the factors at work is associated with more than corresponding additions to aggregate money income and contractions with more than corresponding contractions. It follows that the price level, instead of being not far from constant so long as the general technical efficiency of the factors of production is not altered, is above the normal in times of good employment and below the normal in times of bad employment. So much we have already seen. Provided, therefore, that the excess money income of one moment after its first spending instantly vanished, so that future money incomes were not affected by it, and, in like manner, provided that deficiencies of money income at one moment were irrelevant to later money incomes, the chapter now to be written would not be needed. In real life, however, things are not so simple as this. Besides the immediate reactions studied in the preceding chapter, there is also an aftermath. This calls for analysis.

§ 2. In the language of Chapter IV., so far as expansion is financed by the creation of new balances, money is inserted into my system of tubes; so far as it is financed by a change in the income-velocity of money, some of those tubes are reduced in length. Except in so far as these distortions are offset, further secondary reactions must take place. Not one generation of money income only, but a succession of generations are expanded, just as many generations of men would be expanded if a bounty on large families were accorded to a single generation. Now, since it is obvious that in no circumstances can the distortions be offset instantaneously, we have to ask how speedy an offset is required in order that secondary reactions may be reduced to insignificance. Let us consider first distortions in the form of injections of new money into the system of tubes, not of modifications in the length of any tube. This money at its first spending is, we suppose, placed in the cylinders that stand in the income plane on a particular day or series of days, and is distributed among the several tubes in the same proportions as the money already there. On that day or series of days aggregate money income is, of course, increased by the amount of the new money. The cylinders then move forward round the tubes. If no offsetting action is taken, on any future day that a cylinder into which the new money has been injected appears in the income plane, that day's income is correspondingly increased above what it would otherwise have been. Suppose that the length of a given tube is l days, and that on the first day K units of new money were inserted in it. If an offsetting withdrawal of money takes place from the cylinder standing in the income plane on some day, say the $(l-m)$th day, prior to the lth day, secondary reactions on aggregate income are obviated: for, though the income of the lth day is enhanced by K, the income on the $(2l-m)$th day is contracted by K: and so on over the rest of the future. Thus, though the dating of subsequent incomes is modified, their aggregate amount is not affected. It follows that, if the new money is withdrawn again from all the tubes into which it has been injected after an interval less than the number of days represented by the shortest of the tubes, there are no net secondary reactions. If the interval is more than this, there are net secondary reactions, larger in amount the longer is the interval. For any given interval the magnitude of the reactions can be calculated when the length of the several tubes and the distribution of the money among them is known. If the interval is infinite, if, that is to say, the

new money is not withdrawn at all, the average daily income
of the whole of the future is, of course, increased in a proportion equal to the ratio of the new money to the original
stock standing in the tubes. It is easy to see that analogous
considerations hold good of distortions brought about, not
by injections of new money, but by alterations in the length
of the tubes.

§ 3. With this background of analysis we have now to inquire how far and how rapidly offsetting adjustments may be
looked for in actual life. The answer is quite different according as the initial movement was brought about by real or by
monetary causes. These two sorts of movement must, therefore, be considered separately. This section will be devoted
to the former sort. Let us begin by supposing that on a given
day exceptionally fine weather or an access of optimism
arouses in industrialists as a body a desire to engage more
labour at current real wages than they have been engaging
hitherto. To this end they make use, not only of money saved
by themselves or other people from expenditure on consumption, but also of money withdrawn from existing balances (*i.e.*
via an increase in the income-velocity of money) or created
in new balances. At the end of the day the weather or state
of mind of industrialists returns to what it was before. They
no longer look for special profit in engaging labour. Consequently, they no longer have any inducement, in order to
employ it, to hold a smaller quantity than usual of real resources locked up in money form: and they are no longer prepared to offer better interest terms than usual either to the
banks or to anybody else. The banks, in like manner, finding
the rate of interest what it was before, tend to cut down their
loans to what they were before. In short, the extra money
which was inserted into the system of tubes in response to
the temporary needs of new real investment tends to be
pulled out again. Apart from alterations which may have been
incidentally brought about in industrialists' general attitude
by the associated price movements which have occurred and
are occurring—a matter to be studied in Chapter XII.—this
equilibrating tendency is bound presently to accomplish itself. But it will not accomplish itself instantly. There is certain

to be some time lag. Hence, since some of our tubes are very
short indeed, there is practically certain to be some secondary
creation of money income, and so also some secondary reactions on the price level. This will not be raised above or lowered
below its initial level merely during the time proper to the first
spending of the money injected into or ejected out of income,
but for somewhat longer than that. How rapid the return to
equilibrium will be and, therefore, how large the secondary
reactions on money income and the price level will be it is
impossible to determine *a priori*; nor at present are the statistical data adequate to decide the matter *a posteriori*.

§ 4. It remains to consider movements that have been initiated, not on the real, but the monetary side. When it is a
question of temporary shifts in the supply of money due to
fluctuations in the general economic situation in the outside
world, the situation is much the same as that discussed in the
preceding section. But, besides this sort of movement, there
are also movements initiated by changes in the money supply
of a lasting character, arising, for instance, in a gold standard
world from the discovery of large new gold mines or the adoption by an important country, hitherto on the silver standard,
of a full-value gold money. When this kind of thing happens
we have not to do with the introduction and subsequent re-
moval of a factor that causes movement round an established
position of equilibrium. The new factor is one that makes the
position of equilibrium itself different from what it used to be.
There is, therefore, no tendency for the new money that is
injected into the system of tubes to be presently withdrawn.
On the contrary, other things being equal, it will revolve continually round the tubes, with the consequence described in
the last sentence but one of § 2, namely that money income
is permanently increased in the same proportion as the money
stock.

CHAPTER IX

FORCED LEVIES AND ANTI-LEVIES

§ 1. WHEN the actual rate of bank interest is below the *proper* rate, industrialists are in part financing additional employment with money obtained otherwise than by a reduction of expenditure of themselves and of people from whom they borrow on wage-goods and imported non-wage-goods. This money achieves what may fairly be called a forced levy of wage-goods for use in investment from holders of fixed money incomes. By analogous reasoning it can be shown that, if the actual rate of bank interest is above the *proper* rate, industrialists withdraw money from hiring labour without the expenditure of themselves and the people from whom they borrow on wage-goods and imported non-wage-goods being correspondingly increased. This leaves the wage-goods on offer confronted with a smaller money demand: their prices in general fall, and the possessors of fixed money incomes find themselves securing more of them. There is, if we choose to speak so, an anti-levy operated in favour of rentiers and other recipients of fixed money incomes.[1]

§ 2. If in any short period normal income is I and industrialists inject a sum of money R into the income-expenditure circuit in purchase of wage-goods, the levy they achieve must lie between $\dfrac{R}{I}$ and $\dfrac{R}{I+R}$ times the total real income, as valued in wage-goods, accruing in that period. The former figure, of course, implies that prices do not rise. This is not impossible.

---

[1] It should be noted that, if prices are held up by monopolistic action in spite of reduced money demand, no benefit accrues to rentiers and so on, but stocks are accumulated in dealers' hands.

The injected money *may* buy goods which other people are forced to go without, not by a price rise but simply because, though they have money and are anxious to purchase at the ruling prices, there are no goods left in the shops. In the converse case the anti-levy achieved by rentiers and so on is equal, *prima facie*, to $\frac{R}{I-R}$ times the total real income. The levies and anti-levies thus described I shall call gross levies and gross anti-levies.

§ 3. These gross levies and anti-levies are not all *net*. Business men are accustomed to finance themselves, not merely through the banks, but also by direct borrowings from members of the public. When, however, these persons are mulcted by a forced levy, they naturally are not willing to make such large voluntary loans as they would have made otherwise. Conversely, when they are benefited by an anti-levy, they are willing to make larger voluntary loans. A part of the gross levies and anti-levies that we have been describing is in this way offset. The net levies and anti-levies that emerge under actual monetary systems are to that extent smaller than the gross levies and anti-levies. It may even be suggested that the offset is not merely partial, but of necessity complete, in such wise that there are no net levies or anti-levies at all. Thus, it may be argued, if a man, who would normally have been willing to lend to industrialists 1000 bushels of wheat at 5 per cent, has 400 bushels forcibly taken from him, he will in consequence only be willing to lend 600 bushels; so that his net contribution is no different from what it would have been in any event. This argument, however, omits two important considerations. In the first place, there are a number of rentiers and so on, who would not normally have been making any loans to industry. For these persons, obviously, there can be no offset of this kind when a forced levy is exacted from them. In the second place, it is not true that, when 400 bushels are taken by force from a man who would have been willing to lend 1000 bushels at 5 per cent, he will become willing to lend, at that rate, only 600 bushels. Of the 400 bushels taken from him he will not withdraw the whole from the investment use, but part from that use and part from the consumption use.

For, were he to act otherwise, the marginal utility to him of the bushels he engages in investment would be raised above that of the bushels he devotes to consumption. Hence, though his net contribution to the service of investment will not be increased in consequence of the forced levy by the whole 400 bushels, neither will it be increased by nothing at all. The net levy will be smaller than the gross levy, but it will not be nil. Precisely how large it will be depends on how much the various persons concerned would normally invest and on the comparative elasticities of their desire functions for investment and for consumption.

§ 4. Besides the element just discussed there is also a second element to be deducted from gross levies and anti-levies. In so far as net levies are made for industrialists, the fact that they are made causes the rate of interest, whether in terms of money, or of wage-goods, or of anything else that industrialists are ready to offer for a given quantity of borrowed resources, to be less than it would otherwise have been. This reaction is reflected in the well-known fact that shifts in the bank rate of interest generally lead, after a while, adjustment being made for differences of risk and convenience, to corresponding shifts in the general run of money rates of interest.[1] In the present connection its significance is that, while our rentier, having been robbed of 400 bushels of wheat, is willing to lend voluntarily, say, 800 further bushels at the old rate of 5 per cent, he will not, in fact, be offered 5 per cent, but only, say, $4\frac{1}{2}$ per cent. Consequently, he will lend voluntarily less than

---

[1] This does not, of course, imply that a given shift in the bank rate of interest for short loans will be accompanied by an equal shift in the rate for loans on long term. The long-term shift will, on the contrary, be much smaller than the other. Thus, if we start from a position of equilibrium, with short and long loan rates, adjustment being made for differences of risk and convenience, both at 5 per cent, and if the rate for one-year loans rises to 10 per cent, being expected thereafter to revert to 5 per cent, in order that the long- and short-loan markets shall continue in equilibrium, the rate for an irredeemable loan (*i.e.* the yield on a stock like consols) should *prima facie* rise only to 5·24 per cent. The reaction of cheap money on the yield of long-term securities is, indeed, for reasons, based on the technical character of the market, often, though not always, somewhat larger than arithmetical calculations of this kind suggest. (Cf. Lavington, *Economica*, November 1924, p. 300, and Keynes, *A Treatise on Money*, vol. ii. p. 352 *et seq.*) But it is never nearly so large as the initial shift in short-money rates.

800 bushels. It is as though a demand were confronted by two sources of supply. One of them is expanded. This implies a fall in price, and so a contraction in the supply from the other source; though the supply of the two sources together is, of course, larger than before.

§ 5. Yet a third element must be deducted before the magnitude of the net levies and anti-levies relevant to the present argument is truly gauged. The gross levies and anti-levies, as I have described them, include levies and anti-levies in respect of the general body of wage-earners. Now we shall presently consider separately how the quantity of labour demanded from time to time is affected by those variations in the real rate of wages which the play of the monetary factor brings about. Account of what levies and anti-levies do to real wages is thus taken on the supply side. If account were also taken of it on the demand side, we should be reckoning the same thing twice over. We should be making the levies responsible both for raising the real demand function for labour and for lowering the real wage for which workpeople stipulate. We are entitled to reckon them in either of these aspects, but not in both of them. Thus, when the real demand function for labour swings up, and, in consequence of that swing, the monetary mechanism effects a levy from wage-earners by reducing the real value of the existing money rate of wages, we must suppose that this money rate of wage is instantaneously increased, in such wise that the whole of the levy extracted from wage-earners is, in the same act, returned to them. Since the money income of wage-earners in this country amounts to about two-fifths of the total money income, this point is an important one.

§ 6. The final stage in the analysis has already been in part anticipated in § 4. So far as a deficiency in the actual rate of bank interest below the *proper* rate evokes net forced levies from rentiers and so on for the service of industrialists, it causes all rates of interest, whether in terms of money or of wage-goods or of anything else, to be cut down below what they would have been under the standard monetary system. We must not, indeed, regard the amount of the net forced levy as something given, which affects rates of interest

by a sort of chain process: for the amount of the net forced
levy is, as we have seen, itself partly dependent on the extent
to which rates of interest are affected. None the less, deficiencies in the actual rate of bank interest below the *proper*
rate, by evoking net forced levies, *pro tanto* drag all rates of
interest down. In like manner, by an analogous process,
excesses of the actual rate of bank interest above the *proper*
rate, by evoking net forced anti-levies, push all rates of
interest up. Whereas under standard monetary systems these
deficiencies and excesses could never occur, under actual
monetary systems they do occur.

§ 7. Now it was shown in Part III. Chapter XV. that, other
things being equal, anything which depresses the real rate of
interest (in wage-goods), *i.e.* which enables a given quantity of
wage-goods to be borrowed at a lower rate of interest and a
larger quantity at the original rate, makes the aggregate real
demand function for labour rise; anything which enhances the
real rate makes this function fall. Hence, in so far as under
actual monetary systems deficiencies in the actual rate of
bank interest below the *proper* rate occur in periods when
the aggregate real demand function for labour is rising and
excesses occur when it is falling, failure to establish and
maintain the standard monetary system causes the aggregate
real demand function for labour to fluctuate more widely than
it would otherwise do.

CHAPTER X

REACTIONS ON THE REAL DEMAND FUNCTION FOR LABOUR
FROM THE FACT OF ACCOMPLISHED CHANGES IN THE
GENERAL PRICE LEVEL

§ 1. IN the preceding chapter we were concerned with reactions produced on the demand function for labour at different times by the direct action of certain monetary processes,
when the monetary system established is not the standard one.
These processes *involve* changes in the price level. Broadly
speaking, expansions in the real demand for labour, whether
the impulse to this comes from the real side or from the
money side, are, under current monetary systems, associated
with upward movements in the general body of prices, and
contractions with downward movements. These associations
are at once suggested by the analysis of Chapter VIII. and
exhibited in statistical records. The reactions considered in
Chapter IX., however, did not include those which occur, so
to speak, at the second remove in consequence of changes in
the price level, or, more strictly, in the aggregate money demand function. The present and two following chapters are
concerned with these further reactions. It is necessary to distinguish between the groups of effects due respectively (1) to
the fact of prices having moved from one position to another;
(2) to disturbances associated with the process of movement;
and (3) to expectations of movement. The present chapter is
devoted to the first of these groups.[1]

---

[1] The prices relevant here are, of course, actual prices, not recorded
prices. The prices recorded for any time interval t are, in general, the
prices that are then *contracted* to be paid. Thus the output in time interval
t multiplied by the price level recorded in time interval t does not, in a
fluctuating state, truly represent the money expenditure of the interval.

§ 2. In a world where contracts for deferred payments were all made in terms of a tabular standard, so that they could not be upset by changes in the price level, these changes would not matter. It is true that, prices having risen, the money value of all holdings of commodity stocks would be increased and a book profit would be created for the owners of these stocks, when their current value is set against their money costs of production or purchase. In like manner, prices having fallen, a corresponding book loss would be created for holders of stocks. So long, however, as the volume of stocks was not altered, these book profits and losses would not be "realised". With industry proceeding as before and a constant rate of output flowing into stocks at one end and out at the other, costs would have moved parallel to prices, and there would be no ground for any disturbance. Thus there is no reason to suppose that, if contracts for deferred payments were expressed in a tabular standard, the fact of the price level having undergone changes—apart from the process of and expectation of the changes—would cause the real demand function for labour to be different from what it would have been had the price level remained constant.

§ 3. In the actual world contracts for deferred payments are, in general, expressed in terms of money; so that, if the price level of commodities in general—it does not matter for our present purpose in what precise way that price level is calculated—has changed since the contract was made, what debtors pay and creditors receive in real value in respect of interest and sinking fund is different from what it would have been had the price level remained constant. A raised price level means smaller real payments, a lowered price level larger real payments than would have been needed, *other things being equal*, with a constant price level. It thus appears that realised, and not merely book, gains and losses are brought about: and this is, *prima facie*, a reason for expecting that the real demand function for labour will be disturbed. Attention must, however, be paid to the phrase, *other things being equal*. Under this

---

This in part explains the fact that maxima of recorded price levels often precede the associated maxima of bank balances and notes outstanding. Cf. Mitchell, *Business Cycles, The Problem and its Solution*, pp. 130-33.

is included the condition, "provided that the same contracts are entered into as would have been entered into under a monetary system that kept the price level constant". Now, if impending changes in price level were exactly foreseen by both parties to a contract, the terms of that contract would be adjusted to the foreseen changes, in such wise that, when the changes occurred, the real payments made and received would be precisely what both sides intended—precisely what they would have been with a stable price level and contracts adjusted to that.[1] It is not the fact that changes in the price level occur, but that they occur without being perfectly foreseen, that is responsible for realised losses and gains between debtors and creditors. For this reason, when prices have risen, debtors have usually received a windfall gain at the expense of creditors, and, when prices have fallen, have experienced a corresponding windfall loss. The people who control industry operate in large measure with borrowed funds, and so are, in the main, debtors. Thus, when the price level has risen, they receive a lump-sum benefit; when it has fallen, they are mulcted of a lump-sum fine. We have to inquire in what way that fact, apart from any expectations about the future that it may generate, reacts on the real demand function for labour.

§ 4. There is one reaction of a somewhat special type which it is convenient to deal with separately and at once. When employers in an industry are suffering loss on account of having to pay the old rate of money interest in the face of fallen prices, they may be tempted to undertake a joint contraction of output by tacit or overt monopoly agreements of a sort that reduce the quantity of labour demanded below that quantity the value of whose marginal output is equal to the wage. This sort of effect may, as we saw in Part III. Chapter VII., occur in any depressed industry, whatever the source of the depression. It must, therefore, not be

---

[1] It is not intended to deny that, if the lenders are interested only in boots and the borrowers only in wheat, and if both sides foresee a *relative* rise in the price of boots, *no* contract in terms of money can yield the same rate of interest to both sides in terms of the things in which they are respectively interested. This fact is not inconsistent with the argument of the text.

left out of account when we are considering that particular sort of depression which is induced through fallen
prices. The tendency towards it is enhanced in so far as employers think in terms of money (*i.e.* concentrate attention
on the fact that what they sell is reduced in price, while dis-
regarding the fact that what they buy is also reduced), and
so imagine themselves even more seriously hit than they
actually are. This type of reaction from fallen prices may be
expected, in the presence of large price contractions that have
not been foreseen, to play an important part in industries
where the general conditions make joint action among employers reasonably easy.

§ 5. Apart from this important but indirect reaction, it
appears at first sight that, so long as transfers from debtors
to creditors do not modify the real rate of interest, damage
to business men in respect of past contracts cannot react
adversely on the real demand function for labour. Conditions
of production having remained unaltered, the same number
of men as before will produce any given marginal net product.
Indeed, in so far as their greater poverty makes employers
co-operate with harder work of their own, the same number
of men will produce a larger marginal net product than before.
At the same real wage-rate, therefore, it will pay employers
to hire the same number, or even a slightly larger number, of
men. This result, however, depends on the assumption that
the economic world is absolutely fluid, and that assumption
is not realised in fact. If employers are too severely hit, their
personal credit will suffer and it may prove difficult to renew
the short-time loans by which working capital is financed.
They may be driven into bankruptcy: and, though, of course,
this does not imply the physical disappearance of their fac-
tories and machinery, it does imply the destruction of, or at
any rate serious damage to, *organisation*. Until there has been
time for this to be renewed or repaired, the real demand for
labour will be contracted. In like manner, though less markedly, transfers favourable to business men may be expected
to induce, in the actual world, some slight expansion in the
real demand function for labour.

§ 6. Moreover, the proviso set out in the first sentence of

the preceding section, that transfers from debtors to creditors do not modify the real rate of interest, does not conform to the facts. This is most easily shown by considering the contrary case, that of transfers from creditors to debtors consequent upon prices having been raised. In effect these transfers imply that would-be investors have contrived to raise part of the funds they need in the form, not of a loan but of an involuntary gift. There has been accomplished in their behalf, in so far as they are under obligation to pay fixed interest, a second forced levy from rentiers similar in character to the forced levy described in Chapter IX. This forced levy, like that one, enables a given part of the community's real income to be turned into investment at a lower rate of real interest than would be possible if the levy were not made. That is to say, other things being equal, the real rate of interest is reduced. By parity of reasoning, when transfers of a like type are made from debtors to creditors, the real rate of interest is increased. This implies, as was shown in Part III. Chapter XV., that the aggregate real demand function for labour is lowered.

§ 7. The foregoing analysis, though it allows *some* influence in depressing the real demand function for labour in periods of contraction to the fact that prices *have* fallen, does not allow to it very great influence; and similarly, in periods of expansion, with the fact that prices *have* risen. In view of the common practice of attributing the world economic collapse of 1930–31 in the main to the great contraction in active money and associated fall in the price level, this may seem paradoxical. The explanation is threefold. First, that price fall has been, in part, not a cause of the economic collapse, but a joint effect with it of a general breakdown in confidence, whose origins are largely political. To this extent the price fall is a symptom, not an active principle. Secondly, in this chapter we have been considering only the direct effects of price-falls. In so far as they carry with them expectations of further falls, they exercise indirectly, as will be shown in Chapter XII., very important effects on the real demand function for labour. These indirect effects have played a dominant part in the economic collapse, but they are not under discussion now. Thirdly, it must be remembered that

we are here considering price-falls in relation to one part of
their effects only, namely those produced in the real demand
function for labour. In so far as workpeople's wage policy
holds up the money rate of wages in the face of a reduced
price level, price falls are also indirectly responsible for a
rise in the real rate of wage for which the workpeople stipulate. This matter will be studied in Part V. Chapter IX. The
real demand function for labour being given, the establishment of an enhanced real rate of wage is likely, as was shown
in Part II. Chapter IX., to mean a more than proportionally
diminished volume of unemployment. The fact that prices
have fallen might, therefore, be responsible for a large part
of the 1930–1931 collapse, even though it had not led to any
contraction at all in the real demand function for labour.

CHAPTER XI

REACTIONS ON THE REAL DEMAND FUNCTION FOR LABOUR OF THE PROCESS OF PRICE MOVEMENTS

§ 1. In the preceding chapter we studied the effect on the real demand for labour of accomplished changes in the *general* price level. Nothing was said about inequalities of change as between particular prices. In real life, however, there is always a large amount of friction; and this does not act uniformly. Hence, some prices prove more sticky than others, and *relative* movements take place, some of which are maintained for a considerable time. It seems at first sight that, while this circumstance will affect the comparative real demand functions for different commodities, it is not relevant to the aggregate real demand function for labour as a whole. In fact, however, it is thus relevant. The purpose of the present chapter is to bring this fact into clear light.

§ 2. The real demand function for labour being expressed in terms of wage-good units, it is evident that, in given conditions of productivity, this function will be lowered if the other elements of prime cost rise in value relatively to wage-goods; and that in converse conditions the real demand function will be raised. Now there enter into prime cost, or short-period supply price, substantial elements of cost other than labour cost. Not all salaries, for example, are properly regarded as fixed, or supplementary, costs from a short-period point of view. The element of chief importance here is, however, raw material. If money is withdrawn from the income-expenditure circuit in this country for certain sorts of external cause, *e.g.* because prices have fallen abroad, the withdrawal will probably be associated with a reduction in the prices of imports in general, and, among these, of imports of raw material. In this case, against a fall in the money demand for their product, employers have a partial offset in diminished cost of material. But, if money is withdrawn from the income-expenditure circuit as a result of something that has happened at home, the money prices of imported materials will not have fallen. Thus their real prices in terms of English goods in general will have increased: and so the real demand for the labour which is combined with them in the work of production is contracted. *Per contra*, when money is injected into the income-expenditure circuit, as a result of something that has happened at home, the real demand for labour is expanded.

§ 3. The real demand function for labour will also be lowered if, other things being equal, the value at works of its product falls relatively to wage-good units; and in converse conditions will be raised. Now wage-good items, as bought by wage-earners, are, of course, goods at retail, with the services of wholesalers, distributors and retailers embodied in them. The relation between retail prices and wholesale prices, or—more remotely—prices at works, is complicated by the fact that, since manufacturing is a process in which improvements have more scope than they have in retailing, retail prices may be expected in the long period to rise gradually relatively to the other two. This slow-working movement has no bearing on our present problem. Over and above this, however, there seems little doubt that the prices charged by retailers and distributors for their services are sticky. Professor Bowley, for example, in a recent study of English food prices, has found that retail prices have lagged behind wholesale prices by about two months, after which period 1 per cent changes in wholesale prices are reflected in changes of 0·77 per cent in retail prices.[1] The failure of retail prices to move by as large a percentage as wholesale prices is probably due, in the main, to the fact that the real rates of wages stipulated for—in the industry of distribution as in others—rise when prices fall. It is, therefore, not relevant to the present argument, which is concerned exclusively with demand. But the time lag is relevant. For it a chief cause is, no doubt, that,

[1] *Lloyds Bank Review*, June 1930.

the retail market being imperfect, retailers are able to hold
retail prices in the face of falling wholesale prices until most
of the stocks that they laid in at the higher prices have been
sold. When prices are in process of falling, this time lag implies
that the value of the marginal output *in terms of wage-good
units* of r men at work in industry must be smaller than it
was before the price movement began. Hence, the quantity of
labour demanded at any given real rate of wage, *i.e.* the demand function for labour, must be contracted below what it
then was. When prices are in process of rising, the existence
of the time lag in like manner causes the real demand function
for labour to be expanded above what it was before the movement began.

§ 4. Finally, the wage-good units, in terms of which the
real demand function for labour is constituted, contain the
element house rent. That element is weighted in the cost of
living index for this country at one-sixth. For a number of
years movements in house rents, which, in any event, are likely
to be sticky, have been severely restricted by law. This circumstance obviously affects the relation between price movements and the real demand function for labour in the same
way as the time lag described in the preceding section. It
renders the process of price-falls more adverse, and that of
price-rises more beneficial, to the real demand function for
labour than they would otherwise be.

CHAPTER XII

§ 1. I COME now to the most important route along which the price situation reacts upon the real demand function for labour. The reactions which actual price movements set up have been studied in the two preceding chapters. But, over and above this, when prices have risen or fallen, more particularly if they have been rising or falling for a little time, that fact generates among business men an expectation that they will rise or fall further. This expectation is partly a reflection of our general tendency to expect processes that we observe in action now to continue in action at all events for some time yet. But, whatever the precise way in which the generation of these expectations comes about, there is no doubt at all that they are generated. Prices having risen, business men expect a further rise; prices having fallen, they expect a further fall.

§ 2. Now these expectations of price movements would not in their nature set up any reaction on the real demand function for labour, provided that they and the rate of money interest were appropriately adjusted to one another. Moreover, if all persons concerned, borrowers and lenders alike, always viewed the future through similar glasses, the appropriate adjustment, at all events for commodities capable of being held in store, would necessarily be made. Allowance being made for risk, warehousing and so on, the gap between spot price and future price on the one hand, and the money rate of interest on the other, could not fail to coincide. Business men, therefore, would not, when the expectation is of a general price-rise, experience a stimulus to expand

R

the real demand for labour. In like manner, when the expectation is of a general price-fall, they would not experience a
stimulus to contract the real demand for labour. If, however,
the expectation of price changes is more marked among the
business men who borrow to hire labour than among the
people who lend money to them, this is no longer so. When
prices are expected to rise, the money rate lags in such wise
that the real rate (in terms of wage-goods), which borrowers
reckon to have to pay, declines; in the converse case it increases. In the former case the real demand function for labour
is expanded, in the latter contracted. Thus, to take a simple
illustration, suppose that we start from equilibrium conditions, in which the money rate and the real rate of interest
are both 5 per cent and prices in the future are expected to
remain what they are now. Business men come to expect a
price rise of 10 per cent, but lenders expect no change. By
borrowing 100 units of money business men obtain 100 units
of wage-goods, which, at the end of a year, being used to
employ labour, grow to 105 units. The business men expect
to be able to sell these for $115\frac{1}{2}$ units of money; so that they
reckon, after paying back their loan with interest, to have a
clear gain of $10\frac{1}{2}$ units of money, that is of $\frac{10}{11}$th times $10\frac{1}{2}$
units of wage-goods. It is easy to see on these lines that an
expectation of upward price movements more marked among
business men than among lenders must stimulate the real demand for labour, and that expectations of like character of
downward price movements must depress it. In fact, experience shows, as Professor Irving Fisher has made clear, that
expectations about price movements in either direction are, in
general, substantially more marked among business men than
among the people from whom these men raise loans.

§ 3. Nor is this all. The process that I have been describing
is cumulative and progressive in character. The rise in the
real demand function for labour leads, under non-standard
monetary systems, to a rise in prices. The rise in prices leads
to the expectation of a further rise, which is not offset by an
adequate increase in the money rate of interest. Hence, there
occurs a further expansion in the real demand function for
labour; this involves a further actual rise of prices; this the

expectation of a yet further rise: and so the process repeats itself in a spiral upward movement. A fall in the real demand for labour leads, in like manner, to a fall in prices and a precisely analogous downward spiral movement. Plainly, this cumulative process is of great importance. It means that from small origins large consequences, whether of evil or of good, may be built up. For example, a small injection of money into the income-expenditure circuit in bad times in connection with skilfully chosen public works, or even such an extraeconomic event as a favourable political rumour, *might* lead to a progressive and far-reaching improvement in the employment situation.[1] Marshall must have had these considerations in mind when he wrote: "The chief evil [in industrial depressions] is want of confidence. The greater part of it could be removed almost in an instant if confidence could return, touch all industries with her magic wand and make them continue their production and their demand for the wares of others."[2] In the same spirit Mr. Kinder has observed: "In a community where the individual members are working only half their time, any inducement, though illusory in itself, which sets them to work their full time, may benefit all without necessarily injuring any".[3] He was contemplating the possible effect of an upward price movement brought about by monetary causes.

[1] Cf. my *Industrial Fluctuations*, p. 320.
[2] *Principles of Economics*, p. 711.
[3] *The Effects of Recent Changes in Monetary Standards upon the Distribution of Wealth*, p. 499.

PART V

THE CAUSATION OF UNEMPLOYMENT AND OF CHANGES IN UNEMPLOYMENT

CHAPTER I

INTRODUCTORY

I<small>T</small> is very difficult to arrange the subject matter of this Part in a satisfactory manner. The reason is that fixed quanta of unemployment may result, not only from fixed states of certain determining factors, but also from processes of change in the factors. Thus, as we shall see presently, certain types of *variability* in the relative demands for labour in different centres tend to promote a *constant state* of aggregate unemployment. This fact prevents us from dividing our discussion in a straightforward manner into two parts, one dealing with states of unemployment in relation to states of the determining factors, the other with changes in unemployment in relation to changes in states of these factors. For, if we did this, we should either have to put our discussion of changes in unemployment before we had said anything about states of unemployment, which would be very awkward and confusing; or we should have to study the complex concept of variability in relative demand before we had studied the simpler *variations* in relative demand, out of which variability arises: a quite impracticable proceeding. I am forced by these considerations to a cumbrous and inadequate compromise. In the next four chapters I shall be concerned with states of the determining factors in relation to states of unemployment. I shall then turn in Chapters VI.-X. to changes in certain determining factors that lead to fluctuations in unemployment. In Chapter XI. I shall hark back to states of unemployment, and, finally, in Chapter XII. shall consider the effect, alike on the average amount and on fluctuations in unemployment, of certain rearrangements of the distribution of demand in time.

CHAPTER II

THE STATE OF REAL DEMAND AS A DETERMINANT
OF EMPLOYMENT AND UNEMPLOYMENT

§ 1. IF the rates of real wage stipulated for by workpeople were independent of the average state of the real demand for labour, we should expect the percentage of unemployment to be small in countries and periods where the real demand function for labour stands high and large in countries and periods where the real demand function stands low. Such statistical information as is available does not, however, suggest that high employment and high states of demand are correlated with one another. There is no reason to believe that employment is, on the whole, better in rich countries than in poor. In this country, over the sixty years before the war, during which real income and the real demand for labour were expanded very greatly relatively to population, the general run of employment statistics shows no sensible improvement. The inference is that the average state, as distinguished from variations in the state, of real demand for labour is not relevant in a significant degree to the state of employment. *Changes* in the state of demand are, of course, relevant, but, when once any given state of demand has become fully established, the real wage-rates stipulated for by workpeople adjust themselves to the new conditions. The new conditions thus operate on the wage level and perhaps also, in some degree, on the normal hours of labour, but not on the percentage of unemployment.

§ 2. If this broad conclusion is accepted it follows that long-run Government policies, which, whether by design or by accident, make the state of labour demand permanently better or worse than it would otherwise have been, are not, when once established, either causes of or remedies for unemployment. Thus any lasting expansion in non-wage-earners' desire to devote their resources to the construction of capital instruments (*i.e.* to investment) or of other non-wage-goods will be met, not by an increase in employment, but by a shift of employment out of wage-good industries into the expanded industries, associated with an appropriate relative rise in the real wage rate there.[1] Consider, again, the consequences of collecting, under a system of unemployment insurance, contributions from employers. This involves a depression throughout its length of the demand function for labour by an amount equal to the employers' contribution. Because a portion of non-wage-earners' contribution is collected by this method—as against some method that would not differentiate against employing labour—the volume of employment, *if other things are equal*, must be reduced below what it would otherwise have been. When, however, an insurance system has been established for some time, if the thesis of the preceding section is correct, other things will not be equal. The wage-rate for which workpeople stipulate will have become adjusted to the fact of the employers' contribution. While, therefore, an *alteration* in the amount of that contribution—an increase in it, for example, designed to obviate State borrowing on behalf of the Unemployment Fund —must affect the volume of unemployment until adjustment has been made, a permanent difference in the amount of the employers' contribution will not carry with it any permanent difference in the level of unemployment. In like manner, in so far as the existence of an insurance system, by rendering periods of unemployment less injurious to wage-earners than they would otherwise be, reacts favourably on industrial efficiency, this reaction will be accompanied by corresponding increases in real rates of wage, so that the percentage of unemployment will not be reduced. Yet again, to take an illustration from another field, if the State elects to spend for ever, in the interests of employment, 100 millions a year more than it would have spent otherwise, for some time after this

[1] Cf. *ante*, Part I. Chap. V. § 6.

policy has been inaugurated employment will be, *pro tanto*, bettered. But eventually wage-rates may be expected to adjust themselves to the new demand situation, and, when they have done so, the benefit to employment will be exhausted.

§ 3. Our conclusion, that the long-run effect of expansionist State policies—and under this head must be included not only the undertaking of large-scale public works, but bounties, guarantees of interest and, if successful in their purpose, protective duties—does not touch employment, affords, of course, no argument against the State's *temporarily* adopting these devices as "remedies" for unemployment in times of exceptional depression. For here it is not their long-run, but their short-run, consequences that are significant. Nor need we mean here by "exceptional depression" merely the lower extremity of a normal trade cycle. Thus, though the heavy unemployment that prevailed in this country for the decade following the post-Armistice boom—the intractible million—was not associated with a cyclical depression in the narrow sense, there was, nevertheless, some reason to believe that it was a short-period malady, needing treatment only for a few difficult years. The situation was such that improvements in industrial technique and capital equipment might well have made the normal real demand for British labour expand at more than the usual rate, while, at the same time, owing to the low birth-rate of the pre-war, and, still more, of the war years, the number of the wage-earning population of working age was expanding at much less than the usual rate. This double change must clearly in the near future have made the absorption of the whole body of potential workers at a given wage-rate—real rate and money rate alike—much easier than it would otherwise have been. Thus a temporary campaign maintained for a few years—apart from the great slump that began in 1930—might have proved successful.

§ 4. Moreover, a lasting favourable effect on employment might be produced if the State undertook—and succeeded in its undertaking—not merely to make the real demand for labour higher than it would otherwise have been, but to make it *progressively* higher. The expenditure on public works, the rate of bounty paid to private enterprises, the rates of duties in the protective tariff, or whatever it may be, would have to be raised again and again. If these devices succeeded in expanding progressively the real demand for labour, the time lag that intervenes between the stimulus to and the enforcement of claims to higher wages would enable them to make employment permanently larger than it would otherwise have been. This kind of policy, however, through adverse reactions on the accumulation and retention at home of capital, is liable, if pressed beyond a point, to defeat itself, and has in fact, as a deliberate policy, never been advocated. We need not, therefore, trouble ourselves further with it.

CHAPTER III

§ 1. It was argued in the preceding chapter that the state of demand for labour, as distinguished from changes in that state, is irrelevant to unemployment, because wage-rates adjust themselves in such a manner that different states of demand, when once established, tend to be associated with similar average rates of unemployment. This implies that, from a long-period point of view, the real wage-rates for which people stipulate, so far from being independent of the demand function, are a function of that function in a very special way. With perfectly free competition among work-people and labour perfectly mobile, the nature of the relation will be very simple. There will always be at work a strong tendency for wage-rates to be so related to demand that everybody is employed. Hence, in stable conditions every one will actually be employed. The implication is that such unemployment as exists at any time is due wholly to the fact that changes in demand conditions are continually taking place and that frictional resistances prevent the appropriate wage adjustments from being made instantaneously. In the absence of perfectly free competition among work-people the functional relation, if such exists, between the wage-rate stipulated for and the state of demand need not be of the above simple sort. The goal, so to speak, to which wage-rates are directed, and which, in stable conditions, they would achieve, is not necessarily the level associated with nil unemployment. It may be a level higher than this and implying, even in stable conditions, some measure of unemployment. Moreover, if the goal is of this sort, there is no ground

252

for supposing that it will stand always in the same place. Perfect competition among workpeople is definitely associated with the goal of nil unemployment, but, if the goal is not nil unemployment but some positive percentage, it may well be that this ideal percentage is different at different times.

§ 2. The factor that determines the long-run relation between the real wage-rate stipulated for and the real demand function for labour is best described in a general way as *wage policy*. As was made clear in Part I. Chapter VI., in our parable of the overloaded ship, when real demand is such-and-such and real wage-rate so-and-so, we must not say that the unemployment associated with these conditions is the fault either of the state of demand or of the stipulated wage-rate. It is generated by the relation between the two. In so far as wage policy seeks to *arrange* this relation on some permanent plan, wage policy is a cause determining the volume of unemployment in a sense that the wage-rate stipulated for at a particular time is not. Behind this primary factor, namely the relation existing at particular moments between the real rate of wages stipulated for and the relevant demand function, there stands, as a remoter factor, wage policy—policy designed to produce, or, it may be, producing more or less by accident, certain sorts of relation, in all or some centres of production, between wage-rates and the state of demand. This wage policy is exercised sometimes through collective bargaining on the part of Trade Unions, sometimes through State action establishing minimum rates of pay. It is not necessary, merely because these agencies are employed, that the goal of the policy should be a system of rates higher than those which perfectly free competition among wage-earners tends to bring about. If in fact the goal set were identical with the goal of free competition, the quantity of unemployment for which wage policy made would be nil. No part of the actual unemployment ruling at any time would be attributable to it. There is reason to believe, however, that the goal at which wage policy aims is sometimes, in some centres of production at all events, a wage-rate substantially higher than the rate which, if adopted everywhere, would yield nil unemployment. Several considerations point towards this conclusion.

§ 3. First, in industries that are sheltered from foreign competition, particularly in fundamental industries such as the transport industry, where a stoppage of work would inflict great injury on the general public, wage-earners are in a very strong bargaining position. Even though the demand for labour has an elasticity greater than unity, so that the aggregate earnings in the industry are less with a higher wage-rate than with a lower one, the men may, nevertheless, press—and press successfully—for the higher rate. For adverse reactions on unemployment will not leap to the eye; and, even if they did, the leaders in charge of the bargaining might well prefer smaller aggregate earnings that give good incomes to a comparatively small number of men to larger aggregate earnings made up of a great number of poor incomes. Policy on this matter will depend to an important extent on the nature of the provision that is made for unemployed workpeople. If the unemployed members of a trade union have to be cared for exclusively by that union, so that heavy unemployment means a heavy drain on union funds, this fact will act as a check upon claims for higher wages. If, however, unemployed members are cared for, in the main, at the expense of other people, the union's contribution being no larger when there are many unemployed than when there are few, this check does not operate. There can be little doubt that the system of State-aided unemployment insurance with substantial rates of benefit, which has been widely extended in this country since the close of the war, has enabled wage-earners to maintain rates of wages at a higher level than they would otherwise have been able to do.

§ 4. Secondly, an important influence is exercised by what may almost be described as a technical accident. Under time-wage systems it is impracticable for collective bargains to take full account of small differences of capacity between individuals in any general class. Special arrangements may, indeed, be made for men suffering from some obvious physical defect or for abnormally slow workers; but these are necessarily very rough and imperfect. Consequently the wage per unit of capacity will often be fixed somewhat higher for less able than for more able men. If, in these conditions, the rate

per unit of capacity were set low enough to allow all would-be
wage-earners in the class in question to be employed, the abler
men would be receiving substantially less than their marginal
worth. Naturally this would be resented. In wage bargains
made subject to the condition of a common standard it is,
therefore, likely that a compromise rate will be fixed somewhere intermediate between the marginal worth of the abler
and the less able workers. If this is done the less able workers
are bound to be allotted more than the wage proper to full
employment.

§ 5. Thirdly, public opinion in a modern civilised State
builds up for itself a rough estimate of what constitutes a
reasonable living wage. This is derived half-consciously from
a knowledge of the actual standards enjoyed by more or less
"average" workers. Hence it is to be expected that the lowest
class of workers, who congregate in occupations needing very
little skill or strength, will have a marginal worth, if all of
them are employed, less than what public opinion regards as
a reasonable minimum payment for *any* worker to receive.
Public opinion then enforces its view, failing success through
social pressure, by the machinery of Trade Board legislation.
In these circumstances, unless the receipt of payment in excess of their worth quickly lifts inefficient workpeople's quality
to the level of their pay, or, by quickly stimulating employers
to improved methods, attains equilibrium by an indirect
route, their actual wage will stand above the level to which
free competition tends and at which there is no unemployment.

§ 6. Students of our problem in this country before the war,
while recognising maladjustments of a long-run character
associated with wage policy as one of the factors responsible
for unemployment, in general took the view that the part
played by them was small. Unemployment, for these writers,
was, in the main, a function of industrial fluctuations and
labour immobility—of short-run frictions rather than of long-
run tendencies. In this view they were confirmed by the highly
stable character, on the average of good and bad times, of the
percentage of unemployment recorded by trade unions over
a period of sixty years. In view of this stability, if long-run
factors were playing an important part, they must have been

operating from cycle to cycle in a nearly constant manner. But why should they so operate? Would it not be natural to expect that, if wage policy were directed towards a goal other than that marked out by competition, its resultant would be substantially different at different times? Furthermore, pre-war students found that the level of unemployment tended in good years to approach a standing minimum of some 2 per cent, a figure easily accounted for by the movement of men from one job to another—three days of such movement per annum for the average man gives 1 per cent unemployment— so that, it seemed, little room was left for the operation of a long-run cause. Since the post-Armistice boom, however, the unemployment situation has been very different from what it was before the war. Instead of a percentage of unemployment amounting, on the average of good and bad years, to some $4\frac{1}{2}$ per cent, post-war unemployment has moved about a mean from twice to three times as large as this. This circumstance suggests strongly that the goal of long-run tendencies in recent times has been a wage level substantially above that proper to nil unemployment, and that a substantial part of post-war unemployment is attributable to that fact. In view of the severe dislocations in the economic system of the world, for which the war was directly and indirectly responsible, that conclusion cannot be regarded as certain. It has, however, everyone would agree, considerable *prima facie* probability. Wage policy as a possible long-run determinant of unemployment calls, therefore, at the present time, for closer study than would have been thought necessary twenty years ago.

CHAPTER IV

THE RELATION TO EMPLOYMENT OF CERTAIN FORMS
OF WAGE POLICY

§ 1. THE conditions of real demand are perpetually changing, and, therefore, any given type of wage policy must manifest itself, not in a single permanent scheme of real wage-rates,
but in a succession of schemes that differ from time to time.
Provided, however, that the general form of wage policy is
maintained, the relation aimed at between real wage-rates
and demand conditions will not be thus variable. The broad
tendency of wage policy as a determinant of unemployment
can, therefore, be exhibited by means of a model, in which
short-period demand conditions are taken as fixed and ex-
periment is made with a number of typical wage systems. It
must be understood that the postulate of constancy among
demand conditions stipulates only for an approximate constancy over fairly short periods. For, since the wage system
ruling at one time partly determines the demand system of
future times, the concept of an absolutely constant demand
system confronted with a choice of wage systems is self-
contradictory and, therefore, inadmissible. Throughout this
chapter I postulate that the demand functions for labour in
the occupations where wage-rates are subjected to different
conditions are independent of one another, or, if they are not
independent, that their interdependence is not of such a character as to affect our results. In so far as this assumption is
not justified, our analysis is incomplete: and in fact there is
some reason to believe that the interdependence which actually exists is of a sort to make artificially high wage-rates
more damaging to employment than it would be if there were

S

no interdependence of demand. I also postulate, in order to rule out a troublesome complication, that in all the centres affected employers follow the rule of competition and do not act monopolistically against their customers.

§ 2. With a given short-period demand system and a given number of would-be wage-earners there are an infinite number of arrangements that will permit of exactly all would-be wage-earners finding work, so that there is at once no unemployment and no overlap of unfilled vacancies. Among these arrangements one, however, has a special importance. That is the arrangement under which the real rates of wage (for men of given quality) are uniform for all centres of employment. With a given system of demand functions there is only one rate of wage, which, when established everywhere, can induce nil unemployment and nil unfilled vacancies. Furthermore, in order that even one rate may be capable of doing this, it is necessary that the system of labour distribution among the centres be of a single defined character. The wage-rate which, given these conditions, will induce nil unemployment and nil unfilled vacancies I call the *adjustment rate of wage*. It is convenient to regard this arrangement as a sort of norm, with which other arrangements may be compared. In the present chapter I propose to compare the state of employment under the system of uniform wage-rates set at the adjustment level and its state under a system where, in certain occupations, rates have been pushed up above this level. In the two sections that follow I postulate that there are no reactions from these occupations upon wage-rates elsewhere, but that these stand rigid at the adjustment level.

§ 3. Let us suppose first that labour is perfectly mobile. With the adjustment rate established everywhere there is nil unemployment. We start with this condition, and then suppose that the wage-rate in one of two sets of occupations is pushed up. On the assumption that the demand functions for labour in the two sets are independent of one another, the consequences to employment can be described very simply. In the occupations where the rate is raised above the adjustment rate, the quantity of labour demanded, and so the quantity of employment, is necessarily contracted. The extent of the contraction varies directly with the extent to which the wage-rate has been raised above the adjustment rate and with the elasticity of demand for labour in the occupations affected. In the other occupations the quantity of labour demanded is obviously unaltered. Hence it might seem at first sight that the reduction in employment in the occupations affected exhausts the consequences of putting up the wage. To argue thus, however, is to forget the possibility of unfilled vacancies. With perfect mobility there is a presumption that would-be wage-earners distribute themselves between the affected occupations and others in such wise that the mathematical expectations of earnings there and elsewhere are approximately equal. When this presumption is satisfied, men will be expelled from or attracted into the affected occupations according as the demand for labour there is greater or less than unity over the relevant range. With a demand elasticity greater than unity there is no tendency for men to be drawn into the affected occupations out of the other occupations. Consequently no unfilled vacancies can be created. With a demand elasticity less than unity there is such a tendency. But it may be deflected by arrangements that prevent the presumption just referred to from being satisfied. Arrangements of this sort rule when the holding up of the wage-rate in the affected occupations is accomplished through apprenticeship or other regulations that restrict the entry to these occupations.[1] They also rule if the method of engaging labour there is the permanent staff method, so that nobody who fails to find employment now can hope to find it presently, and is, therefore, at once—as with unsuccessful candidates for the Civil Service—driven to seek work elsewhere. In these conditions no men are drawn from outside to attach themselves to the affected occupations; for the mathematical expectation of earnings there to a person already engaged in them does not measure the prospect they offer to a person not so engaged. When, however, the elasticity of demand for labour in the affected occupations is less than unity and labour is engaged

---

[1] Verbally it might be more in conformity with common usage to speak of these rules as limitations upon labour mobility. For my purpose, however, it is convenient to define mobility in such wise that rules of this sort are *not* conceived as impeding it.

by methods under which outsiders have an equal chance with insiders, the excess wage-rate ruling there will draw men from other occupations into attachment to these occupations. These men, or rather a number of men equal to their number, will then stand idle in the affected occupations as well as the men who have lost their jobs there. That is to say, the reduction in aggregate employment is equal to the reduction in employment in the affected occupations *plus* a further reduction, due to the withdrawal of some men from employment in other occupations and measured by the number of unfilled vacancies that are created in these other occupations.[1]

§ 4. So far we have postulated perfect mobility of labour. Let us now postulate perfect immobility. In these conditions it is still *possible* that, with the adjustment rate of wage, as defined above, uniformly established everywhere, there will be nil unemployment and nil unfilled vacancies. Such a state of things could, however, only come about if, by a sort of miracle, labour were distributed among the various occupations in the precise way in which, with perfect mobility, free competition would cause it to be distributed. In practice it is quite certain that labour will not be distributed precisely in this way; though, if the system of demand functions has been fairly stable over a long period, some approach towards that form of distribution will, no doubt, have been achieved through the choice of occupations made by new recruits into industry. Hence in practice the establishment everywhere of the adjustment rate of wage implies the existence in some occupations of unemployment and in others of unfilled vacancies. Hence, if the wage-rate in certain occupations is raised above the adjustment level, it no longer follows that unemployment is created. If the occupations in which the rise takes place already contain unemployed men, that must, indeed,

---

[1] If we write V for the adjustment wage, $(V + h)$ for the wage established in the affected occupations and $\phi(w)$ for the quantity of labour demanded there at a wage w, the reduction in employment in the affected occupations $= \phi(V) - \phi(V + h)$, and the reduction of employment in the aggregate $= \dfrac{h}{V}\phi(V + h)$. With unitary elasticity of demand over the relevant range in the affected occupations these two quantities are obviously equal. If the elasticity of demand is less than unity, the latter is larger than the former: in the reverse case smaller.

happen. But, if they contain unfilled vacancies, it need not happen. The wage-rise may simply destroy some or all of the unfilled vacancies and leave employment unchanged. Employment cannot, indeed, be larger than it would have been with uniform wage-rates at the adjustment level; but it is not necessarily smaller.

§ 5. I pass to a third case. With labour perfectly immobile there is no tendency for the pushing up of wage-rates in particular occupations to react in reducing them in other occupations. But, with labour perfectly mobile, if in the other occupations free competition among workpeople prevails, the ejection of labour into them from the occupations where the rates have been raised, or the ejection out of them of labour attracted to those occupations, will modify their wage-rates in such wise that in them nil unemployment and nil unfilled vacancies continue to rule. The effect on employment in the aggregate needs in these conditions further study. Employment in the occupations where the real wage-rate has been pushed up is affected in precisely the same way as in the conditions contemplated in § 4. But employment in other occupations, and so employment in the aggregate, may be affected differently. If the conditions are such that men move out of these other occupations into the affected occupations, they are in fact not affected differently. For all the men left in the other occupations would have been employed on the hypothesis of the preceding section, just as they are all employed now. But, if the conditions are such that men move out of the affected occupations into the others, these men on the present hypothesis find work, whereas on the previous hypothesis they did not. Thus the net effect on employment is less unfavourable. If methods of engaging labour in the affected occupations are of such a sort that insiders and outsiders are on the same footing, and the demand for labour in these occupations has an elasticity greater than unity, some men pass out of them to seek—and find—work elsewhere. Hence aggregate employment is reduced in consequence of the wage-movement less than employment in the affected occupations. The ratio, total contraction of employment divided by contraction in the affected occupations, is smaller the more

elastic is the demand for labour in the affected occupations.[1]
With a perfectly elastic demand, employment in the affected
occupations is reduced to nil, but aggregate employment is not
diminished at all—that is, there is nil unemployment. If the
method of engaging labour in the affected occupations is of
the type ruling in the Civil Service, whether the elasticity of
demand for labour in them is greater or less than unity, all
the men displaced from employment in them are also displaced from seeking employment in them, turn to other
occupations, and, on the assumption taken in this section,
there find employment. Aggregate employment is, therefore,
again not diminished: aggregate unemployment is again nil.

---

[1] This ratio, in the symbolism of the preceding footnote, is

$$\frac{\frac{h}{V}\phi(V+h)}{\phi(V)-\phi(V+h)}.$$

With a linear function this reduces to $-\left\{\dfrac{\phi(V)}{V\phi'(V)}+\dfrac{h}{V}\right\}=\left\{-\eta+\dfrac{h}{V}\right\}$. This is
obviously smaller, the smaller (numerically) is η, and, since it cannot be
negative, its lower limit is 0.

CHAPTER V

§ 1. THE problem of this chapter is to compare, for a given arrangement of demand functions, the state of employment under a system of wage-rates uniform at w and under a system where the average rate is w, but the actual rates, w_1, w_2 and so on, in some or all of the several occupations, differ from w. The term average is used with the signification that if a_1, a_2 be the quantities of labour employed in the several occupations,

$$\frac{a_1 w_1 + a_2 w_2 + \ldots}{a_1 + a_2 + \ldots} = w.$$

§ 2. Let us begin by supposing that there are no unfilled vacancies either under the uniform wage system or under the discrepant system. In these circumstances the quantity of employment in each occupation is always equal to the quantity of labour demanded there. Hence, if we write ϕ_1, ϕ_2, etc., for the demand functions in the several occupations, under the discrepant system

$$= \frac{w_1 \phi_1(w_1) + w_2 \phi_2(w_2) + \ldots}{\phi_1(w_1) + \phi_2(w_2) + \ldots} = w.$$

We have then to determine in what conditions aggregate employment under the discrepant system, namely, $\{\phi_1(w_1) + \phi_2(w_2) + \ldots\}$ is greater or less than aggregate employment under the uniform system, namely, than

$$\phi_1(w_a) + \phi_2(w_a) + \ldots$$

§ 3. A full solution of this problem would involve complications which it is not practicable to tackle here. It is, however, possible to indicate its general character by means of a highly simplified special case. Let us suppose that there are two centres of demand only. We start with a uniform wage w and aggregate employment $\phi_1(w) + \phi_2(w)$. The wage-rate in the first centre is then raised by h. In order that the average rate in the two centres together may be kept the same, the wage in the other centre must be reduced by k. We then have: original employment $= \phi_1(w) + \phi_2(w)$; employment after the change $= \phi_1(w+h) + \phi_2(w-k)$. Provided that the functions are linear, the gain of employment is, therefore, $= h\phi'_1 - k\phi'_2 = G$. Now we are given

$$\frac{(w+h)\phi_1(w+h) + (w-k)\phi_2(w-k)}{\phi_1(w+h) + \phi_2(w-k)} = w:$$

that is, $h\phi_1(w+h) = k\phi_2(w-k).$

We, therefore, have the means of determining in what conditions the gain of employment is positive and in what negative.

$$\text{For } h = k\frac{\phi_2(w-k)}{\phi_1(w-h)}.$$

$$\therefore\ G = k\left\{\frac{\phi_2(w-k)}{\phi_1(w+h)}\phi'_1 - \phi'_2\right\}$$

$$= k\phi_2(w-k)\left\{\frac{\phi'_1}{\phi_1(w+h)} - \frac{\phi'_2}{\phi_2(w-k)}\right\}.$$

Write η_1 for the elasticity of demand in respect of wage w in the first centre and η_2 for the corresponding elasticity in the second.

The above equation then becomes

$$G = \frac{k\phi_2(w-k)}{w}\left\{\frac{\eta_1}{1+\eta_1\dfrac{h}{w}} - \frac{\eta_2}{1-\eta_2\dfrac{k}{w}}\right\}.$$

This is positive or negative according as $\left\{\dfrac{\eta_1}{1+\eta_1\dfrac{h}{w}} - \dfrac{\eta_2}{1-\eta_2\dfrac{k}{w}}\right\}$

is positive or negative. Hence, for linear functions, when h and k are very small, G is negative, that is to say employment is smaller under the non-uniform system than under the uniform if the demand in the low-wage centre is less elastic in respect of the wage-rate w than the demand in the high-wage centre, and is larger in the opposite case. When h and k are not very small, employment is smaller under the non-uniform system if the demand in the low-wage centre is less elastic than the demand in the high-wage centre, and also if the demand in the low-wage centre is the more elastic, but its elasticity does not exceed the elasticity of demand in the high-wage centre by more than a certain finite amount, which is larger the larger are h and k. Employment is larger under the non-uniform system than under the other if the elasticity of demand in the low-wage centre exceeds the elasticity of demand in the high-wage centre by more than this certain finite amount. It follows that, in all circumstances, with linear functions, when a non-uniform wage system is converted into a uniform one with the same average wage, aggregate employment will be increased if the demand in the hitherto low-wage centre is in any degree less elastic (in respect of the new wage-rate) than in the other; and will be diminished if it is *substantially* more elastic.

§ 4. With non-linear functions no simple general results are obtainable. But there is still a presumption that, if the demand is less elastic in the hitherto low-wage centre than in the other, the substitution of a uniform for a non-uniform system with equal average wage will involve an increase in aggregate employment; and that, if the demand is substantially more elastic in the hitherto low-wage centre, it will involve a diminution in aggregate employment. This presumption can, in the absence of special knowledge, be extended to the case of many centres. The average real rate of wage, in the sense defined in § 1, remaining constant, if wage-rates are raised in centres of abnormally inelastic demand, aggregate employment is likely to be increased; whereas, if they are raised in centres of abnormally elastic demand, aggregate employment is likely to be diminished.

§ 5. When unfilled vacancies are brought into account, the condition that the average wage-rate shall be the same under the discrepant as under the uniform system has a different implication. Let us now write W_a for the uniform wage,

hitherto represented by w, when unfilled vacancies are ruled
out, and W_b for the uniform wage when they are admitted.
In respect of this latter case write $u_1, u_2 \ldots$ for the numbers
of unfilled vacancies in each several occupation under the
discrepant system and T for the total number under the
uniform system. Let w_1, w_2 and so on have the same values
as before. Then we have, not

$$\frac{w_1\phi_1(w_1) + w_2\phi_2(w_2) + \ldots}{\phi_1(w_1) + \phi_2(w_2) + \ldots} = W_a,$$

but
$$\frac{w_1\{\phi_1(w_1) - u_1\} + w_2\{\phi_2(w_2) - u_2\} + \ldots}{\{\phi_1(w_1) - u_1\} + \{\phi_2(w_2) - u_2\} + \ldots} = W_b.$$

Our problem is to determine the relation between

$$[\{\phi_1(w_1) + \phi_2(w_2)\} + \ldots - \{u_1 + u_2 + \ldots\}]$$

and
$$\{\phi_1(W_b) + \phi_2(W_b) + \ldots - T\}.$$

§ 6. Under the discrepant wage-system the aggregate
quantity of labour demanded will be the same as we found it
to be in our preceding discussion. In general, however, W_b
will not be equal to W_a: so that under the uniform wage
system the quantity of labour demanded will not be the same
as we then found it to be. In the absence of detailed information we are unable to say whether W_b will exceed or fall
short of W_a, and whether, therefore, $\{\phi_1(W_b) + \phi_2(W_b) + \ldots\}$
will fall short of or exceed $\{\phi_1(W_a) + \phi_2(W_a) + \ldots\}$. If, then,
starting from a system of discrepant wages, we raise rates in
centres of inelastic demand and lower them in centres of
elastic demand, in such wise as to establish a system of uniform rates at the same average level, the presumption is less
strong than it is in the conditions postulated in §§ 3-4 that
the aggregate quantity of labour demanded will be increased.
In the converse case the contrary presumption is, in like
manner, less strong. If, however, for the bulk of important
occupations under the discrepant wage system the quantity of
unfilled vacancies is small relatively to the quantity of labour
demanded, W_b will approximate very closely to W_a. This does
not necessarily imply that $\{\phi_1(W_b) + \phi_2(W_b) + \ldots\}$ approximates very closely to $\{\phi_1(W_a) + \phi_2(W_a) + \ldots\}$. Still the
damage done to our presumptions is *pro tanto* mitigated.

§ 7. Granted, however, that, when a discrepant wage system is transformed into a uniform system with the same average wage, the aggregate quantity of labour demanded will probably be increased or diminished according as the occupations in respect of which wage reductions take place are predominantly of elastic or predominantly of inelastic demand, we must not step straightway to a like presumption about the aggregate quantity of employment. For even when the sum of the u's, and *a fortiori* the difference between this sum and T, is small relatively to the aggregate quantity of labour demanded, this difference may well be large relatively to the difference between the aggregate quantity of labour demanded under the discrepant and the aggregate quantity demanded under the uniform wage system. The effect of the shift from the one system to the other upon the quantity of unfilled vacancies may thus be much more important than its effect on the quantity of labour demanded; so that in the total reaction on aggregate employment the latter effect is swamped.

§ 8. If labour is perfectly immobile, the effect of a shift from a uniform to a non-uniform system of wage-rates (spread round the same average) upon the number of unfilled vacancies obviously depends on the way in which labour is initially distributed among the several centres in relation to the general conditions of demand and the scheme of wage-rates. Clearly, the situation may be such that no unfilled vacancies will exist either with the uniform or with the non-uniform system. In this case the aggregate quantity of labour demanded is, under both systems, identical with the aggregate quantity of employment. When conditions are not of this kind it may happen either that there are less unfilled vacancies under the uniform system than under the other, or that there are more unfilled vacancies under the uniform system. Hence, a shift from a uniform to a non-uniform system or *vice versa* may be either more or less favourable to aggregate employment than it is to the aggregate quantity of labour demanded. Thus suppose that we start with a system of unequal wages. If initially there is no unemployment in the high-wage centres, a reduction of rates there cannot increase employment—it can only increase unfilled vacancies—and, if initially there are some unfilled vacancies in the low-wage centres, the raising of the rates there will exhaust part, and may exhaust the whole, of its effect in decreasing them rather than in decreasing employment. More generally, with immobile labour, a part or all of the favourable effect on employment that would otherwise occur, and also a part or all of the unfavourable effect, may be wiped out. The favourable effect will be more restricted, the fewer are the unemployed men initially in the high-wage centres; and the unfavourable effect will be less restricted, the fewer are the unfilled vacancies initially in the low-wage centres. It is impossible to say *a priori* that the net effect will be favourable or unfavourable.

§ 9. In so far as labour is mobile between the several occupations a further consideration comes into account. Suppose, for simplicity, that labour is perfectly mobile. If the wage-rates that have to be raised in order to convert the discrepant system into a uniform system belong to occupations of inelastic demand, aggregate earnings are increased in the occupations affected, while they are diminished in the other occupations. Hence, in accordance with the argument of Chapter IV. § 3, men move into the occupations where wage-rates are being raised and out of those where they are being lowered. This movement *cannot* destroy any unfilled vacancies. If in the occupations in which wage-rates are being lowered there is a sufficient store of unemployed men to draw upon, it will not create any. But, if there is not such a sufficient store of unemployed men, it will withdraw from the occupations where wage-rates are being lowered some men who, apart from the movement, would have been employed there, and thus will create some unfilled vacancies. In that case the sum of unfilled vacancies is affected less favourably than it would have been if labour had been perfectly immobile; and, therefore, the likelihood of aggregate employment being increased is smaller.

§ 10. Our discussion so far has been general. It has, however, a particular application to the employment situation of this country since the war. In the decade following the post-Armistice boom the average percentage of unemployment over good and bad years together was markedly higher—some 6 per cent higher—than the corresponding percentage before the war. It has often been suggested that this excess was mainly attributable to wage-rates being held too high to allow of normal employment in existing conditions of production and demand. On the other hand, it has been answered that, though, no doubt some wage-rates were too high in this sense, wage-rates on the average were not too high, but the evil was due to a wrong distribution of high and low wage-rates, coupled with a wrong distribution of labour: so that, if wage-rates had been equalised and labour distributed aright, the pre-war level of employment could have been maintained with as least as high an average real rate of wage as in fact prevailed.[1] What is to be said of this issue? It is certain that the wage-rates ruling in different occupations before the war were much more nearly equal, for men of given quality, than those that ruled subsequently. To restore pre-war relative levels would, therefore, have meant to approach much more nearly to equality. Now the industries in which wage-rates underwent a relative fall were unsheltered industries, in many of which, on account of exposure to foreign competition, the demand for labour is highly elastic: and those in which wage-rates underwent a relative rise were, in the main, sheltered industries of fairly inelastic demand. The argument of § 4 has suggested that to reduce wages in industries of inelastic demand and at the same time to raise them in industries of elastic demand, in such wise as to keep average rates, in the sense here defined, constant, is likely to mean diminished

---

[1] It is worthy of note, though the fact is frequently not realised, that at the present time such maldistribution of labour as exists can no longer be accounted for as an aftermath of war. "Steel-smelting, etc., pig iron and shipbuilding alone of the industries which grew largely in the war are now in the list for heavy unemployment: for all three, the decline of exports is a sufficient explanation of continuing depression, though they all show some improvement from 1924 to 1929. All the other large industries which, taking men and women together, increased their numbers in the war— general engineering, electrical engineering and marine engineering; motor vehicles, cycles and aircraft; chemicals, oil, glue, soap, etc.; and theatres, music halls and cinemas—have by 1929 got back to having less than the average unemployment. Conversely, industries conspicuously contracted in the war—pottery, glass bottles, tin plates, cotton, building, public works and dock, harbour, river and canal service—are now conspicuous by heavy and, as a rule, increasing unemployment." (Beveridge, *Unemployment—A Problem of Industry*, p. 355.)

aggregate demand for labour and so, even though labour is redistributed in such wise as to prevent the emergence of any unfilled vacancies, diminished aggregate employment. Hence, even with this condition satisfied, if wages had been merely equalised and the average level retained, employment would probably have been cut down more in the actual low-wage industries than it was expanded in the actual high-wage ones; so that aggregate employment would have been smaller, and not larger, than it in fact was. But this is not all. It is well known that in the high-wage industries of the post-Armistice period the percentage of unemployment prevailing was relatively small, while, since large unemployment had been a factor making for wage-reduction in the low-wage industries, in those industries it was relatively large. Hence, had wage-rates everywhere been brought nearer to the average, in order to obviate the occurrence of unfilled vacancies—in actual conditions the number of these vacancies was almost certainly insignificant—a substantial amount of labour transference might have been needed. In the absence of such transference the aggregate quantity of labour demanded in the new conditions would not all have been translated into employment: and the situation would, therefore, have been damaged more seriously than the argument so far has suggested. In fact, in view of the known difficulty of transferring men from the unsheltered to the sheltered industries, no extensive redistribution of labour would have been likely to take place except by slow degrees. Our general conclusion then must be that, as a remedy for the heavy unemployment of the post-war period, a mere correction of wage inequalities would probably have proved, not merely unavailing, but actually harmful. This would have been so even were labour perfectly mobile, and in actual conditions the argument is *a fortiori*. To reduce unemployment from the side of wages it would have been necessary, after wage inequalities had been reduced and labour appropriately redistributed, *also* to reduce the average rate of real wages.

§ 11. This thesis is *compatible with* the further thesis that real wages in *all* occupations were too high, in the sense that, if they had been equalised at a level calculated to absorb the abnormal post-war unemployment, the rates in *all* occupations would have had to be lower than they were. But it does not *imply* that thesis. On the contrary, it may be that in some occupations rates would have been higher than they were. In that event it would follow that in some of the occupations where employment was most seriously contracted—for, in general, it was in these occupations that wages were lowest—employment might have needed to be cut down still further. It would follow too that wage-earners in these occupations had a much stronger economic case—not merely a much stronger sentimental case—for resisting wage-cuts than their colleagues in the undepressed industries.

CHAPTER VI

FLUCTUATIONS IN THE QUANTITY OF LABOUR DEMANDED IN A
SINGLE CENTRE IN RELATION TO SWINGS OF REAL DEMAND
AND OF REAL WAGE-RATES IN THAT CENTRE WHEN THE
DEMAND FUNCTIONS IN OTHER CENTRES ARE STABLE

§ 1. I now turn, in accordance with the programme sketched
in the introductory chapter of this Part, to study *fluctuations*
in unemployment. In the preceding chapters wage policy has
been envisaged as establishing one or another sort of wage
system in relation to a given system of demand functions.
Whatever the system of demand functions may be, if it is
established long enough, we conceive of wage policy adjusting
the wage system to it in such a way that the quantity of
labour demanded bears a fairly constant relation to the
number of men seeking work. Thus, if demand conditions
were stable, it would not greatly matter to the quantity of
labour demanded what those conditions were. In real life,
however, the system of demand functions is always in process
of change. Wage policy, even though its general tendency and
intention is constant, cannot adjust itself instantaneously to
each momentary state of this process. Consequently, alterations in the system of demand functions are liable to involve
expansions and contractions in the quantity of labour demanded, even though wage policy is directed in a long-run
manner to make this quantity stable. Moreover, short-run
shifts in the real rate of wages stipulated for may occur from
time to time, so to speak, automatically, and not merely as
a response to shifts in demand conditions. A change in the
quantity of labour demanded comes about if there is a shift
in the real demand function, or a shift in the real wage-rate

stipulated for, or shifts, that do not exactly cancel one another, in both these things. The purpose of the present chapter is to study, in respect of a single occupation, the relation of these two kinds of shift to fluctuations in the quantity of labour demanded in that occupation. When conditions are such that the quantity of unfilled vacancies is constant, our analysis will at the same time describe the relation of the two kinds of shift to the quantity of employment in the occupation.

§ 2. If between two times the state of the real demand function has remained stationary, the whole of whatever fluctuation in the quantity of labour demanded has taken place is caused immediately by such change as there has been in the real rate of wage stipulated for, and ultimately by the factors determining this. If the real rate of wage stipulated for has remained stationary, the whole of whatever fluctuation has taken place is caused immediately by such change as there has been in the real demand function, and ultimately by the factors determining that. In the former case, if we write for the demand function $F(w)$ and for the real wage-rates at the two times W and $W(1+m)$, the change in quantity of labour demanded, which is caused by the shift of wage-rate, is measured by $F(W) - F\{(W)(1+m)\}$. In the latter case, if we write $F(w)$ for the demand function in the first period, $\psi(w)$ for that in the second period, and W for the real wage-rate in both periods, the change in the quantity of labour demanded, which is caused by the shift in the demand function, is measured by $F(W) - \psi(W)$. The implications of these movements have already been studied in Parts II. and III. It is obvious that, when the wage-rate shifts and the demand function remains constant, the resultant fluctuation in the quantity of labour demanded is larger, the larger is the wage shift and the more elastic, over the relevant range, is the demand function: and that, when the demand function shifts and the wage-rate remains constant, it is larger, the larger is the horizontal range through which the demand function swings at the level of the ruling wage.

§ 3. It does not, however, always, or even usually, happen that, as between two times, only one of the two elements in

T

the complex determining the quantity of labour demanded alters. When both alter, *provided that a certain condition is satisfied*, the total effect on the quantity of labour demanded must always be equal to the sum of the effects which the alteration in each item would have produced had the other remained stationary. We can, therefore, divide such variation in the aggregate quantity of labour demanded as has actually occurred into two parts, one of which is *immediately* due to the shift in the real rate of wage stipulated for and the other to the shift in the real demand function. The requisite condition is that the relation between the new demand function and the old is of a particular kind; *i.e.* is such that, when the two demand functions are depicted by curves, the horizontal distance between them is the same at the level of the second wage-rate as it is at the level of the first. This condition we may call, for brevity, the condition of parallelism.

§ 4. Let us postulate that, over the range relevant to our problem, the demand curves are straight lines—in which case, of course, horizontal parallelism implies also vertical parallelism. If the wage-rate moves downward by p and the demand curve moves upward by q, of the resultant expansion in the quantity of labour demanded $\dfrac{p}{p+q}$ parts are due to the wage movement and $\dfrac{q}{p+q}$ parts to the demand movement. If the wage-rate moves downward by p and the demand curve downward by q—it being postulated that $p > q$—it follows that the effect in contracting the quantity of labour demanded due to the downward movement of the demand curve by q is offset by the effect in expanding the quantity due to the downward movement of the wage-rate by q: so that the whole of such expansion as actually occurs is caused by the excess $(p - q)$ of the downward movement of wage-rate stipulated for over the downward movement in the demand curve. Writing K for this expansion, we find the wage movement responsible for a virtual expansion $\dfrac{p}{p-q}$K; the demand movement for a virtual contraction $\dfrac{q}{p-q}$K; the balance of the wage movement over the demand movement for the actual expansion K. These results are, it will be observed, independent of the slope of the demand curve, though, of course, the absolute value of K is a function of the slope.

§ 5. The condition of parallelism is not one that is very likely to be satisfied in real life. If any type of movement could properly be called normal, this title should rather be accorded to those movements in which all parts of the curve shift, not through equal absolute, but through equal proportionate, vertical distances. With movements of this type the elasticity of demand in respect of each quantity of labour demanded is the same with the old curve as with the new; and the upper of any two demand curves thus related necessarily slopes more steeply than the lower. Except, however, when the condition of parallelism is satisfied, wage movements not only affect the quantity of labour demanded directly, but also modify the way in which any given movement of the demand curve affects it: and conversely. Hence, the effect of given alterations in both the real wage rate stipulated for and the real demand function is not equal to the sum of the effects of each of the two alterations introduced alone. The wage change by itself would cause the quantity of labour demanded to increase by a: the change in the demand function by itself would cause it to increase by b: both changes together will *not* cause it to increase by $(a + b)$. In some conditions the combined effect will be larger than the sum (regard being had to sign) of the separate effects in isolation, in other conditions it will be smaller than this. It is, therefore, not possible to divide any actual change in the quantity of labour demanded into two parts, one of which is immediately due to wage change and the other to demand change.

§ 6. Further light on the general situation can be thrown as follows. Let the wage-rate in the first period be W, the wage-rate in the second period $W(1 + m)$, the quantity of employment in the first period $F(W)$ and the quantity in the second period $\psi\{W(1 + m)\}$. Write a for the change that would follow from the wage change by itself: b for that which would follow from the change in the demand curve by itself: and c for that which actually follows from the two together. Then, with linear functions, we have

$$a = m\mathrm{W}\mathrm{F}' \qquad \qquad \qquad \text{(I)}$$

$$b = \psi(\mathrm{W}) - \mathrm{F}(\mathrm{W}) \qquad \qquad \text{(II)}$$

$$c = \psi\{\mathrm{W}(1+m)\} - \mathrm{F}(\mathrm{W}) = \psi(\mathrm{W}) - \mathrm{F}(\mathrm{W}) + m\mathrm{W}\psi'$$

$$= b + m\mathrm{W}\psi' = b + a\frac{\psi'}{\mathrm{F}'}. \qquad \qquad \text{(III)}$$

In what follows, ψ' and F' being both negative, I call one greater than the other when it is numerically greater. Hence, first, when a and b are both positive, c also is positive, and $c >$ or $< (a+b)$ according as $\psi' >$ or $< \mathrm{F}'$. Secondly, when a is negative and b positive, c may be either positive or negative. In the former event it is a smaller positive, in the latter a larger negative, quantity than $(a+b)$ if $\psi' > \mathrm{F}'$: and conversely if $\psi' < \mathrm{F}'_1$. Thirdly, when a is positive and b negative, c may be either positive or negative. In the former event it is a larger positive, in the latter a smaller negative, quantity than $(a+b)$, if $\psi' > \mathrm{F}'$; and conversely, if $\psi' < \mathrm{F}'$. Fourthly, when a and b are both negative, c also is negative, and c is a larger negative quantity than $(a+b)$ if $\psi' > \mathrm{F}'$; and less in the converse case. Now $\psi' > \mathrm{F}'$ when the second demand curve slopes less steeply than the first; and $\psi < \mathrm{F}'$ in the converse case. Where two demand curves are so related that the elasticities of demand in respect of a given quantity of employment are the same in both, the upper of the two curves necessarily slopes more steeply than the lower one. Therefore, when we have to do with an upward movement, *i.e.* when b is positive, $\psi' > \mathrm{F}'$; when we have to do with a downward movement, *i.e.* when b is negative, $\psi' < \mathrm{F}'$.

§ 7. Inability to divide actual changes in the quantity of labour demanded into two parts, which can be attributed to wage movements and to movements of the demand curve respectively, does not carry with it inability to specify what *difference* would be made to the change in quantity of labour demanded if one or other of these two movements were eliminated while the other remained. That calculation can be made. Thus let the wage-rate move from W to W$(1+m)$ at the same time that the demand function moves from F(W) to

$\psi(W)$. The change in the quantity of labour demanded that actually occurs $= \psi\{W(1 + m)\} - F(W)$. If the wage movement did not take place, but the other did, the change in this quantity would be $\psi(W) - F(W)$. Therefore the difference made to the change by the wage movement is $\psi\{W(1 + m)\} - \psi(W)$. In like manner, if the demand movement did not take place, but the other did, the change in the quantity of labour demanded would be $F\{W(1 + m)\} - F(W)$. Therefore the difference made to this quantity by the demand movement is $\psi\{W(1 + m)\} - F\{W(1 + m)\}$.

§ 8. We must be careful not to step from this result to the inference that, by estopping the wage movement and doing nothing else, we should necessarily cut down the change in the quantity of labour demanded by precisely $\psi\{W(1 + m) - \psi(W)\}$; and that, by estopping the demand movement and doing nothing else, we should cut the change down by precisely $\psi\{W(1 + m)\} - F\{W(1 + m)\}$. This would only be so if (1) shifts in the real wage-rate stipulated for had no causal influence on the position of the demand function, and (2) shifts in the demand function had no causal influence on the rate of real wage stipulated for. It may be that in real life the former of these conditions is usually satisfied. It must be borne in mind, however, that a reduction in the real wage-rate in one occupation may induce a reduction in other occupations that are more or less competitive with that one, and that, if this happens, the demand function in the first occupation will tend to contract. In some circumstances this consideration has large practical importance. The latter of the above two conditions frequently fails. A fall in the demand function *tends* to bring about, through the pressure of unemployment, a fall in the real wage-rate for which wage-earners stipulate. As a consequence of this tendency the net effect in changing the quantity of labour demanded of a given swing of demand is *pro tanto* mitigated, and the effect of estopping the swing *pro tanto* reduced.

§ 9. One final caution may be added. When the condition of parallelism rules, the sum of the changes in the quantity of labour demanded, that would be made by estopping the changes both in demand movement and in wage movement, is, of course, equal to the change that has actually occurred. In this case, if we know that the change is c and that, by estopping the wage movement alone, we should reduce it by b, we also know that, by estopping the demand movement alone, we should reduce it by $(c - b)$. Apart from the secondary reactions described in the last section, it is impossible, by cutting off the one cause, to reduce it otherwise than by the actual change that has occurred *minus* the difference that would be made by estopping the other cause. When, however, the condition of parallelism, even though the one cause is in no degree a cause of the other cause, is not satisfied, this limitation does not hold. A state of things may exist in which we could keep the quantity of labour demanded practically stationary *either* by stabilising the demand function without interfering at all with wage movements *or* by stabilising wage-rates without interfering at all with demand movements. A proof that the one policy would be completely successful is no proof that the other would fail. Conversely, a state of things may exist in which we could do little towards keeping the quantity of labour demanded stationary *either* by completely removing demand fluctuations and leaving wage fluctuations *or* by completely removing wage fluctuations and leaving demand fluctuations, and yet could do a great deal by slightly reducing both sorts of fluctuation. A proof that either policy singly would have negligible consequences is no proof that both together would have negligible consequences.

CHAPTER VII

FLUCTUATIONS IN AGGREGATE UNEMPLOYMENT IN RELATION
TO SWINGS OF REAL DEMAND IN A SINGLE CENTRE WHEN
THE DEMAND FUNCTIONS IN OTHER CENTRES ARE STABLE

§ 1. In this chapter I propose to examine the effect on aggregate employment—and so also on aggregate unemployment —of a shift in the demand function proper to a single occupation, it being assumed that this demand function and the other demand functions are independent of one another. I contemplate a state of things in which all the other functions save only this one are stationary. I postulate that no general outside factor is at work to modify the real rates of wages for which workpeople stipulate; and that these rates, if they change, change only in response to the swings in real demand. On this basis I shall consider first the case in which the wage system, whether a uniform or a non-uniform system, is perfectly rigid, and, secondly, the more complicated case in which the system is in some degree plastic.

§ 2. If, with a rigid wage system, labour is absolutely immobile, it is clearly impossible for a shift in the demand function in one centre—we are premising, it will be remembered, that the demands of the several centres are independent—to influence the number of unfilled vacancies in the other centres. Therefore, if unfilled vacancies are affected at all, this can only be in that centre where the demand function has moved. With an *upward* swing of the demand curve in that centre aggregate employment is increased by the increase in the quantity of labour demanded there *minus* the excess of the number of unfilled vacancies there after the change over the number

279

there before the change. If there were some unfilled vacancies
there before the change, aggregate employment will, of course,
not be increased at all. In other terms, the limit of possible
increase in aggregate employment is the quantity of unemployment that was present in the centre before the change
occurred. With a *downward* swing of the demand curve in the
centre affected, aggregate employment is diminished by the
amount of the decrease in the quantity of labour demanded
there *minus* the excess of the number of unfilled vacancies
there before the change over the number there after the
change. If there are some unfilled vacancies there after the
change, this implies that aggregate employment has not been
affected at all, but that the whole effect of the downward
swing in demand has spent itself in doing away with unfilled
vacancies. *Per contra*, if there were no unfilled vacancies before the change, none of the effect of the downward swing can
have been spent in this way: and aggregate employment must
have been affected to precisely the same extent as the quantity of labour demanded.

§ 3. With a perfectly rigid wage system and labour not
absolutely immobile the situation is modified. If the demand
function in a particular centre swings upward, aggregate employment may increase by more than the number of men
initially unemployed there; for some men may be drawn into
employment there from unemployment in the other centres.
That is to say, movement of labour from unemployment elsewhere into the centre of improved demand enables a larger
part of the increase in the quantity of labour demanded there
to be translated into employment, as against unfilled vacancies,
than could have been so translated in the absence of movement. If the demand function in a particular centre swings
downward, aggregate employment may diminish by less than
the number of men forced out of employment there: for, if,
before the change, unfilled vacancies existed elsewhere, some
of the displaced men may enter these vacancies. That is to say,
movement of labour out of the damaged centre enables a
larger part of the decrease in the quantity of labour demanded there to be translated into destruction of unfilled
vacancies, as against creation of unemployment, than would

have been possible if the only unfilled vacancies accessible to it were those existing in the centre itself.

§ 4. With a perfectly rigid wage system, if there is initially no unemployment outside the centre in which demand swings, it is obvious that the state of labour mobility makes no difference to the effect on aggregate employment of *upward* swings of demand there. It is similarly obvious that, if there are initially no unfilled vacancies outside this centre, the state of labour mobility makes no difference to the effect on aggregate employment of *downward* swings there. This latter point has relevance to important practical issues. It may be put otherwise by saying that, with the wage system rigid, when demand for labour in one centre contracts, whatever the state of labour mobility, aggregate employment must fall by the amount of the reduction in the quantity of labour demanded in the contracted centre *minus* the unfilled vacancies, if any, that initially existed in that centre. Thus, if the demand for labour in coal mining or shipbuilding falls off and there are no unfilled vacancies elsewhere, it is useless, in a regime of absolutely rigid wage-rates, to transfer unemployed coal miners away from mining districts or unemployed shipbuilders away from shipbuilding districts. No addition whatever is made to employment as a whole. These men—or an equivalent number of other men—remain unemployed: they merely appear in a different district or as attached to a different industry.

§ 5. With a wage system which is not absolutely rigid we must reckon with the fact that a swing in demand upwards or downwards in one centre may lead to a change in the wage-rate for which people stipulate in that centre and, perhaps, also in other centres. Clearly the reactions here may be complicated. The main point, however, can be brought out without much difficulty. Let us suppose that our starting-point is a state of affairs in which no unemployment and no unfilled vacancies exist anywhere. *Expansions* of demand from this starting-point in general have a nil effect on employment. In the section that follows I shall inquire what happens when the real demand for labour in a particular centre or centres *contracts*. Contractions and expansions from other starting-points produce a series of consequences which, in the light of what has been and is about to be said, the reader will readily work out for himself.

§ 6. When, in the conditions contemplated, the demand function for labour in the particular centre contracts, full employment can be maintained either if nobody moves and the wagerate in the contracted centre is greatly reduced, or if men move freely from the contracted centre and wage-rates in all of the centres are slightly reduced. In like manner, if aggregate employment has to be reduced to some extent, the magnitude of the reduction can be kept down either by a large reduction in the wage-rate in the contracted centre *plus* no movement of labour, or by a small reduction of wages everywhere *plus* a substantial movement of labour. Of these two routes the former is theoretically open in all conditions; the latter only if labour moves with some degree of freedom. The former route is, however, a very difficult one to follow far. The extent to which wage-rates anywhere are free to fall depends in part on the bargaining strength of employers and employed. But the resistance against wage-cuts grows with their magnitude: and, in a country with a system of unemployment insurance and Poor Law relief, is, after a point, absolute. It follows that, provided rates of real wages are in some degree plastic, the damage to aggregate employment resulting from a contraction of labour demand in particular centres is likely to be much smaller if labour can move freely out of those centres and offer itself at others than if it is immobile. In the latter case the whole process towards wage reduction is concentrated at the one point, where an enormous reduction, which wageearners are certain to refuse, would alone suffice; and no pressure at all is exerted at other points. In the latter event adult men move away from that point, pressure is exerted at other points, and there is some prospect that the small reductions, which, if spread over a wide area, would suffice to absorb the unemployed, will in fact be accepted. The natural *prima facie* inference is that, if the demand for labour in a particular industry or group of industries undergoes contraction, the weakening of obstacles that hinder labour from moving away from these industries may indirectly, by inducing wage reductions and so creating demand for labour elsewhere, accomplish a good deal to reduce the aggregate volume of unemployment.

§ 7. There is, however, a very serious practical difficulty in the way. If there are initially no unfilled vacancies in the undepressed industries—still more, if there is an appreciable percentage of unemployed men attached to them— unemployed coal miners and shipbuilders will have little inducement to seek work there and will not in fact do so. Hence they cannot exercise pressure to make wage-rates there fall. For no employers' association in a sheltered industry would dare to argue that wage-rates in that industry ought to be reduced, not because an abnormal number of the workpeople attached to that industry are out of work, but because a reduction would enable displaced coal miners and shipwrights to be absorbed into it. Thus there is an impasse. Displaced coal miners and shipbuilders will not seek work in other industries because there are no vacancies there: and there are no vacancies there because the coal miners and shipbuilders do not seek work there and so do not exert that pressure which might reduce wages and so create vacancies. The impasse is not, indeed, quite so serious as it appears to be at first sight. For, whatever be the case with adults, new recruits flowing into industry will not concentrate their thoughts upon whether or no actual vacancies exist in this or that occupation. They will rather, in a vague way, look to the comparative mathematical expectation of earnings in different occupations. Since, *ex hypothesi*, there has been a special slump in demand in certain occupations and not in others, the comparative mathematical expectation in the others must have improved. Hence, there is a continuing tendency for wage-earners to flow towards the other industries, thus exerting pressure towards wage reductions there. This process, however, works slowly. It may well be that the prospect of such reductions, and so of the absorption of some of the unemployed into industry, would be improved if transfers out of the depressed occupations were fostered, so to speak, artificially by State action.

CHAPTER VIII

FLUCTUATIONS IN AGGREGATE EMPLOYMENT IN RELATION TO COMPENSATORY SWINGS OF DEMAND IN DIFFERENT OCCUPATIONS

§ 1. IN this chapter I shall trace the effect on unemployment of a variation in relative demand, as between two or more occupations, aggregate demand being assumed constant. By this it is meant that, the several demand functions being treated, as in the preceding chapter, as independent, the particular functions at one moment are $\phi_1(w)$, $\phi_2(w)$ and so on, and at another moment $\psi_1(w)$, $\psi_2(w)$ and so on; but that $\{\phi_1(w) + \phi_2(w) + \ldots\} = \{\psi_1(w) + \psi_2(w) + \ldots)\}$, or more generally, if we suppose the working population to have expanded in the proportion m, that $m\{\phi_1(w) + \phi_2(w) + \ldots\} = \{\psi_1(w) + \psi_2(w) + \ldots\}$ for all values of w. Changes of this type may be expected to come about if the tastes of people of given incomes are shifted from one thing to another, or if income is transferred from people with one set of tastes to people with another set. I postulate that, at the start of the movement to be studied and also at the end of it, the real wage-rate ruling in all of the occupations, between which a relative variation occurs, stands at the adjustment level. The associated movements need not, of course, be instantaneous, but may be spread over longer or shorter periods of time. They must, however, be compensatory, not only in respect of the whole period occupied, but also in respect of each several part of it.

§ 2. When compensatory swings of demand of the type just described take place, adjustment to the new situation is partly accomplished by a deflection of the stream of new recruits coming into industry away from the less towards the more favoured occupations. What happens in detail depends in large part upon the speed with which the shift in relative demand takes place—the magnitude of the interval over which it is spread—as compared with the normal rate of occupational wastage. That rate depends, of course, on the length of the employee's industrial life. Thus, if in any occupation a representative workers' industrial life is thirty-three years, and if the occupation has hitherto been neither expanding nor decaying, there will be a wastage from it every year of 3 per cent of the number employed in it. Suppose then that the shift of demand is such as to require a 15 per cent addition to the numbers at work in one occupation and a 15 per cent reduction in those at work in another, and that this shift takes place gradually over a period of five years. The whole of the necessary adjustment *could* be accomplished by a deflection in the stream of new recruits, without any man who has ever been at work having to move at all. If this in fact happens, at each instant during the process of the movement the distribution of labour will be precisely adjusted to the conditions of demand at that instant. The optimum distribution will gradually shift and the actual distribution will shift along with it without any failure or lag. No unfilled vacancies and no unemployment will occur. With shifts in relative demand that require contractions in the number of workers employed in the declining occupations in excess of the wastage that occurs in them during the time the shift is taking place, the position is different. Suppose, as before, that the shift of demand is spread over five years, but that the contraction required in the declining occupations (and so also the expansion required in the others) is 30 per cent. As before, a 3 per cent contraction *could* be secured every year by a deflection in the stream of new recruits. Even if the whole 3 per cent is in fact secured in this way, complete adjustment cannot be reached till five years after the demand has become stabilised at its new level. During the first of the five years over which the shift is spread there will, unless some other method of adjustment also is invoked, be 3 per cent less men in the expanding industry and 3 per cent more in the contracting industry than, so to speak, there "ought to be".

During the second year the corresponding figure will be 6 per cent; and it will increase continually over the period of the shift till at the end of it, it stands at 15 per cent. Thereafter, during the following five years the figure will decrease continually till, at the end of that period, it becomes zero. More exactly, there will be a series of deficiencies and excesses equal to 3 per cent, 6 per cent, 9 per cent, 12 per cent, 15 per cent, 12 per cent, 9 per cent, 6 per cent, 3 per cent, 0 per cent of the original number of men in the expanded industry. In real life it is not to be expected that the flow of new recruits will distribute itself in the ideal manner we have so far been supposing. Youthful wage-earners, and the parents who help to direct their choice of jobs, are necessarily very ignorant of the comparative prospects of different openings. Hence the measure of adjustment that is in fact attained through deflection of recruits is certain to be much less than the measure that is theoretically possible. None the less, some fairly substantial measure of adjustment may be looked for.

§ 3. At this point an important comment must be made. So far we have been tacitly assuming that the population of working age is stationary, and that a change in relative demand means an increase in the absolute number of wage-earners demanded at a given wage in one centre accompanied by an equal decrease in the absolute number demanded at another centre. If, however, the population of working age is expanding or contracting and absolute aggregate demand is moving parallel to it, so that at a given wage-rate the same *proportionate* number of the population is in demand, we have a stationary aggregate demand, not in an absolute sense, but, so to speak, per head of the population. With aggregate demand stationary in this sense, a relative variation in demand between two occupations must be interpreted to mean, not that the absolute number demanded at the one centre increases to the same extent that the absolute number demanded at the other decreases, but that *the percentage of the total working population* demanded at the one centre increases to the same extent that the corresponding percentage demanded at the other centre decreases. It is apparent that, with an expanding population of working age, this sort of relative change will not, unless it exceeds a certain magnitude, imply any reduction in the absolute number of men demanded at the contracted centre; and that, the larger the rate of expansion, the larger the proportionate change in relative demand can be without any absolute contraction in demand occurring anywhere. Thus in general, if the population of working age is expanding, a larger proportionate change in the numbers of men employed in different occupations can be effected in a given time by the deflection of new recruits than would be possible with the population of working age stationary.[1] More generally, the more rapidly the population of working age is expanding, the more easy it is for given relative variations in demand to be met by deflections in the flow of new recruits, in such wise that no question of unemployment can arise. It follows that the check to the rate of growth in the population of working age, which, on account of the low birth-rate during and following the war, must soon be strongly manifest in this country, will reduce the scope of this innocuous method of meeting relative variations in the demand for labour.

§ 4. Let us now put aside this method of adjustment, premising that whatever is to be accomplished by means of it is in fact accomplished, and concentrate on such part of the relative swings of demand as has to be met otherwise. What happens to employment during the course of the relative variations obviously depends in large measure upon what

---

[1] It should be noted that the rate of increase of the population of working age may in different circumstances bear very various relations to the rate of increase of the population as a whole. Thus, if the progress of medical science were to diminish the death-rate at all ages within the working period, while leaving the death-rate at other ages stationary, and if the birth-rate were unaltered, the expansion of population that resulted would be concentrated on persons of working age: this part of the population would come to constitute a larger proportion of the whole. On the other hand, if the progress of medical science reduced the death-rate chiefly among children, particularly if it diminished the rate of infant mortality, or if the birth-rate increased, the expansion of population would be concentrated on persons below working age; their numbers would, until the new lives began to reach working age, expand relatively to the total population. In like manner, it is easy to see that a high birth-rate in the year 1 makes for a small ratio of working population to total population for the next fourteen years, and that thereafter its effect is transferred from the child population to the working population, in such wise that it makes for a larger ratio.

happens to the rates of real wages ruling in the occupations
between which relative swings take place. I shall consider
first the extreme case in which these rates are held absolutely
rigid.

§ 5. The quantity of employment ruling at each moment is,
as we have seen, equal to the aggregate quantity of labour
demanded *minus* the quantity of unfilled vacancies. It is
convenient, therefore, to consider these two elements separately. Let us begin with the former of them. At first sight
it appears that, with wage-rates rigid, when the aggregate
demand function for labour is given, the aggregate quantity
of labour demanded cannot be affected by relative movements
of particular demand functions. If the rate of wage in all
occupations is the same, this is true. But, if the wage-rates
ruling in different occupations differ—and our postulate that
initially there is nil unemployment and nil unfilled vacancies
does not preclude this—it is not, in general, true. This can be
made obvious by symbols. Thus let the wage-rates at two
centres—we suppose for simplicity that there are only two
—be respectively W_1 and W_2. Our overriding proviso tells
us that $\phi_1(W_1) + \phi_2(W_1) = \psi_1(W_1) + \psi_2(W_1)$, and also that
$\phi_1(W_2) + \phi_2(W_2) = \psi_1(W_2) + \psi_2(W_2)$. But, unless $W_1 = W_2$, it
does not follow necessarily from this that $\phi_1(W_1) + \phi_2(W_2) =$
$\psi_1(W_1) + \psi_2(W_2)$, which is the condition of constant aggregate
quantity demanded. This condition will, indeed, be satisfied
in a number of important cases. Thus, whatever the values of
W_1 and W_2, it will always be satisfied when the transitions
that occur take the form of swings parallel to themselves of
the demand schedules that move, in such wise that $\{\phi_2(W)$
$- \psi_2(W)\}$, and, therefore, also $\{\psi_1(W) - \phi_1(W)\}$, is constant
for all values of W. It will also be satisfied for some other sorts
of transition in respect of particular values of W_1 and W_2.
In fact our overriding proviso is not incompatible with the
condition being satisfied. But it does not insure that it will
be satisfied: and, except in the special case of transitions
by parallel swings, the chance that it will in fact be satisfied is exceedingly remote. It is important that this fact
should be held clearly in mind. In view, however, of our
ignorance of the forms of actual demand functions, it does not

seem possible to draw any practical inferences from it. For the purpose of the present analysis, therefore, I shall postulate that the variations in demand functions that take place are by way of parallel horizontal swings, so that the above difficulty does not arise. In these conditions the aggregate quantity of labour demanded at a given real wage-rate remains the same whatever swings in relative demand take place.

§ 6. It follows that swings can only diminish employment —in contracting occupations—to the precise extent in which they create unfilled vacancies in expanding occupations. Unemployment is, in fact, created through the transformation of so much employment into an equal quantity of unfilled vacancies. How much unemployment is thus created depends upon the degree of freedom with which the wage-earners attached to the declining occupations can move, in response to the changes in relative demand conditions, to the expanding ones, i.e. upon the mobility of labour.[1] If labour is absolutely immobile, there will be in the expanded centres, at each moment, whatever number of unfilled vacancies the transferred new recruits have not sufficed to occupy: and in the contracted centres there will be an exactly equal number of unemployed men. As we imagine labour less and less immobile—more and more free to move—it is clear that the number of unfilled vacancies and the associated number of unemployed men will be progressively reduced. In the limit with mobility perfect, i.e. when movement is not only entirely free but also occupies no time, the number would become nil. This limit, however, is really ultra-theoretical, because the conception of movement occupying no time is an impossible one. Ruling out this impossibility, we obtain a genuine limit as follows. Even when movement is restricted by no obstacles either of ignorance or of cost, when mobility, in short, is as perfect as can be conceived—there will, in any year, be a number of man-days of unemployment equal to the number of men transferred during that year multiplied by the average number of days occupied in the process of transfer. Thus, if, of the total number of employees, h per cent are transferred during a year and the

---

[1] For an elaborate discussion of the meaning and significance of labour mobility, cf. *Economics of Welfare*, Part III. chap. ix.

average act of transfer occupies three days (out of a working year of 300 days), the annual percentage of unemployment among wage-earners will be equal to $\frac{1}{100} h$. Plainly, however, this only mitigates, and cannot offset, the favourable effect of movement on unemployment; for the men who are unemployed because they are in movement must, with absolutely rigid wage-rates, have been unemployed anyhow. They are now, each of them, unemployed for three days instead of, in general, a much longer period.[1]

§ 7. In the extreme case opposite to that examined in §§ 5-6 wage-rates are absolutely plastic. In this case, if labour is absolutely immobile, swings in relative demand are obviously incapable of creating either unfilled vacancies or unemployment. They are thus completely innocuous, just as they are with wage-rates absolutely rigid and labour perfectly and instantaneously mobile. These two conditions are, of course, very different in their general consequences. If the latter is satisfied, real wage-rates in all centres stand at every stage at the adjustment level, and labour is always distributed in the optimum manner relatively to the state of demand and the distribution of income. If the former condition is satisfied, real wage-rates will not, in general, stand at the adjustment level, and labour will not be distributed in the optimum manner. It is further probable that less capital will be created than under the other arrangement, with the result that the demand for labour in the future is less than it would have been. So far, however, as employment at the time is concerned, there is nothing to choose between the two sets of

---

[1] It is this type of case—compensatory upward and downward swings of demand, (temporarily) rigid wage-rates and some measure of labour mobility—that Mr. and Mrs. Webb probably have in mind when they write of Employment Exchanges: "Experience proved that, even in London, at a time when thousands were unemployed, there were opportunities for the taking on of more hands, which employers forwent because they could not, in the absence of machinery of this kind, discover quickly and without trouble exactly the kind of labour that they required. By enabling these opportunities to be taken, instead of being let slip, the Labour Exchange may, to some slight extent, and with regard to certain specialised kinds of skill, even increase the volume of employment. Even to enable each employer to begin new jobs a day or two earlier than would otherwise have been possible, meant, by adding several days to the productive period of each year, an actual increase of production, and, therefore, an increased demand for labour" (Webb, *English Poor Law History*, Part II. p. 662).

conditions. If labour is not absolutely immobile, but is mobile in some degree, since movement occupies time, swings of relative demand necessarily create some unfilled vacancies and so some unemployment—the unemployment of men in movement between jobs. In like manner, any improvement of mobility, other than improvements that involve a shortening of the time occupied by a given act of movement, is *pro tanto* injurious to employment. Improvements that involve such a shortening of time have a double effect. On the one hand, since quicker movement means less cost in loss of wages, they cause more men to move: on the other hand, they cause each act of movement to involve less unemployment. Hence their net effect on the volume of unemployment cannot be determined with certainty.

§ 8. The wage systems of real life are neither absolutely rigid nor absolutely plastic. We have found that, with absolutely rigid wage-rates, there will be more unemployment if labour is perfectly immobile than if it is perfectly mobile: and that, with absolutely plastic wage-rates, there will be more unemployment if labour is perfectly (but not instantaneously) mobile than if it is perfectly immobile. With wage-rates that are neither absolutely rigid nor absolutely plastic, but of some unspecified intermediate character, no general statement on these matters is possible. With wage-rates, however, of that considerable rigidity which rules in England there can be no serious doubt that, the more mobile labour is, the smaller, in the face of given swings of relative demand schedules, the volume of unemployment is likely to be.

§ 9. Hitherto we have tacitly assumed that the degree of plasticity in wage-rates and the degree of mobility of labour are independent of one another. In fact greater plasticity is likely to go with smaller mobility; for the reason that, the more difficult it is for unemployed men, at a time when their industry is depressed, to move away to work elsewhere, the greater is the pressure on the general body of wage-earners in that industry to accept reductions in wages. It follows that higher mobility affects unemployment in a double manner: (1) directly when the degree of plasticity of wage-rates is taken as given, and (2) indirectly by lessening this degree. The direct way, we have seen, is almost certain in practice to lessen unemployment; the indirect way, to increase it. The second reaction *may* outweigh the first. It is, however, in my judgement, very unlikely to do so.

CHAPTER IX

FLUCTUATIONS OF EMPLOYMENT AND CORRELATIONS
BETWEEN REAL DEMAND AND REAL WAGE MOVEMENTS

§ 1. In Chapters VII. and VIII., when we were considering shifts in the real demand functions for labour over a small range of occupations, it was proper to suppose that the rates of real wages stipulated for either remained constant or, if they altered, altered only as a consequence of, and in response to, alterations in the demand functions. With widespread shifts of demand functions, such as characterise the so-called trade cycle, it is no longer proper to suppose this. The monetary factor, whose influence over real demand movements was discussed in Part IV. Chapters IX.-XII., intervenes. The manner of its operation is tolerably well known; but a general account must, nevertheless, be given here.

§ 2. Let us imagine an economy in which wage-rates are all contracted for in kind. In such an economy inertia would operate to stabilise real rates of wage in the face of changes in real demand conditions. Employers and employed seldom recognise any principle in accordance with which real wage-rates should be governed. They seldom even agree that the rate ruling in some given period was "right" relatively to the conditions of real demand that then prevailed. Consequently, when these conditions improve, employers will not forthwith welcome an increase of rates: when they worsen, workpeople will not welcome a decrease. There is thus always a resistance on one side or the other to wage changes appropriate to demand changes. This resistance is fortified by three factors. The first is doubt as to how long the new state of real demand will last; if it is only a flash in the pan, to alter what is perhaps a complicated system of mutually adjusted rates will not be worth while. "To adjust wages to temporary fluctuations, to know whether such fluctuations are likely to prove temporary or not, to choose between a higher proportion of unemployed for a few months or more and all the creaking of a cumbrous machine which widespread changes of wage-rates must cause, demands an economic sagacity which, in fact, the world does not possess." [1] The second factor is more important. Employers are unwilling to grant real wage increases in good times for fear that, if they do so, they will be unable to recall them when the good times pass: workpeople are unwilling to accept reductions in bad times for fear that employers will refuse to rescind them when the bad times pass. The third factor is the difficulty experienced on both sides in ascertaining and setting out in a clear way suitable tests as to what good times and bad times are. These considerations are relevant alike to improvements and to worsenings in the conditions of real demand. In the case of worsening conditions there are also further factors making for a refusal of real wage-rates to fall. In this country the workpeople's resistance is strengthened and rendered more effective by the unemployment insurance system. Pressure of unemployment in an industry, as an instrument for persuading men to accept wage reductions, has become much less important than it used to be in the absence of this system. Moreover, wage-earners opposing reductions of real wages can reckon now on much public sympathy, even in times of serious depression.

§ 3. These factors of inertia, which, in an economy where wage-rates were always contracted for in kind, would tend to keep real wages stable in the face of changing demand, in a money economy tend to keep money wages stable. To a great extent people—employers and employed alike—think in money. Our income is our money income, and it requires an effort to realise that, provided the price of the things we buy with money has halved, we are really no worse off with a money income that is also halved. If the conditions of real

[1] Loveday, *Britain and World Trade*, p. 136.

demand were stationary and known to be stationary, and the
only variable factor was the quantity of money available
for expenditure, the custom of basing wage contracts for
long terms on a cost of living sliding scale might, after a time,
win wide acceptance. But, in fact, real demand frequently
fluctuates. For either side to accept a cost of living scale as a
long-term regulator of wages means to surrender the right
of seeking adjustment to these fluctuations. This circumstance militates against such a far-reaching use of scales as
would effectively cure us of our money complex. Thus, except
in periods of very violent price oscillations, employers in
general fight strongly against upward movements in money
rates of wages and workpeople against downward movements.
Money wage-rates show themselves in practice highly resistant
to change.

§ 4. This translation of wage inertia, so to speak, from real
rates to money rates of wages has, of course, no effect if the
prices of wage-goods are stable. If these prices are not stable,
it has a different effect according as downward price movements go with enhancements or with depressions of the real
demand for labour. In so far as downward price movements
and enhancements of real demand are associated, the translation will promote stability of employment. Thus, if the
prices of wage-goods fall because the methods of producing
these goods have improved, to hold the money rate of wage
at its old level allows the real rate to increase in proportion to
increased productivity, so that the quantity of employment
can remain unchanged. The real rate of wage is allowed to
move so that it maintains equality with the marginal net
product of the original number of wage-earners. In short, the
translation of inertia from real wage-rates to money wage-
rates causes real rates to move in a manner compensatory to
movements in the real demand functions. In actual life, however, experience shows that, as a general rule, downward price
movements go with contractions in the real demand for labour
and upward price movements with expansions. The reason is
that variations in the real demand function for labour due to
changes in desires and expectations about capital goods and
other non-wage-goods take place on a much larger scale, and

play a much larger part in short-period economic movements, than variations due *solely* to changes in the productivity of wage-good industries. Hence, in general, the translation of inertia from real wage-rates to money wage-rates causes real rates to move in a manner not compensatory, but complementary, to movements in the real demand function. Real wage-rates not merely fail to fall when the real demand for labour is falling, but actually rise; and, in like manner, when the real demand for labour is expanding, real wage-rates fall. The result, of course, is that the quantity of labour demanded, and so the volume of employment, is substantially more variable than it would be, other things being equal, in an economy where wage-rates were contracted for in kind.

§ 5. To this general statement one point should be added that is of significance analytically. It is tempting at first sight to say that such and such an upward movement of real demand is associated with such and such a rise in the price level; that, the money rate of wage being given, this causes such and such a fall in the real rate of wage stipulated for; and that this, in turn, the elasticity of the real demand for labour being given, causes such and such a rise in the quantity of labour demanded, and so in the volume of employment. A chain sequence of this type does not, however, truly represent the facts. For when, in consequence of a given expansion of real demand, money demand expands by so much, the extent to which the price level rises itself depends on the extent to which employment and production are increased. We cannot say that, the larger the price rise, the larger will be the fall in the real rate of wages, and, therefore, the larger the increase in employment; for, the more elastic the real demand for labour, and, therefore, the larger the increase in employment, the smaller, other things being equal, the rise in the price level will be. Thus, when inertia keeps the money rate of wage constant, the monetary factor does not affect the real rate of wage stipulated for in such and such a way and, through this, affect the aggregate quantity of labour demanded in such and such a way. Rather it affects the whole complex of balancing forces, and thereby brings it about that the real rate of wage stipulated for and the aggregate quantity of labour demanded are *both* modified. These movements, though bound together in a rigid nexus, are not successive links in a causal change, but joint effects of a process that stands behind them.

CHAPTER X

THE SIGNIFICANCE OF STATISTICAL CORRELATIONS BETWEEN CHANGES IN EMPLOYMENT AND IN REAL WAGE-RATES

§ 1. WHEN defined changes in the quantity of employment in some industry or group of industries are recorded, and also the associated changes in rates of real wages, it is natural to inquire whether any manipulation of statistics can inform us to what extent the employment changes would have been different from what they are if the associated changes in real wage-rates had not taken place. The type of manipulation which immediately suggests itself is that of calculating correlation coefficients. This method of attack has been made familiar by M. Jacques Rueff. I propose to consider here, not the particular application of it which M. Rueff has made to recent English statistics, but the general significance of the method.[1]

§ 2. If it were known that shifts of wage-rate and shifts in other factors relevant to employment were independent of one another, the occurrence of perfect correlation between wage movements and employment movements would make

---

[1] In conformity with the general scheme of analysis followed in this book, the index of real wages must, of course, be fashioned by dividing the index of money wages by the index of cost of living. In M. Rueff's work and the later work based upon it the index used is money wage-rate divided by wholesale prices, so that, when, with money wages constant, wholesale prices fall, the real wage-rate rises. As will be shown presently, variations in wholesale prices divided by cost of living are a factor relevant to the real demand function for labour (i.e. the demand function in terms of wage-good units). Thus M. Rueff's statistics relate unemployment movements, not to pure changes in real wage-rates as understood here—and understood generally—but to movements of a quantity that depends partly on real wage-rates and partly on the real demand function for labour. They cannot, therefore, display the relation between changes in unemployment and changes in real wage-rates in a strict sense.

it highly probable that, over the period under review, absence of wage movements would have involved absence of employment movements, *i.e.* that, if we write c for the average of actual employment changes, a for the average of employment changes that would have occurred in the absence of demand movements, and b for the average of employment changes that would have occurred in the absence of wage movements, a is equal to c. It would not prove this absolutely, because it is conceivable that variations in real demand conditions should be taking place—as it were by accident—in such a way as to produce throughout additional effects on employment bearing the same constant proportion to those produced by the wage movements. Plainly, however, that this should happen, despite the premise of independence, over a period of any length is exceedingly improbable. The equality $a = c$ throughout the period, if it were realised, would imply, of course, that the real demand function for labour had not moved at all: thus carrying with it the further inference that $b = 0$.

§ 3. The presence of a very high, but not perfect, correlation between wage movements and employment movements would, in like manner, make it highly probable that, on the average of our period, a did not differ from c by much: or, in other words, that, if the wage movements had not taken place while everything else remained the same, the *predominant part* of the employment movement would have been eliminated. This would carry the inference that (1) demand movements had occurred only rarely, or (2) that they had been small, or (3) that, though not small, they had been of such a sort that their presence, in the absence of wage movements, would have made little difference to employment.

§ 4. The foregoing discussion rests on the assumption that wage shifts and shifts in other factors relevant to employment occur independently of one another. In fact, however, we know that shifts of wage-rates and shifts in demand conditions are not independent, but are related in two ways. On the one hand, as was pointed out in Chapter VI. § 8, shifts in real demand, *via* their effect on employment, sometimes induce shifts *in the same sense* in the real rate of wage for which workpeople stipulate. On the other hand, periods of depression, which are associated with contractions of real demand, are also associated with reductions in the price level, and these, in turn, owing to friction, are associated with increases in the real wage-rates for which workpeople stipulate. That is to say, shifts in real demand are associated with shifts in the *opposite* sense in the rate of real wage for which workpeople stipulate. There can be little doubt that in modern industrial communities this latter tendency is predominant over the former. Hence a very high correlation between real wage-rates and unemployment may be present; and yet it is not *very* unlikely that the observed variations in unemployment are *mainly* due—they are almost certain to be due in considerable measure—to the direct action of changes in the conditions of real demand. The point may be put more concretely thus. Over the period 1920 to 1930 money rates of wages in this country on the average remained approximately constant, but price levels, both wholesale and retail, varied. Upward and downward movements in the (retail) price level imply, as a matter of arithmetic, proportionate downward and upward movements in the real rate of wages. But they also frequently *indicate* downward and upward movements in the real demand for labour. Since the indication is only rough and general, we cannot calculate the coefficient of correlation between indices of the real demand movements and the unemployment movements. We cannot, therefore, say whether this coefficient, if it could be calculated, would be larger or smaller than the coefficient actually found between real wage-rate movements and unemployment movements. Hence we cannot affirm with any confidence that the main part of the recorded changes in employment would not have taken place had the recorded shifts of real wage-rates been estopped.[1]

§ 5. If this be so, the appearance of a high correlation

---

[1] It may be noted in passing that M. Rueff's correlations have sometimes been cited as evidence, not merely that the *fluctuations* of unemployment in this country since the war have been caused by inverse fluctuations in the rate of real wages, but also that the very high average *level* of unemployment that has prevailed during that period has been due to real wages being held "too high". A moment's reflection, however, shows that they can have no bearing whatever on that matter.

between changes in real wage-rates and changes in unemployment has less significance than M. Rueff attaches to it. The
appearance in any period of a very low correlation—a condition with which M. Rueff's argument is not concerned—
would, however, have considerable significance. It would indicate that the complex of wage movements, *plus* such demand movements as were linked up with them in the manner
indicated in the preceding section, had made little difference
to the employment movements: and it would suggest, as a
probable inference, that demand movements not thus linked
to wage movements had been the predominant factor at work.
It is thus interesting to find that, whereas in England since
the war the correlation between real wages and unemployment has been high, in Germany it has been very low: and to
note, in connection with this circumstance, that Germany has
been exposed to a large disturbing factor on the side of the
real demand for labour that has not been present in England,
namely large fluctuations in the influx of foreign investments.[1]

[1] Cf. International Institute of Statistics, 1930, *Real Wages and Employment*, p. 8.

CHAPTER XI

THE STATE OF UNEMPLOYMENT IN RELATION TO THE VARIA-
BILITY OF RELATIVE DEMAND IN ANY SET OF CENTRES
WHEN THE AGGREGATE REAL DEMAND OF THE SET IS
CONSTANT

§ 1. WE must now, in accordance with our programme, hark
back from fluctuations in unemployment to the state of unemployment. We have to consider the relation of this state
to the variability of the relative demand for labour as between different centres. To isolate this matter for separate
study, let us imagine that we are confronted with a number of
centres in which the aggregate demand function for labour is
stable, but the several separate demand functions, presumed
independent of one another,[1] fluctuate. If we suppose these
fluctuations to take place by way of parallel horizontal movements, the relative variability of demand in the system of
centres is conveniently measured by the average of the average
deviations from the average of the quantity of labour demanded at any given wage-rate in the several centres. Let us
write $\dfrac{t}{2}$ for this measure and n for the number of centres.
There must then at all times be certain centres in the sum of
which the quantity of labour demanded at any given set of
wage-rates exceeds the average quantity demanded there by
$\dfrac{nt}{4}$; and certain other centres in the sum of which the quantity

[1] We ignore here the fact that, if an upward swing of demand in a
non-wage-good industry A creates unfilled vacancies, the associated downward swing in other non-wage-good industries will, because wage-goods
are not absorbed, be smaller than it would have been if the upward swing
in A had created employment.

302

so demanded falls short of the average quantity demanded there by an equal amount.

§ 2. I postulate, as conditions reasonably conformable to those of real life: (1) that, from a short-period standpoint, the rates of real wage in all our centres are, when once they are established, rigid; (2) that the total number of would-be wage-earners, through the flow of new recruits, is distributed, as between the centres under study and other occupations, in such wise that the mathematical expectation of earnings over good and bad times together is the same in the average of them as it is elsewhere; (3) that, subject to the above conditions, there is free competition among both employers and employed. It is convenient, though not essential to our analysis, to postulate further that there is some one occupation outside our set of centres in which the demand function for labour is stable.

§ 3. In the conditions postulated in § 2 it is impossible for the wage-rate ruling in our set of centres to be such as to allow of there being in any centre any unfilled vacancies at the time of its minimum demand or any unemployment at the time of its maximum demand. Hence in the average centre the maximum possible quantity of unemployment *plus* unfilled vacancies over the average of good and bad times there is t. Therefore, over the sum of all centres, the maximum possible permanent pool of unemployment *plus* unfilled vacancies is nt. The minimum possible permanent pool is obviously nil. Hence two problems present themselves for consideration. First, when n and t are given, how is the magnitude of the total pool of unemployment *plus* unfilled vacancies, which we know lies somewhere between nil and nt, determined? Secondly, how is the division of the total pool between unemployment and unfilled vacancies determined? These two questions have now to be examined in turn.

§ 4. Suppose first that within our set of centres labour is absolutely immobile. It then necessarily happens that in the average centre the sum of unemployment *plus* unfilled vacancies varies over a range $2t$, and so, on the average of good and bad times, amounts to t. Therefore in the sum of all the centres there is a permanent pool of employment *plus* unfilled vacancies equal to the maximum possible amount, namely, nt. Suppose, secondly, that within our set of centres labour is absolutely mobile. It follows obviously that the pool of unemployment *plus* unfilled vacancies is permanently nil, stands, that is to say, at the lowest possible amount. Suppose, thirdly, that labour within our set of centres is neither perfectly mobile nor perfectly immobile, but partially mobile. The permanent pool of unemployment *plus* unfilled vacancies will then lie somewhere between the two limits, approaching the lower or the upper one according as this partial mobility is greater or less. It follows that, whatever the wage situation is, anything that makes for immobility will expand, and anything that makes for mobility will contract, the size of the complex pool. The lack of adequate arrangements for transferring men from points of temporary short demand to points of temporary high demand is responsible for this pool being very large in dock and wharf labour, works of construction and building. Since, furthermore, the pool of unemployment cannot exceed the complex pool of unemployment *plus* unfilled vacancies, it follows that obstacles to mobility expand, and improvements in mobility contract, the limits within which the pool of unemployment must lie. If the postulates of § 2 are satisfied, with perfect mobility the complex pool is nil, and the pool of unemployment is, therefore, also nil.

§ 5. At first sight it may seem that these results have nothing to do with rates of wages. Our second postulate in § 2 has, however, required that the expectation of earnings on the average of our set of centres shall be equal to the wage-rate ruling in a stable occupation outside them. The substitution of perfect mobility for perfect immobility of labour within our set of centres, involving, as it does, employment for people hitherto unemployed, requires, if it is to destroy the complex pool, to be accompanied by a reduction in wage-rates from something above the stable outside level— say w—to that level. Failing such a reduction, an inflow of labour from outside will take place into our set of centres, and a pool, this time consisting exclusively of unemployment, will be re-created. Moreover, it is easy to see that the absolute quantity of unemployment in the new pool must exceed the absolute quantity of it in the old. For, the wage-rate being given, the quantity of employment divided by the number of men attached to any one of our centres cannot be reduced. That is to say, the proportion of unemployment there is unaltered; which implies, since more men are attached there, that the absolute quantity of it is increased. Hence, in the situation here contemplated, the substitution of mobility of labour for immobility in our set of centres, though a *necessary* condition for the destruction of the complex pool, as for the reduction of the part of it comprising unemployment, is not a *sufficient* condition. It is also necessary that the appropriate wage reductions shall not be obstructed. These reductions do not imply any injury to the collective interest of wage-earners in our centres. For, though certain of them are paid a lower rate of wages, increased regularity of employment in general more than compensates for this, and aggregate real earnings are increased.

§ 6. Let us turn to the division of the complex pool between unemployment and unfilled vacancies. The non-mathematic reader is likely to suppose that, the postulates of § 2 being given, this division is determined, and can be calculated for him by his mathematical colleagues. This, however, is not so. With the conditions that have been laid down there are not sufficient equations to determine the unknowns. Equilibrium can be established in our set of centres either with higher wage-rates and more unemployment or with lower wage-rates and less unemployment. To show that this must be so, let us take the simplest possible case. Suppose that, outside the set of centres, in the occupation where demand is stable, this demand is also perfectly elastic, so that the wage-rate ruling there is a constant W. Suppose further that, in each member of our set of centres, for half of the time (bad times) the quantity of labour demanded at any wage $w = F(w)$, for the other half of the time (good times) $= \psi(w)$. Let the quantity of labour attached to each centre be x; the quantity of unfilled vacancies in times of good demand v, and the quantity of unemployment in bad times u. We then have the three equations

X

(1)
$$\frac{w}{2} \cdot \frac{F(w) + \psi(w) - v}{x} = W;$$

(2)
$$\psi(w) - v = x;$$

(3)
$$F(w) + u = x.$$

Thus there are four unknowns, w, x, v and u, but only three equations.

§ 7. It may perhaps be argued that, though the distribution between unemployment and unfilled vacancies in any one of our centres is indeterminate, if there are a large number of centres, for all of them together this is not so, but the pool must be, or at all events is likely to be, divided about equally between these two elements. This, however, would only be true if the assertion that the distribution is indeterminate meant that all distributions over the range of possibility are equally likely. It does not mean this. When I say that the distribution is indeterminate, I am confessing ignorance; when I say that all possible distributions are equally likely, I am professing knowledge. We are not entitled to make this use of the principle of insufficient reason. It is, therefore, impossible to decide by any *a priori* method how much of the total pool will consist of unemployment and how much of unfilled vacancies. Nor, when the process of counting tells us in what way it is in fact divided at any particular time, are we entitled to infer that it will also be so divided at other times. A considerable degree of caution and scepticism seems proper to this subject.

§ 8. The proposition that the distribution of the pool between unfilled vacancies and unemployment is indeterminate does not, of course, mean that it is not determined by causes; only that it is not determined by those causes of which account is taken in our equations. Within the limits set by those causes there is in play the comparative bargaining strength of employers and employed. Employers' strength tends to promote lower wages and unfilled vacancies: workpeople's strength higher wages and unemployment. *A priori* either side might be the stronger.

§ 9. We have not experience of a state of constant aggregate demand such as has been contemplated in the preceding argument, but only of the fluctuating aggregate demands of actual life. That experience, for what it is worth, suggests that in those many-centred industries of unstable demand, mainly dock labour and building, to which in this country the investigations conducted in this chapter are chiefly relevant, the workpeople have, paradoxical though it may seem, usually proved themselves the stronger party; and that the main part of the complex pool has usually consisted of unemployment. It is not, indeed, true, as is sometimes asserted, that the wage-rate actually established is high enough to attach to each centre all the men needed to satisfy the peak of demand there. This would imply that the pool never contains *any* unfilled vacancies. In general, however, there can be little doubt that the unfilled vacancies division has been much smaller than the unemployment division, and that no great error would result from ignoring it. If it is ignored, the conclusion set out at the end of § 4 about the effect of improvements in mobility on the limits within which the pool of unemployment must lie holds good also of the actual size of that pool.

CHAPTER XII

THE POSSIBLE EFFECT ON FLUCTUATIONS IN, AND ON THE TOTAL QUANTITY OF, UNEMPLOYMENT OF REARRANGEMENTS OF REAL DEMAND IN TIME

§ 1. In this chapter I postulate that real wage-rates are every-where rigid and equal—the consequences of lapses from rigidity can be readily assessed on the lines indicated in earlier chapters,—and that, over a specified period of time, the sum-total of all demands for labour is constant; but that the distribution in time of some of these demands may be altered. Such alterations are *prima facie* liable to affect both the way in which the volume of employment fluctuates between different parts of the period and also its average and aggre-gate amount in the whole period. Three sorts of alteration have to be distinguished. First, in a particular centre the demands of different parts of the period may be rendered more equal by transferences of a part of the demand from boom times in that centre to depressed times there. Secondly, the demand in a particular centre, that has hitherto been fairly stable, may be rendered unstable in such wise as to provide large demands in that centre at times of poor demands in other centres, and *vice versa*. Thirdly, the time-distribution of the demands of a particular centre may be so altered that the large demands there, which have hitherto coincided with large demands in other centres, are shifted to times of small demand in other centres.

§ 2. The third of these three cases is the simplest and may conveniently be considered first. If labour is perfectly im-mobile between the particular centre and others, it is obvious that, as a consequence of the change of system which that case contemplates, the extent to which unemployment fluctuates will be reduced. Ten per cent of unemployment in the particular centre is made to coincide with 4 per cent in the sum of all other centres, and 4 per cent with 10 per cent, instead of 10 per cent coinciding with 10 per cent and 4 per cent with 4 per cent. This may be regarded from some points of view as a social gain. But the average and aggregate quantity of unemployment over our period is not affected at all.

§ 3. If labour is perfectly mobile between the particular centre and others, the effect of the change of system will be to lessen the gap between the combined demand of the sum of all centres for labour in good times and the combined demand of all centres in bad times. Before the change the aggregate quantity of labour demanded in bad times was $F(w)$. Therefore, if x be written for the number of men seeking employment and u for the quantity of unemployment, $\{x - F(w)\} = u$. In like manner the quantity of labour demanded in good times was $\{F(w) + t\}$. Therefore, if v be written for the quantity of unfilled vacancies, $\{F(w) + t - x\} = v$. After the change a quantity of demand a is transferred from good times to bad. Therefore in bad times the quantity of unemployment is reduced by a or by u, whichever is the smaller; and in good times the quantity of unemployment is increased by $(a - v)$ or by nothing, whichever is the larger. Hence, if $a < u$ and $< v$, aggregate unemployment over good and bad times together is reduced by a. If $a > u$ and $< v$, it is reduced by u. If $a < u$ and $> v$, it is reduced by v. If $a > u$ and $> v$, it is reduced by $(u + v - a)$, which may be either positive or negative, and must be negative if $v = 0$. Thus in the first two cases unemployment must be diminished provided that initially there was some unemployment in bad times: in the third case it must be diminished provided that initially there were also some unfilled vacancies in good times: in the last case it must be *increased* if initially the unfilled vacancies were nil, or, being greater than nil, fell short of a defined figure. Hence in general it is probable, but not certain, that average and aggregate unemployment over good and bad times together will be diminished. In all cases where unemployment is affected at all the extent to which it fluctuates will be diminished.

§ 4. We may next consider my first case—an alteration of time-distribution that equalises the demand in a particular centre between good and bad times there, while leaving the combined demand of both sorts of times in that centre unaltered. With labour absolutely immobile, this arrangement will diminish fluctuations in employment as a whole if good times in the particular centre coincide with good times elsewhere and bad times with bad: in the converse case it will increase them. The effect on average and aggregate unemployment in other centres will obviously be nil. The effect on aggregate and average employment in that centre, and so in the sum of all centres together, is determinable by precisely the same analysis as that set out in the preceding section, x, a, u and v being now taken to refer to that centre alone instead of, as in the section cited, to the sum of all centres. Thus in general it is probable, but not certain, that a policy of equalising demand between good and bad times in a particular centre will diminish average and aggregate unemployment over good and bad times together.

§ 5. If labour is perfectly mobile between the particular centre and other centres, this policy will lessen or will increase the gap between the combined demand for labour of the sum of all centres in general good times and general bad times according as good times in our particular centre coincide with general good times or with general bad times. When they coincide with general good times, the analysis of § 3 is again precisely applicable. Whereas in that section we contemplated a transfer from general bad times to general good times of the difference a between the high and low demands of a particular centre, we now contemplate a like transfer of the difference between the high (or low) demand of a particular centre and the average of demand there, namely $\dfrac{a}{2}$. Everything that was said in the section cited, alike of the effect on average and aggregate unemployment and of the effect on the extent of fluctuations, is, therefore, applicable here. When good times in the particular centre coincide with general bad times, the preceding case is simply inverted, and opposite consequences follow.

§ 6. There remains, thirdly, my second case. We have to consider the effect of destabilising demand in a particular centre, which, for simplicity, I shall suppose hitherto to have been completely stable, in such wise as to increase demand there in general bad times at the expense of decreasing it in general good times. If labour is perfectly immobile between the particular centre and others, it is obvious that the extent to which aggregate unemployment fluctuates will be reduced. The effect on the average and aggregate quantity of unemployment in the sum of all centres can be set out thus. First, suppose that initially there were v unfilled vacancies in our centre. The total quantity of employment in that centre in general good and bad times alike was $x - v$. Demand then is increased by a in general bad times and decreased by a in general good times. It is obvious that the increase of demand, since there are already unfilled vacancies, cannot create any employment: but the decrease can create unemployment, provided that $a > v$. Thus aggregate unemployment is increased by nothing or by $(a - v)$, whichever is the larger; it cannot be diminished. Secondly, suppose that initially there is u unemployment in our centre. The result of destabilising demand there in the manner contemplated is to diminish unemployment in general bad times by a or u, whichever is the smaller, and to increase it in general good times by a. Thus, if $a < u$, unemployment in the aggregate is unaffected: if $a > u$, it is increased by $a - u$. As before, it cannot be diminished. If initially there were neither unfilled vacancies nor unemployment, it is plainly increased by a.

§ 7. If labour is perfectly mobile between the particular centre and other centres the policy of destabilising demand in the particular centre in the manner contemplated has the effect of narrowing the gap between the combined demand of all centres in general good times and the combined demand of all in general bad times. The consequences, alike to aggregate and average unemployment and to the extent to which unemployment fluctuates, are the same as those described in § 3. For we are simply transferring a certain quantity of demand from general good times to general bad times. If we write a for the difference after the change between the high demand and the low demand of the particular centre, this quantity is measured by $\dfrac{a}{2}$, and the parallelism with the argument of § 3 is apparent.

§ 8. Up to this stage of the discussion we have supposed all the other centres outside our particular centre to be homogeneous and bound together by perfect labour mobility. When this supposition is abandoned, serious complications are introduced. Thus the possibility is opened up that labour may be mobile between our particular centre and certain centres and at the same time immobile between that centre and certain others; and it becomes a relevant fact that expansions in demand in the sum of all these centres may be associated with contractions of demand in certain of them; and *vice versa*. Thus our particular centre may be represented by a Government building roads or a local authority building schools. Labour may be mobile between this centre and other centres engaged in building and navvying work, but not at all mobile between this centre and centres engaged in coal mining or engineering: and the good times in the group of centres interested in building and navvying work may not coincide with the good times of these centres and all other centres combined. In a situation of this kind, when we wish to determine the effect of happenings in our particular centre on the average and aggregate quantity of unemployment, the state of those centres from which it is cut off by labour immobility has no relevance. The foregoing analysis is, therefore, applicable, subject to those centres being left out of account. Thus, if it is a question of the effect on the average (and aggregate) amount of employment in all centres of equalising the demand in a particular centre between good and bad times there, the critical question is, not whether good times in that centre coincide with good times in the sum of all other centres, but whether they coincide with good times in the sum of those centres with which it is linked by labour mobility. When, however, we wish to determine the effect of happenings in the particular centre on the extent to which the amount of employment in all centres fluctuates, we cannot thus disregard what is taking place in the disconnected centres, but must bring this into account after the manner of the preceding sections.

§ 9. One further very important consideration remains. As was shown in the concluding chapter of Part IV., movements initiated on the real side are liable, under actual monetary systems, to set up movements on the money side, which, once started, are cumulative and self-propagating and which in turn react on the real side. One consequence of this is that shifts of given pieces of real demand from one time to another often involve shifts in total real demand much larger than themselves. The effect on the volume of unemployment is further accentuated by reactions on real wage-rates in the manner described in Chapter IX. It follows that temporal adjustments of particular demands, such as we have been considering, are likely to have a steadying influence on employment, much larger than might be looked for at first sight. This, however, is not all. Even though no reactions on the average level of real wages takes place, it may happen that, not only the range of fluctuation, but also the average and aggregate volume of unemployment will be favourably affected. This may happen, not merely in the manner contemplated in the preceding sections, through a decrease in the average and aggregate number of unfilled vacancies, but also, quite independently of unfilled vacancies, through an increase in the average and aggregate quantity of labour demanded. The reason for this is that the economic system is not always equally sensitive to monetary impacts or equally ready to be touched off into an upward or downward spin. Opportunity may, therefore, arise to take a piece of real demand from a time when its presence or absence makes little difference, and to inject it into industry at a moment so chosen that a downward spin is stopped or an upward spin initiated. The existence of this possibility is, of course, readily perceived. But to turn it to practical account may well need more knowledge and greater skill than are as yet available.

INDEX

315

THE END

Printed in Great Britain by R. & R. CLARK, LIMITED, *Edinburgh.*